THE AUTHOR   Andrew Fisher was born in Scotland and now works and lives there as archivist to the Duke of Buccleuch and Queensberry and as administrator of Drumlanrig Castle. He is the biographer of William Wallace and a regular contributor to magazines, radio and television on Scottish history.

SERIES EDITOR   Professor Denis Judd is a Fellow of the Royal Historical Society and Head of the School of History at the Polytechnic of North London. He has published over 20 books including biographies of Joseph Chamberlain, Prince Philip, George VI and Alison Uttley, historical and military studies, stories for children and two novels. He has reviewed extensively in the national press and in journals, and has written several radio programmes.

The front cover shows 'Macbeth' by John Martin. By kind permission of the National Galleries of Scotland.

Other titles in the Series

A Traveller's History of France
A Traveller's History of Italy
A Traveller's History of Greece
A Traveller's History of Spain
A Traveller's History of Russia and the USSR

D0029672

A Traveller's History of Scotland

A Traveller's History of Scotland

ANDREW FISHER

Series Editor   DENIS JUDD
Line Drawings   *JOHN HOSTE*

INTERLINK BOOKS
An Imprint of Interlink Publishing Group, Inc.
NEW YORK

First American edition published 1990 by

INTERLINK BOOKS
An imprint of Interlink Publishing Group, Inc.
99 Seventh Avenue
Brooklyn, New York 11215

Published simultaneously in Great Britain by The Windrush Press 1990

Text © Andrew Fisher
Preface © Denis Judd 1990

All rights reserved. No part of this publication may be
reproduced, stored in a retrieval system, or transmitted
in any form or by any means, electronic, mechanical,
photocopying, recording or otherwise, without the
prior permission of the publisher.

Library of Congress Cataloging-in-Publication Data
Fisher, Andrew, 1935–
    A traveller's history of Scotland / Andrew Fisher.
    1st American ed.   p.   cm.
    Includes bibliographical references.
    ISBN 0–940793–59–8
    1. Scotland—History.   I. Title.
DA761.F57   1990
941.1—dc20   90–34709
                                      CIP

Printed and bound in Great Britain

Contents

Preface

Few nations have a prouder or more stirring history than Scotland. Since the Roman invasion of Britain, the Scottish people have been engaged in the apparently impossible, indeed contradictory, mission of maintaining their independence against imperial encroachment and being themselves colonisers and expansionists. In the process they have forged an international image – part steely reality, part dreamy Celtic-cum-Hollywood myth – that is striking in both its simplicity and its complexity.

Among the instantly recognisable symbols of Scotland are the bagpipes, Scotch whisky, the tartan bonnet, the haggis, the claymore and, of course, the kilt. But Scotland is also a country of paradoxes. It possesses some of the world's finest highland scenery and some of its harshest urbanised landscapes. It combines the romance of rural clanship with a history of uncompromising proletarian struggle in its industrial cities – against the blue of the lochs and the hills must be set the red flags of the Clyde and the Lanarkshire coalfields. There is Glasgow Rangers football club, but also Glasgow Celtic; there is Bonnie Prince Charlie, but also John Knox; there is Harold Macmillan, but also Ramsay MacDonald – or, better still, Keir Hardie.

A capacity to resist, and to survive, is central to Scotland's history. Imperial Rome built Hadrian's Wall more as an acknowledgement of defeat than an assertion of power. The Norsemen were contained and deflected. Even the English, with their vastly superior numbers and their capacity for patient organisation and statecraft, achieved no permanent conquest and subjugation. The Act of Union did not mark Scotland's unconditional surrender to Anglo-Saxon supremacy, but rather admitted the Scottish people to a working partnership in an expanding global enterprise. The St Andrew's cross was incorporated into the Union Jack, but Scots enterprise was unleashed throughout the British Empire. Scotland lost a separate parliament, but put a disproportionate number of her sons into 10 Downing Street. Scotland had been a Mother Country almost from the start of Britain's great expansion overseas – there was, after all Nova Scotia as well as New England – and her peoples flooded into the Canadian prairies, the great cities of the United States, the Australian wilderness and the green valleys of New Zealand. The British Raj, Britain's presence in tropical Africa, South-east Asia and the South Pacific were each partly sustained by Scottish soldiers, administrators, engineers, traders and missionaries.

Yet Scotland has never been willing to sacrifice her separate identity in the cause of cooperation with the rest of the United Kingdom. Her ancient universities considered themselves the equal, if not the superiors, of Oxford and Cambridge, the Scottish legal and educational systems retained important differences from those south of the border, and every year the dark blue shirted players of Scotland's football and rugby teams passionately seek to beat the old enemy – the English.

I have read no better account of Scotland's history than this one. It is clear, fascinating and comprehensive. It begins with the bedrock of geography, and ends with a Scotland disaffected with Thatcherism and with the Scottish National Party once more in the ascendant. The author has a keen eye for detail and a proper sense of proportion – witness his analysis of the importance of Association Football in Scotland. For travellers to the ancient, noble, varied and beautiful kingdom of North Britain, this book will be an excellent guide.

Denis Judd
London, 1990

CHAPTER ONE

The First Scotland

The Shaping of the Land

It is impossible fully to understand the history of a country without reference to its geographical features and position. The former dictate the extent and nature of the constraints which people faced and thus to a degree their ability to colonise and develop, as they would wish, the environment into which they have moved; the latter determines and conditions their relations with their neighbours and the world at large. Scotland is no exception to this general rule. Its physical structure, the setting which was so influential in many of the events described in the following pages, evolved over many millions of years, long before the now familiar and evocative name of the country itself came into existence. Settlers came late to Scotland and had no part to play in the shaping of its appearance; they inherited a land over which they had no control and of which no knowledge could be left to them. From the dawn of geological time the creation of the land occurred in the course of continuous change, often remarkable, sometimes cataclysmic, at the end of which Scotland stood where it stands now. The last of the Ice Ages which continued to hold Scotland in its grip as recently, in geological terms, as 12,000 years ago was preceded by a number of geological and climatic changes. There was a slow but irreversible northward drift of the vast continental landmass, made up of America and Europe, of which Scotland was a fraction. The land suffered from spectacular upheavals caused by earthquakes and typhoons, extremes of temperature unimaginable today, the formation and disappearance of deserts, the activity of volcanoes since dormant, the scouring effects of constant erosion, the laying down of sand and mud in the oceans, the hardening of sediment into hills and mountains, and the spread of lush, tropical, impenetrable vegetation in which reptiles lived.

People were prevented by the climate from achieving in Scotland what was being done elsewhere. At a time when cave art was flourishing in areas of France west of the Rhône and south of the Loire, in Spain in the provinces of Cantabria and Andalusia and in Italy in the vicinity of Rome and Palermo with graphic depictions of humans and animals, adventurers had already crossed over the Bering Straits from Asia into America. Scotland, by contrast, was virtually uninhabitable, with much of the land buried under the ice as it had been on previous occasions. By approximately 10,000 years ago, however, the ice was finally in retreat to the north. With less inclement and destructive weather came first the vegetation and then the forests which rapidly covered most of Scotland. The birch, the pine, and the oak predominated in the different regions. The availability of food brought animals from the south and west and from the continent of Europe to which Scotland, like the rest of Britain, was still joined. Many of the species to be found in the Scotland of the post-Ice Age are now gone, for example the boar, the wolf and the reindeer, which have left traces in caves near Inchnadamph in Sutherland, and the predecessor of the great 'Caledonian Bear', believed to be as large as the grizzly bear of North America.

There remained one process necessary to complete the emergence of the land of Scotland. As the melting of the ice-sheets gradually raised sea-levels, in some cases submerging the coastal outlines, in others producing new features, what we know as the North Sea was formed. In the subsequent flooding the land-bridge between the south-east of England and mainland Europe was replaced by the Straits of Dover. Scotland was henceforth the northern part of an island, open not merely as before to penetration from the south and from western Europe but, no less important in its history, from the north and from Ireland.

The First Settlers

The land which awaited its earliest known immigrants contained many elements recognisable to today's visitor – the lochs, the glens and the mountains were there. The distinction between the Highlands and the Southern Uplands, so marked even now, was exaggerated in the aftermath of the last Ice Age. The great mountain chains of the Highlands, cut in two by Glen More (a name repeated throughout the north to indicate a 'big valley'), and reaching at their highest point to some 1,200 metres (4,000 feet), belonged to a zone which, originating in the Silurian Age of 4,000,000 years ago, stretched from north and west, through the English Lake District and into Wales. Today the Highlands are a source of wonder and pleasure, but to the incomers of the Mesolithic or Middle Stone Age, they were a forbidding and impassable barrier. The Southern Uplands were formed during the same geological period as the Highlands from the reduced remains of a mountain chain covering the country from the south-west to the north-east. Our perception of them is misleading in the context of the Mesolithic Age. These Southern Uplands would have presented a daunting obstacle to the first hunters and fishers who ventured north from England. When it is realised that the interior of Scotland was either bog or marsh with the higher ground forest or scrub, we shall not be surprised to learn that the earliest immigrants appeared to have lived in coastal areas or on offshore islands.

It is likely that the warmer intervals between the Ice Ages had attracted people who established routes along the western, Atlantic edges and along the eastern, North Sea edges of the land. These routes continued to be favoured in the post-Ice Age period and for thousands of years afterwards as men and women clung to the safety of what was known. Excavations on the islands of Rhum, Islay and Jura, and on the mainland at locations in Aberdeen, Inverness and Fife, have in recent years revealed the remains of a number of campsites, the homes of people dependent for their existence on such items of food as they could obtain by hunting, fowling and fishing, supplemented by beachcombing and the gathering of plants, nuts and edible berries. They were thus accustomed to the nomadic life necessary if they were to unearth fresh resources once the old ones had been exhausted. For that reason it is perhaps inaccurate to refer to these peoples as 'settlers', although they created through their repeated visits to Scotland the suggestion of a permanent way of life formerly lacking. However rudimentary their skills, they became adept at utilising what was at hand; they could not afford to disregard any potential source of materials or food. Weapons for hunting and protection could be fashioned from microliths, flakes of stone minute in size and hafted in wood or bone; clothes were made from the hides of animals killed by these same weapons. Such tools as they disposed of could be used to scrape, cut, and dig, and to hollow out boats for fishing or travel. Discoveries of pins, harpoons, and fish-spears in a cave near Oban indicate the uses to which bone could be put and remind us that the cave offered an alternative to the campsite as a home. Wood from the many varieties of trees provided fuel for fires, offering warmth, a focal point for the group, and a deterrent to aggressors, whether animal or human. We cannot tell whether, in time, there was building in wood; the perishable nature of the medium means that traces above ground do not survive. Where wood has survived in the form of post-holes, for example, at Balbridie not far from the River Dee in Aberdeen, a date around 5,500 years ago must be assigned. Life, like the land was poor, despite the improvement in the climate which allowed higher average temperatures than those of today. Inevitably, the quest for better conditions led men to forsake the relative safety of shoreline and island to brave the interior. By the end of the Mesolithic Age, that is about 6,000 years ago, the way of life of the fisher and hunter, short, precarious, even dangerous, had spread across almost the whole of Scotland. But after some 4,000 years it was about to be replaced by a more secure and stable existence, that of the farmer.

The Neolithic Age

The Neolithic or New Stone Age, which lasted some 2,000 years, from 4000 to 2000 BC, was introduced into Scotland by immigrants who naturally travelled along the coastal routes favoured by their Mesolithic predecessors. With them these immigrants brought cattle and sheep to supply milk and meat, and cereals, notably wheat and barley, an indication that they intended to cultivate and therefore to stay. They were already experienced in the techniques which they had introduced into Scotland and being capable of a measure of foresight denied to the fisher and hunter, their effect on the land of which they were beginning to take possession was consequently the greater and more durable. Whether they succeeded peacefully in establishing themselves or whether there was a stage in which they forcibly dislodged those already there it is impossible to say, but in the true sense they deserve to be called 'settlers'. Agriculture implied clearance, and colonisation required substantial dwellings and villages in stone instead of the transitory campsites of the previous inhabitants.

A number of houses built in the Neolithic Age have survived, the most remarkable being that on the island of Papa Westray in the northern part of Orkney where the farm at Knap of Howar, preserved under a blanket of sand, dates back some 5,500 years. Just as well preserved, in the same way but on a larger scale, is the village of Skara Brae on the Bay of Skaill, again in Orkney. The village, hidden beneath the sand for 4,000 years, was uncovered in 1850 by a fierce storm coming in from the Atlantic. It consists of a unique group of interconnected stone houses, each with stone beds, cupboards, and other furniture. Skara Brae, the most perfectly preserved village of its period in Europe, probably housed as many as 50 people, in circumstances which suggest a strong sense of community. The site was continuously occupied for 600 years before its abandonment, probably the result of some natural disaster.

The settled life style of the farmers of the Neolithic Age did not, however, preclude change. Two practices demonstrate this. The first is the transition, increasingly evident towards the end of the era, from communal to individual burial. Originally, Neolithic people buried their dead collectively in chambers covered with cairns of stones often considerably larger than the chambers themselves. A fine example of a chamber is that at Maes Howe in Orkney, 11 metres high and 92 metres in circumference. Here, as elsewhere, bones from previous burials would be shifted to allow space for those from new burials. Here, too, inside the communal chamber would be placed pottery bowls, either simple or more ornate, and cups, some with handles – as part of a ritual, its meaning no longer clear to us. The most stylish form of pottery, the beaker, did not appear in Scotland from Europe until near the end of the Neolithic Age. Its origins are the subject of much debate – the beaker may have been imported with a new wave of immigration or simply through trade. Whatever the reason, the beaker came to Scotland at the same time as the spread of individual burial. Although communal burials continued, there was a tendency towards the individual grave marked perhaps by a cairn. At the same time as this development there occurred the second significant practice, evidence of which can also be discovered in connection with burial. This was the provision in the chamber or grave of objects worked in metal. As pottery had perhaps been placed in a chamber for ritualistic reasons, so metal objects, initially of bronze, would now as a matter of course accompany the individual to his grave as a token of esteem or of the pre-eminent position he had occupied in the society to which he had belonged. It is these two practices, the replacement of communal inhumations by individual burial or even cremation and urn burial, of which there is abundant evidence, and the increasing and significant uses of metal, which mark the next stage in the history of Scotland. The people did not at once and for ever abandon the sites and practices of the past. In Argyll, for example, in the Kilmartin valley, and in Orkney at the Ring of Brodgar, custom dictated as before the holding of burials. It is unlikely, therefore, that the people of Scotland were aware of a sudden change in their circumstances but they were now entering into a period of expansion greater than before.

The Age of Metals

As the Neolithic Age merged gradually into the early part of the Bronze Age, the climate was already beginning to deteriorate. It had now become colder and wetter and this was to have an inevitable and damaging impact on life in Scotland. Cultivation became more difficult, crops could no longer be guaranteed, and the population could not escape the possibility of starvation. This may help to explain why so much of the material recovered from this time consisted of weapons, in particular axes and spearheads. Communities now needed to protect themselves from others under threat of starvation and bronze, a hard metal, was well suited for the making of weapons. While copper could be mined locally, for example from the deposits in the south-west of the country, tin was scarcer. The need to import it ensured a continuity of contact with Cornwall, an important supplier of tin and also one of the strongholds of the Celts who were to appear in Scotland by the middle of the first millennium BC. As the Scottish bronze trade expanded, there was an increase in imports from Europe as well as from Cornwall; a market existed in Scotland for the exotic that matched the demand for locally made products. In such a mundane way, through trade rather than as the result of invasion, as was formerly believed, Scotland was drawn into events on a wider front. The Bronze Age in Scotland lasted for some 14 centuries with an acceleration in the production of weapons and other items between 900 and 600 BC. When the people learned how to temper iron to make it as hard as bronze, it replaced the latter for the making of weapons. Iron, because it was common, was cheap whereas bronze was rare and consequently more expensive. By 600 BC the use of bronze was almost entirely limited to jewellery.

THE CELTS

It was during the Iron Age that, in all probability, the people known to us as the Celts established themselves in Scotland. Their reputation is a considerable one despite the fact that their numbers in the Iron Age may have been relatively small. That reputation is to some degree the result of their opposition to the Romans whose campaigns against them in Europe were chronicled by Julius Caesar and in Scotland by Cornelius Tacitus. The Celts lived in tribes with an economy based on crops and animal husbandry. But it was for their fighting qualities that they had first been noted in Europe, with their invasion of northern Italy and the capture of Rome in 390 BC. Their westward move had brought them from France to England before they descended upon Scotland and then Ireland. Their religion, organised by the Druids and involving human sacrifice, appalled the Romans and led to its extirpation in Britain in the reign of Nero.

All this rather simplifies what was in fact a complex situation involving a life style which included an oral tradition of learning, a well-developed legal system, close-knit family and social obligations and a language which, with regional variants, allowed the Celtic inhabitants of Scotland to converse with those of England, Wales, Cornwall, Ireland, and northern France. So tight was the relationship between the Celts of England and those of France that it forced Caesar to cross the Channel in two attempts to break it. Perhaps because of their history as much as because of their changing conditions, the Celts were conscious of the importance of strong defensive positions. In Scotland they took part – it would be incorrect to say that they introduced the idea – in the building of hill-forts. The larger ones may mark tribal capitals, for the majority of the people lived in farmsteads built not according to defensive criteria but as the fertility of the land allowed. Hill-forts are common in the Lowlands but rare in the Highlands. There the fortification was more often the broch, a circular tower of dry masonry with cavity walls, examples of which have been found in Orkney and Shetland and on the mainland in Sutherland and Caithness. Although the broch is now usually dated to the first century AD, that is after the Roman invasion, it reflects a much older tradition. Other types of fortification included the ring-fort or the dun (a name which has persisted in a variety of locations throughout Scotland), or the artificial island of stones and tree-trunks called the crannog, one of which has been discovered at Ardanaiseig on Loch Awe in Argyll. Their efficacy and the resistance of the native population of Scotland to invasion were to be tested by the arrival, in the latter part of the first century AD, of the most formidable incomers Scotland had yet known, the Romans.

The Roman Invasion of Scotland

It is to the Roman historian Cornelius Tacitus (55–120), living and working through the events of which he wrote, that we owe the earliest account of the land and people of Scotland. The inevitable progress of the Romans into the northern part of Britain, once they had subdued the southern in the aftermath of Claudius' invasion of 43 AD, was chronicled by Tacitus in his biography of his father-in-law, Gnaeus Julius Agricola, which appeared about the year 98. Tacitus' devotion to the memory of his father-in-law has ensured that it is Agricola who is generally credited with the establishment of the Roman presence in Scotland. It is not unlikely, however, that the Romans had penetrated into Scotland, albeit in a limited way, before the advent of Agricola. His predecessor as governor of the province of Britain in the years 71–74, Quintus Petilius Cerealis, under whom Agricola served as commander of the Twentieth Legion, had overrun much of Yorkshire and Lancashire in his campaign against the Brigantes and reached Carlisle (Roman Luguvallium). Recent excavations suggest that he then dispatched strong reconnaissance forces into the territory of the Novantae in the south-west of Scotland. Cerealis was recalled to Rome in early 74 and whatever intentions he had for Scotland did not concern his successor, Sextus Julius Frontinus. If we are to accept the brief account of his governorship in Tacitus' biography, Sextus Julius Frontinus concentrated on the reduction of the Silures in south-west Wales. He certainly did more than Tacitus suggests against the Orovices, but he did not move towards Scotland.

Agricola was not content with reconnaissance into Scotland as Cerealis had been; he was determined on conquest during his period as governor (78–85). In his first campaign, in 80, he advanced through the territories of the Selgovae, of the middle and upper Tweed, and the Votadini who inhabited the area from Northumberland to the Forth, with two columns as far as the line of the Forth. He even sent a detachment to the Tay. The next year, back at the Forth–Clyde isthmus, he laid roads and built forts. It was no more than a temporary defensive frontier to hold the tribes of the Caledonian confederacy to the north in check while Agricola turned his attention to the Novantae of the south-west in 82. To deal with them he crossed the Solway, catching them by surprise, and swept through Dumfriesshire, Galloway and the southern part of Ayrshire, erecting forts at Dalswinton, Glenlochar, and probably Gatehouse of Fleet. He must have been tempted to cross the Irish Sea but either on the orders of the emperor, Domitian, or because of continued resistance from the tribes of the south-west, he decided against it.

He was not yet done with Scotland, however. He had already employed his fleet in an exploration of the west coast and the islands, in the hope of discovering an easier and less dangerous route to the Highlands than that by land. In this he was disappointed, and when in 83 he marched north – his army supplied from the sea – he went along the eastern plain, his route traceable by the forts he had built at Ardoch, Strageath and Cardean. At Inchtuthil in Perthshire, seven miles from Dunkeld, he built a legionary fortress, a secure base for further advances. His intention was to bring the tribes of the northernmost part of Britain, which the Romans called Caledonia, to a pitched battle and to break

Cape Wrath
Duncansby Head
Butt of Lewis
OUTER HEBRIDES
Stornoway
HARRIS
The Minch
Moray Firth
AUCHINHOVE
Inverness
Mons Graupius
AD84
SKYE
CALEDONIAN TRIBES
Barra Rum
Eigg
STRACATHRO
Coll
Fort William
CARDEAN
Dundee
Tiree Mull
INCHTUTHIL
FENDOCH
BERTHA *Firth of Tay*
DALGINROSS
STRAGEATH
BOCHASTLE
ARDOCH
Firth of Forth
CAMELON
Edinburgh
JURA
ANTONINE WALL
CRAMOND
INVERESK
CASTLECARY
OXTON
Islay
CASTLEDYKES
EASTER HAPPREW
VOTADINI
NEWSTEAD
ARRAN LOUDON HILL
CAPPUCK
Ayr CRAWFORD
OAKWOOD
CHEW GREEN
Mull of
MILTON
RAEBUMFOOT
HIGH
Kintyre
ROCHESTER
NOVANTAE
SELGOVAE
BLAKEHOPE
BROOMHOLM
DALSWINTON BIRRENS
HADRIAN'S WALL
WARD LAW
SOUTH
GATEHOUSE
CORBRIDGE
SHIELDS
EBCHESTER
50 miles
KIRKBRIDE Carlisle
OLD CARLISLE OLD PENRITH
50 kms
Penrith
BRIGANTES

Legionary fortress
Large fort
Milliary or Ala fort
Normal fort
Fortlet
Marching camp
Occupation uncertain

The Romans in Scotland

their resistance. This he did to brilliant effect at a site still the subject of a debate, which Tacitus refers to as Mons Graupius – the earliest recorded battle in the history of Scotland. Tacitus' description provides us with one of the most enduring stereotypes of the inhabitants of Scotland: brave but undisciplined in warfare. According to Tacitus, one of the leaders of the Caledonians, a certain Calgacus, created another stereotype, this time of the Romans themselves; the Romans, Calgacus opined, were a people who 'create a desert and call it peace'. In the battle itself the Caledonian tribesmen acted in keeping with the Roman historian's view of them, abandoning the higher ground to rush at the enemy, only to be routed when Agricola loosed against them the four cavalry regiments, which he had held in reserve for just such an opportunity. It is recorded that 10,000 of the Caledonians died for the loss of no more than 360 Roman soldiers.

Agricola had cowed Scotland in a series of memorable campaigns culminating with Mons Graupius. The battle was, however, fought late in the season and Agricola could not follow it up. His fleet was sent to sail round the north of Britain to prove that it was indeed an island, and while engaged on this enterprise the Romans explored the Orkneys and received their submission. Agricola himself returned south, to be recalled to Rome in 85 by Domitian. The legionary fortress which he had built at Inchtuthil was abandoned and with it any realistic hope of a permanent occupation of Scotland. It was the first in a series of withdrawals from Scotland which extended over three centuries as the Romans sought the means to hold the country, without, as they had done in England, garrisoning it.

The Building of the Walls

After Agricola's departure to Rome for a triumph which Domitian, jealous of Agricola's achievements if we are to believe Tacitus, had arranged for him, the Romans maintained a presence in Scotland with the line of the Forth and Clyde as the frontier. Below this line there was much reconstruction of forts, with Dalswinton in the west and Newstead in the east the key positions. By 100 they had, however, effectively abandoned their original plan. Their inclination, as always, was to mark their boundaries and this they did with the building of Hadrian's Wall between 122 and 128. Hadrian, who succeeded Trajan as emperor in 117, arrived in Britain in 121 for a detailed tour of inspection. Having decided upon his policy he appointed Antonius Platorius Nepos as governor in the next year with instructions to carry it out. The wall, 73 miles (122 kilometres) in length, stretching from Bowness on the Solway to Wallsend on the Tyne, and made of stone and turf, had 16 larger forts with smaller forts or 'milecastles' every thousand paces. It was a remarkable construction, much of it visible today, attracting understandable attention from the historian and archaeologist and admiration from the tourist. However, the decision to build it in the first place was essentially an admission of the ambivalent attitude of the Romans to the problem of Scotland. Unable to impose their authority permanently on the country, they seemed unwilling to leave it alone, despite the threat from its tribes. Hadrian's Wall, a symbol of an empire to which Scotland could never be made to conform, was intended to bar

Emperor Hadrian

Slab commemorating the construction of the Antonine Wall

the Scottish tribes from Roman Britain and to permit the Romans to undertake from its shelter those periodic descents upon Scotland which they could not resist. Inevitably in the case of the former it ultimately failed, as we can now appreciate, but not before the latter had been attempted under various emperors.

Within less than 20 years of the start of the wall and within a few months of the death of the inspiration behind it, Hadrian's successor as emperor, Antoninus Pius, had instructed the governor of Britain, Quintus Lollius Urbicus, to push the Roman frontier back into Scotland. This Urbicus did and himself built a wall, at the narrowest part of Scotland, between Bridgeness on the Forth and Old Kilpatrick on the Clyde, a distance of 37 miles (60 kilometres). The Antonine Wall, made of turf and about 9 feet in height (3 metres), was evidence of a new Roman determination to bring Scotland, or at least the Lowlands into the empire. It proved impossible to maintain the fiction of Roman occupation. The wall, completed in about 144, was overrun by the tribes of the Maeatae and the Caledonii at least twice during the next 40 years and retaken by the Romans on each occasion. Realism, lack of manpower, and strategic demands combined to force the Romans to withdraw again from Scotland before the end of the second century. So weak had their authority become, even in the north of England, that elements of the Scottish tribes had penetrated beyond Hadrian's Wall to join with the Brigantes in the sack of York in 197.

In the Emperor Septimius Severus the Romans found, briefly, a second Agricola. Under him the restoration of Hadrian's Wall was put in hand as a prelude to his own visit to Britain. He arrived in 208 at the suggestion of the governor, Senecio. Severus, resolved to subdue those Scottish tribes, the Maeatae of Strathearn and the Caledonii of the Central Highlands, who had allied themselves with the Brigantes in the rising of 197, imported experienced troops from the continent. From a base at Cramond, Severus' army, either under his own leadership or that of his son Caracalla when Severus himself was ill in 210, reached as far as the north-east. Both the Maeatae and the Caledonii were defeated but Severus knew that he had not accomplished his purpose. He was preparing another expedition to Scotland when he died at York in 211, a fortunate event for the tribes against whom it was to be directed. Severus was ambitious enough to envisage the reoccupation of at least some of the country and had demonstrated that he was competent enough to succeed. As it was, he had left Hadrian's Wall once again secure and Scotland itself, with its tribes still recovering after Severus' death, enjoying a period of peace and some prosperity. The growing number of village settlements in the south-east of the country in the century after his death testified to this. Scotland, then, was free of the Romans with the exception of those outpost forts which were maintained with difficulty immediately to the north of Hadrian's Wall. They can have presented no serious obstacle to the tribes of Scotland. These tribes were about to exact their revenge on the Romans, breaching or outflanking the great wall which had been erected to pen them inside their own country.

The Enemies of the Romans

The year 297 is of considerable significance in the history of the relationship of Scotland with Rome since it brings the earliest written mention of the Picts. In collusion with the Scots, the Picts now profited from the opportunity given them by the decision of Allectus, the pretender to supreme power, to evacuate the garrison of Hadrian's Wall in order to employ them in his struggle with Constantius. The name of the Picts was to recur with alarming frequency in Roman records. Allectus failed in his enterprise against Constantius and, after his defeat and death near Silchester in 296, Constantius emulated Severus with an expedition into Scotland, punishing the Picts as his predecessor had punished the Maeatae and the Caledonii. Neither Constantius, who died at York in 306, nor any of his successors, including his celebrated son, Constantine, could indefinitely stem the attacks which were besetting the empire from a number of directions. The province of Britain, the outermost limit of the empire in the west, could not hope to escape the trend of events. The periodic references to the restoration and rebuilding of the wall, for example, under Constantius in 305 when it was said admiringly that he had 'restored the position', and under Count Theodosius in 370 as part of the military and political reorganisation of Britain, are a measure of the damage done to it by raiders from Scotland. The Romans were forced too often to react to events; their ability to determine them was being undermined by pressure from the north. While the wall was garrisoned, it was possible to resist that pressure, but when it was evacuated by claimants to the imperial throne, like Allectus and later, in 383, Maximus, it ceased to deter the Picts whose raids exceeded in ferocity those of the other tribes.

In 367 the inconceivable (from the Roman point of view) happened when a Conspiratio Barbarica – an alliance of the tribes occurred. The Picts again breached the wall; the Scots, still pirates based in Ireland, were assaulting the west coast, as were the Attacotti, a tribe of uncertain origin but possibly from Ireland or the Western Isles of Scotland; and further south, there were landings by the Saxons on the east coast of England, the Litus Saxonicus, heavily populated but vulnerable from the sea. In such circumstances the end of the Roman province of Britain could not be long delayed. The Romans counterattacked with great effect in 370 and 392. They used their west coast fleet from its bases in Wales and Lancashire to intercept attackers from Ireland, and sought to turn the tribes of Lowland Scotland into allies against the more savage ones from the north. Such tactics were no more than a temporary expedient; the Romans could only postpone what was now inevitable. In 410 the separation of the province of Britain from Rome came about.

THE END OF ROMAN OCCUPATION

We can see now that the Romans could never conquer Scotland and make it part of the province of Britain. It is a measure of their failure in Scotland that it is so bare of the signs of their influence. In England they left a civil government which survived their departure as well as towns and villas. None of this they bequeathed to Scotland. If they produced in the tribes of Lowland Scotland a desire to participate in their culture, there is a lack of evidence to prove it. Their language, like their culture, so important in England as in mainland Europe, found no home in Scotland. Forts, roads and defensive structures are the mark of a military and impermanent solution to the intractable problem of Scotland. The Romans were defeated by the climate, the terrain, the financial demands on their resources, without a guarantee of an adequate return, and continuing hostility of the native population; the struggle for power in Rome itself had resulted in instability and lack of continuity in policy in Scotland. The future of Scotland was being decided without them.

CHAPTER TWO

A Land of Kingdoms and Christianity, 400–900

The Peoples of Scotland

Well before the unwelcome arrival of a letter from the Emperor Honorius to the anxious citizens of the province of Britain acknowledging the hopeless reality of their situation, Scotland, in common with the rest of Europe, was already witnessing the disintegration of the Roman Empire in the west. The emperor advised his subjects in Britain to look to their own defences and thus prepared them for their eventual separation from Rome. A new order was being created. Raid and invasion led to settlement and colonisation through the rise of individual nations and kingdoms which some centuries in the future would unify into a single kingdom, that of Scotland. The name was derived not from any tribe indigenous to the country but from one of Irish extraction. The Romans, in their references to the various groupings which made up the population of Scotland, had described them by tribal names. Among them were the Novantae, Selgovae, Votadini and Caledonii (their title originating from the part of the country north of the Antonine Wall), names which today are known to relatively few. When however, the great Northumbrian scholar and historian, Bede, invariably thought of as 'the Venerable' since his death in 735, was at work on his most famous book, *The Ecclesiastical History of the English People*, which he brought to a close in 731, he did not write about tribes. He referred to four distinct peoples whom he called Picts, Scots, Angles, and Britons. Bede, upon whose writings later historians drew extensively, was identifying the inhabitants of Scotland in a manner recognisable to us. The history of

Scotland in Bede's time and for some 400 years before was the history of these four peoples. From their continuing interaction and with the addition from the eighth century onwards of a fifth factor, from Scandinavia, came the kingdom of Scotland.

THE PICTS

As we have already seen, the first appearance of the Picts in recorded history was in the year 297, in the reign of Emperor Diocletian, when the writer Eumenius mentioned a raid beyond Hadrian's Wall by Picts and Scots. Whether the two had previously acted in concert against the Romans is unknown. However, it is unlikely that 297 was indeed the earliest occasion on which the Picts had struck at the Romans, in whose demonology their place was henceforth assured. Of the four peoples of Scotland we know least of the Picts, despite their undoubted contribution to its history. This is in part the consequence of a natural reliance on Roman sources for information, since they do not always clearly distinguish between individual units within a larger group. It was their practice to apply the name of the largest tribe to others with a separate identity. This was the case, for example, with the Caledonii; the primacy accorded to them by the Romans, it may be argued, is undeserved when they are compared to the Picts. It is thus unclear whether the 'Painted Men' of Eumenius, much given to personal adornment with jewellery and tattooing, were by then a distinct entity or one of a loose collection or confederacy of tribes of the type which had faced Agricola at Mons Graupius. Even the readiness with which we call them 'Painted Men' may come from a misconception. The word 'Picti' may be rather an equivalent of the Celtic word 'Priteni', used to describe the inhabitants of Britain in the fourth century BC and later, under the influence of Latin, changing to 'Britanni'. Nor can we pronounce with confidence on when the Picts came to Scotland, although it is possible that their arrival may have preceded that of the earliest Celtic immigrants.

PICTISH CULTURE

No reconstruction of their language can be attempted, since no Pictish literature has been passed down to us. We do not know what they called themselves; in this sense the term 'Picts' may cover several racial and cultural groups. Their sculptured stones, on sites which underline the importance to them of areas like the Tay valley, Moray and Fife, portray animals both wild and domesticated: the bull of the Aberdeen Angus strain, the wolf, the Celtic horse, the deer and the eagle among them. They also show weapons, armour and costume, tools such as the hammer and pincers, individual figures of hunters and soldiers and mythological, sometimes disturbing creatures like the dog-headed and spiral-tailed dragon, and Christian crosses with elaborate designs. That these Pictish stones represent a remarkable achievement, unequalled among the other peoples of Scotland at the time, is undisputed; the symbols which decorate them convey messages which intrigue and baffle scholars.

The two original Pictish kingdoms of the 'northern' and 'southern' Picts were united in a single, extensive kingdom by the late sixth or early seventh century. It covered Scotland north of the Forth–Clyde line, excluding Argyll, but including the Orkneys, where some of the most impressive stones have been found, and, perhaps, the Shetlands. At that time the Picts had not lost the warlike attributes of their ancestors from Roman times. In the seventh century the main threat to the territory of the Picts came from the Angles of Northumbria who, having defeated the Scots in 603, moved northwards and over the Forth. Here the Angles were able to impose a settlement on the southern half of the Pictish kingdom. In 685, however, at Nechtansmere, generally identified as Dunnichen south-east of Forfar in Angus, they were crushed by the Picts under Brude, son of the Pictish king, Bile, and their king, Egfrith, was slain. This catastrophe was revealed, we are told, in a vision granted to the Northumbrian saint, Cuthbert, then on a visit to Carlisle. So heavy were the losses inflicted by the Picts that the Angles were forced to call a halt to their expansion into Pictland and the southern boundary of the kingdom of the Picts was re-established on its previous line. Freed from the threat posed by the Angles, the Picts were able to resume their interrupted struggle with the Scots of the kingdom of Dalriada, their former allies against the Romans. It has been suggested that Dalriada was created when the Scots, at the instigation of the Britons of Strathclyde who sought a barrier against the Picts, took Argyll from the latter. If this was so, it would help to explain the intense rivalry between Picts and Scots. This situation would also confirm the strength of the Pictish

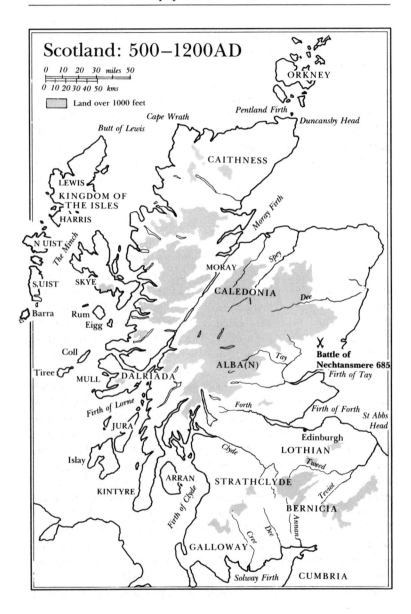

Scotland: 500–1200AD

0   10   20   30   *miles* 50

0 10 20 30 40 50 *kms*

Land over 1000 feet

ORKNEY

Pentland Firth   Duncansby Head

Cape Wrath

Butt of Lewis

CAITHNESS

LEWIS

KINGDOM OF
THE ISLES

HARRIS

Moray Firth

N UIST

The Minch

Spey

MORAY

S.UIST   SKYE

CALEDONIA

Dee

Barra   Rum

Eigg

Coll

Tay   **Battle of
Nechtansmere 685**

Tiree

MULL   DALRIADA

ALBA(N)   *Firth of Tay*

Firth of Lorne

Forth   *Firth of Forth*   St Abbs
Head

JURA

Edinburgh

Islay   *Clyde*   LOTHIAN

Tweed

ARRAN

Teviot

KINTYRE   STRATHCLYDE

Firth of Clyde   BERNICIA

Cree   *Dee*   *Annan*

GALLOWAY

Solway Firth   CUMBRIA

kingdom since the Scots and the Britons were not natural allies. After Nechtansmere, the Picts appear to have been in their ascendancy. In the middle of the eighth century, their king, Oengus or Angus, was recognised as their overlord by the Scots of Dalriada. The reign of Oengus (731–761) saw the Pictish kingdom at perhaps its peak of authority. Oengus defeated the Britons of Strathclyde in 756 and, an indication of his realistic approach to politics, did so in alliance with the Angles of Northumbria. Under the successors of Angus, shadowy figures not all of whose names are known to us, the Picts maintained their superiority over the Scots until the ninth century when with the accession of Kenneth MacAlpin as king of the Scots the position was brutally and permanently reversed.

THE SCOTS

We read in the Roman accounts that before the end of the fourth century, when the Twentieth Legion had been withdrawn from Chester and the fort of Caernarvon had been evacuated, Scots from Ireland were taking advantage of the situation to settle in Wales. They settled in Pembrokeshire, the Gower peninsula, and in the Lleyn peninsula of Caernarvonshire. It is reasonable to suppose that the rest of their compatriots were descending on Scotland with like purpose at the same time, although it cannot be said that such arrivals were in accordance with a general plan. The settlements in Wales did not remain independent but in Scotland, albeit almost a hundred years later, there was a powerful Scottish presence in Argyll, the kingdom of Dalriada. The Scots of Argyll, Gaelic speaking, took the name of their kingdom from their homeland in Antrim in Northern Ireland. In 500 the connection with Ireland was strong; Domangart, son of Fergus, son of Erc, king of the Scots of Irish Dalriada was also king of the Scots of Argyll. The tradition of the link with Fergus, son of Erc, and the value of a close relationship with Ireland were important to the Scots of Dalriada as they strove to hold on to their territory on the west coast of Scotland. As late as the ninth century they were able to call on the aid of the Irish in their wars with the Picts, although the two kingdoms had long been distinguished as Irish and Scottish Dalriada.

The Scots of Dalriada, ambitious and aggressive, added much of

Galloway to Argyll and the Western Isles, including Iona – the importance of which as a centre of Christianity was becoming evident under St Columba – before turning their attention to the east of Scotland under their king, Aedan MacGabran, who ruled from about 574 to 608. They may have been motivated by the need to provide for a growing population as well as by the desire for territorial aggrandisement but, once committed to a thrust to the east and over the Forth, they could not avoid conflict with the Picts and the Angles of Northumbria. Initial successes were followed by defeat at the hands of both the Picts and the Angles. The territory gained was quickly lost and the political importance of the Scots now diminished. Their advance across the central belt of Scotland and north-eastwards had, however, produced an interesting situation. As their influence in political and military terms waned, their language and culture, crucial factors in their eventual supplanting of the Picts, gained ground. The defeat of the Picts by the Scots in the ninth century came about so abruptly that it is difficult to comprehend.

The Picts, inhabitants of an extensive kingdom for centuries, lost it in circumstances which suggest an intrinsic weakness, hidden because of the greater weaknesses of the other kingdoms of Scotland in the period between the mid seventh and early ninth centuries. The defeat of the Picts was more than a military one. One cause of instability, it has been stated, lay in their complicated system of succession which allowed descent matrilineally, resulting in numbers of potential claimants. One who appears to have been able to use the system to his advantage was Kenneth MacAlpin. By the time of his accession as king of the Scots, in 843, the Picts were in some difficulty from external forces. They had already suffered extensively from irruptions from Scandinavia and a serious defeat at the hands of the Danes in 839. It is likely the Scots had called up reinforcements from Ireland as early as 836, thus tipping the balance further in their favour. Kenneth MacAlpin's claim to the kingship of the Picts, whether or not it was superior to that of the other potential claimants, bestowed an element of legitimacy on his determination to rule the Picts as well as the Scots. In a similar way, his predecessor of the seventh century Aedan had enjoyed the blessing of Columba in his expansionist policy. Kenneth MacAlpin was ruthless in

Kenneth MacAlpin

his methods; a story of his luring some of the Pictish chiefs to a banquet only to slaughter them perhaps reflects with some accuracy his reputation among contemporaries. The Picts had been subdued by about 847 and he united them with the Scots in the new kingdom of Alba, once the name given by the Romans to that land north of Hadrian's Wall which they had failed to bring under their control. Alba was now the name given to Scotland north of the Forth over which Kenneth MacAlpin ruled from his capital at Scone until his death in 858 when he was succeeded by his brother, Donald.

THE ANGLES

The Angles came to the province of Britain from their homeland in Europe, identified by Bede as 'Angelen' and corresponding with modern Angeln at the base of the Schleswig–Jutland peninsula. Unlike the Picts and Scots they came not as enemies of the Romans, but at their invitation. The use of foederati or federates, that is, allies from barbarian tribes introduced into the empire to defend its frontiers in return for subsidies and grants of land, was tried as a matter of expediency in the third century. It was now developed from an expedient into a practice and the Angles were imported into England in the course of the next century.

At some stage in the fifth century, impossible to date, the relationship between the Angles and the post-Roman government of the province changed into the more familiar one of invasion and settlement. Two other tribes, the Saxons who came from the area between the rivers Weser and Elbe, and the Jutes whose territory was in the northern part of the Schleswig–Jutland peninsula, were also involved. The progress of the Angles northwards through eastern England and thus in the direction of Scotland was slow. The resistance of the native British population was considerable and it is even possible that it reached such a peak that about the year 530 some of the invaders fled back to their German homelands. In 547, however, under their king, Ida the Flamebearer, they captured the British fortress of Dinguardi, now Bamburgh, which became the capital of their kingdom of Bernicia. This was to be the springboard for further expansion westwards into the land of the Britons and northwards into the Lowlands of Scotland. What Ida had begun, Ethelfrith, who became king near the end of the century, continued but to greater effect. His victory over the Scots in 603 was an event of such consequence that, according to Bede, from that time until 731, when Bede completed the *Ecclesiastical History*, 'no king of the Scots (has) dared to come against the English in battle'.

At Degsastan, probably Dawston in Liddlesdale, the king of the Scots, Aedan MacGarban, lost almost the whole of his army. Among the many dead at Degsastan was his son, Domangart lost like this brothers, Artuir and Echoid Find, who had died in battle against the southern Picts. Aedan, it should be noted, had been so disturbed by the advance of the Angles into the south-west of Scotland that he and his army undertook what was a remarkable march for that time, of some 120 miles. They marched from Aedan's capital at the fortress of Dunadd or Dunatt which was situated on the Crinan isthmus of the Kintyre peninsula, in a disastrous attempt to halt the advance. This march was surpassed, however, in 616 by Ethelfrith who having defeated Aedan, led his army across England from his capital at Bamburgh to Chester (approximately 175 miles) to inflict a severe beating on the Britons of north Wales. This was perhaps part of a general strategy to drive a wedge between them and their natural allies, the Britons of the kingdom of Rheged and Strathclyde. Ethelfrith was killed not long after Chester, a victim of an internal struggle for the kingship of Northumbria. Although this event was one in a series of similar political upheavals which would, in the long run, seriously weaken Northumbria, it did not impede the momentum of the Angles' expansion into Scotland. The British kingdom of Strathclyde was deprived of that part of its territory which stretched deep into England; at some unknown date in the seventh century the land between the Solway and the Mersey passed under the dominion of the Angles. At the same time as they were exercising their lordship over the Britons to the west, the Angles, under Ethelfrith's immediate successors, Edwin, Oswald, and Oswy, had strengthened their hold on the Lothians of Scotland. Nechtansmere put an end to their ambitions north of the Forth; their losses there meant, as Bede would later put it, that the kingdom of the Angles of Northumbria had 'narrower bounds'. But if their kingdom was indeed more limited in territory than it had been before Nechtansmere, the influence of the Angles on Scotland would persist in one remarkable way long after their grip on the southern part of the country had slackened.

The eighth century saw a diminution of the authority of Northumbria. The kingdom was not only torn with internal strife of the kind which had brought about the death of Ethelfrith, but it was beset by raids from Scandinavia. The language of the Angles, however, had become so entrenched in Scotland that it was able to survive these and other events and to emerge as a potent force in the continuing history of Scotland. Its fate was in complete contrast to that of the other languages of Scotland. Pictish, established in Scotland for centuries before the introduction of English, may well have been in decline before the accession of Kenneth MacAlpin altered the political complexion of the Pictish kingdom, and would eventually disappear. The other languages of Scotland, of Celtic origin, would likewise know a decline and, in recovering, would become the tools of minorities. The language of the Angles, Germanic in origin and a relative newcomer to Scotland, gained and maintained the primacy which it has not subsequently lost.

THE BRITONS

Of the four peoples of whom Bede wrote in his *Ecclesiastical History of the English People*, it was perhaps the Britons who were most radically affected by developments in the period between the Roman departure from Britain to 731, the year in which Bede closed his account. Their culture and language suffered an almost total extinction in the east of Britain, from the south-east of England to the Forth in Scotland. Not even the often unquestionably heroic resistance associated with the name of Arthur, the ubiquitous commander or even king, could prevent that catastrophe. The pressure from Angles, Saxons and Jutes was not to be denied, dislodging the Britons and forcing them into retreat where it did not exterminate them. The vigorous language of these Germanic invaders put down its roots in the areas of political change and settlement. The Britons, gradually withdrawing into Cornwall, Wales, the north-west of England and the west of Scotland south of the Clyde, had quickly divided the land into a number of kingdoms, the boundaries of which varied according to circumstances. Even that line of British resistance was to be broken on occasion, most notably by the Battle of Chester in 616 to which reference has been made. Ethelfrith's decision to march to Chester may have been an answer, long delayed, to the Battle of Ardderyd, thought to be Arthuret, eight miles to the north of Carlisle. Here, in 573, the Britons of the kingdom of Rheged, under the leadership of Rederich, fought for their religion and their own survival. Victorious, Rederich joined Rheged, its capital probably in Luguvallium or Carlisle, with the kingdom of the Britons of south-west Scotland, to form Strathclyde. Its new capital was at Alcluith or Dun Breatann, the fort of the Britons, modern Dumbarton. It was in Ethelfrith's interests to sever the connection of this kingdom of Strathclyde with the Britons of Wales and this he succeeded in doing.

The kingdom of Strathclyde in its form under Rederich did not in any case survive. Ethelfrith's successors brought the English part, that is Cumbria, under their control. Scottish Strathclyde, roughly the shires of

Ayr, Dumbarton, Lanark, Renfrew and Stirling was to enjoy a lengthier and somewhat more distinguished if no less turbulent history. Its independence was often challenged, by the Picts, the Angles of Northumbria, and by raiders from Scandinavia. Under such attacks it could play only a subordinate role in events, although it was not entirely without some impact. A short resurgence of the power of the Britons, coinciding with the decline of Northumbria, allowed the Britons of Cumbria to unite with their kinsmen in Scotland. A similar episode occurred in the tenth century but was brought to a conclusion at the Battle of Brunanburgh, a site somewhere in the north of England. The lands of the Britons of Strathclyde had been devastated by Athelstan, king of Wessex and Mercia and acknowledged as king of all the English between 926 and 939. Therefore the Britons entered into an unlikely alliance with Olaf, king of the Vikings of Dublin, who sought to reclaim from Athelstan the kingdom of York, as well as with the Picts and the Scots whose lands had also been ravaged by Athelstan. Unfortunately they suffered defeat at Brunanburgh. Eight years later, Strathclyde, once again devastated by a king of the English, this time Edmund, Athelstan's half-brother, was handed over by him to Malcolm I, king of the Scots and the descendant of Kenneth MacAlpin.

Christianity in Scotland

Edward Gibbon, in *The Decline and Fall of the Roman Empire*, advanced five causes of the growth of Christianity in the Roman Empire. These were: the zeal of the early Christians; the doctrine of a future life; the miraculous powers ascribed to the early church; the purity and austerity of the morals of the early Christians; the union and discipline of the Christian Church. Which of these five causes might have had the greatest effect in bringing about the conversion of Scotland to Christianity must be a matter of opinion. No doubt each of them had its part, its relative importance decided by the perceptions of those to whom the new religion came in a number of guises and from a number of sources. The triumph of Christianity had been achieved in the Roman Empire at a time when it was already well into the process of disintegration. This was not, of course, universally recognised and the final victory of Christianity over its many rivals was far in the future. So likewise did Christianity come to a Scotland which was passing through a prolonged state of change and disturbance, much of it violent. The adoption of Christianity as the religion of the Roman Empire by the emperor, Constantine, was a significant factor in its success.

In Scotland there was no such single authority as an emperor and therefore no single figure capable of imposing Christianity on the country and its peoples. It is true, nonetheless, that in Scotland, in some instances, the success of Christianity was closely linked to its identification with the ruling power. Thus, Columba owed his acquisition of Iona to the king of the Picts, Brude son of Maelchon, his patron and admirer. Subsequently, Columba brought his authority to bear on the choice of a king of the Scots, selecting Aedan MacGarban who met with defeat at the hands of the Angles at Degsastan in 603. The zeal of the early Christians to which Gibbon draws our attention was not absent in those who proselytised for their faith in Scotland. Without it, and without their accompanying courage, those Christians, for example, who left Ireland to minister in an unknown, possibly hostile Scotland could not have survived. It is unknown whether Christianity came to Scotland first from Ireland, so often the origin of developments. It may equally have come from England, over Hadrian's Wall, with soldiers sent to defend the wall or to man an outpost fort. Carlisle, with its long Christian tradition, probably had its own bishop in Roman times but there is no way of establishing whether his zeal was of a kind to take him beyond the wall to what he would consider barbarian and dangerous territory. Trading with the Continent offers a third possibility, no more certain than any other. Our ignorance of how Christianity first reached Scotland extends to that period. All that can be said is that the arrival and spread of Christianity in Scotland was the world of many men, only a few of whose names have come down to us. It is these few who appear from the shadows as the founders of Christianity in Scotland.

NINIAN

From Bede we learn of Ninian whom he recalls as 'a most reverend bishop' who had received his training at Rome. Ninian worked in the early fifth century among the southern Picts, that is, as Bede again leads

St Ninian

us to believe, those who lived below the Grampians. Ninian is unlikely to have been content to minister only to the Picts and at some stage he came to Galloway, where he founded the monastery of Whithorn, 'Candida Casa', in or about the year 397. His reputation was considerable in the north of England as well as in the south-west of Scotland but his ministry among the Picts may not have been as successful as has been supposed. In Fife, where he preached, the inhabitants reverted to paganism and had to be converted back to Christianity at a later date. It is perhaps because he is the earliest Christian missionary of whom we have any real knowledge, however slight, that his reputation remains unassailable.

KENTIGERN

Like Ninian, who was born in Cumberland, Kentigern or Mungo, the patron saint of Glasgow, has a connection with that part of England.

According to a biography written in 1185 by one Jocelyn, a monk of Furness, Kentigern was forced to flee from Glasgow because he was being persecuted by the enemies of Christ. Kentigern moved south, intending to seek refuge among the Britons of Wales, his co-religionists, but spent some time in Cumberland converting many to his faith. That achieved, he left the district. While he was away, the Battle of Arthuret took place, the sword completing what the Bible had begun. The king of Rheged, Rederich, sent for Kentigern who took his place in the new kingdom of Strathclyde which was being created. Kentigern did not return to Glasgow for some time after his recall by Rederich. Instead, he established his see in Dumfriesshire, at Hodelm or Hoddom. Once back in Glasgow, he was responsible for a see which may have stretched from there as far as Westmorland. A tradition, recounted in another twelfth-century life of Kentigern, suggests that he met with Columba but evidence to confirm this is lacking. Kentigern, whose name means 'hound-lord', as his other name Mungo, means 'hound', is said to have lived to an advanced age. If we accept his connection with the Battle of Arthuret, fought in 573, his return to Glasgow and the start of his long tenure as bishop must have occurred about 580.

COLUMBA

Our information about Ninian is unsatisfactory and while we know more about Kentigern and his work in Glasgow, 'the green hollow' beside the Clyde, it is not until we come to Columba that we can speak with any confidence about the progress of Christianity in Scotland. Our knowledge of Columba derives from a life of the saint written by a successor as abbot of Iona, Adamnan, who died about 704. Adamnan had access to oral tradition about his illustrious predecessor as well as to an earlier biography of him. If we ignore the element of miracle and legend, found in all comparable works, we can hope to obtain a fuller picture than that available about Ninian and Kentigern.

Columba was of Irish extraction and his Gaelic name was Calumcille, 'dove of the church'. He left Ireland in or about 563 after a quarrel with King Diarmait. In the aftermath of the quarrel there occurred a great battle, at Cuildremne, at which there was much slaughter. After the battle, Columba with twelve companions crossed to Iona and, on land granted by Brude, King of the Picts, built a monastery, the most celebrated in Celtic Christianity. Columba was an inspirational figure, who travelled widely in Scotland and also back to Ireland. He appears to have seen the importance to his religion of political factors and his journey to Ireland may have had political overtones as did his intervention in the choice of a king of the Scots. Much of his success in Scotland and elsewhere was the result of his belief that the monks of Iona must go out into the world and live among the people. From his monastery on Iona he was able to influence other monasteries on the mainland, in Dalriada and in the Pictish kingdoms. His prestige depended, in part, just as much upon the miracles with which he was credited as upon his undoubted learning. After the death of Columba in 597, monks from Iona continued his work. They were particularly active in Northumbria to which they were invited by King Oswald, in 634. There they founded the monastery of Lindisfarne where Aidan was consecrated bishop and from which he built up the strength of the Celtic church in Oswald's kingdom. Twenty years after Aidan's death, an even more remarkable figure, Cuthbert, was in charge of Lindisfarne, symbolising the traditions of the Celtic church which had by that time come into conflict with the traditions of Rome. It is possible now to see that the cult of Columba, for such it was, obscured the work of many of his contemporaries, such as another Irishman, Moluag, and that of later missionaries, again from Ireland, with names like Maelrubha, Corindu, and Itharnan. These men and others who, like Columba, came to Scotland from Ireland were all part of the connection with Ireland – the crucial factor in the coming of Christianity to Scotland.

The Celtic Church and Rome

The mission of the monks of Iona under Aidan was at first encouraged by Oswald's successor as king of Northumbria, his brother, Oswy. Oswy shared Oswald's fondness for Iona for the two had spent time there while exiled from Northumbria. It was during Oswy's reign, however, that the primacy of the Celtic Church in Northumbria came to an end and the church of Rome began to force it into retreat. Oswy was aware that in Northumbria there were differences among the clergy as to their devotion either to Rome or to the Celtic Church, and he also discovered that his own wife favoured the traditions of Rome. Therefore, he sought the advice of the clergy. At the Synod of Whitby, in 664, the case for the Celtic Church was argued by Colman of Lindisfarne, that for Rome by Wilfrid, bishop of Ripon. The basis of their disagreement was the calculation of the date of Easter; in its adherence to an old system Iona was running counter to the thinking of the rest of the Christian Church. Even in the community of Iona itself there was division on the issue. In the end it was Wilfrid who was able to convince Oswy of the soundness of his reasoning. The Northumbrian Church as a whole now accepted the usages of Rome. Colman, recognising the inevitable, left Lindisfarne for Iona. Even Cuthbert, late in his life, saw the need for unity within the Church. That could only be achieved through Rome and the refusal of Iona to conform created some difficulty. In 717, Nechtan, king of the Picts, is said to have expelled the monks of Iona from his kingdom because of their stubborn defiance of Rome. But it was a last flurry of resistance; the supremacy of Rome was by then too obvious for Iona to ignore. In the previous year the monks had already agreed, persuaded by the arguments of the English monk, Egbert, to accept the Roman calculation for Easter.

Throughout this period there had been no break by the Celtic Church of Scotland from Rome, even on Iona. The advantages of acknowledging the authority in Rome were irresistible. Acceptance of Rome did not, however, mean unification with the Church in England; the two remained distinct.

CHAPTER THREE

Newcomers and Nationhood, 900–1286

The Fury of the Northmen

In the last decade of the eighth century the northern part of Britain from the kingdom of Northumbria, round the coast of Scotland to the Western Isles, began to be subjected to attack by raiders from Scandinavia. It is convenient and usual to refer to these warriors and pirates as 'Vikings', a term of which the origin has been lost. They came from Norway, Denmark, and Sweden, first to attack and then to settle. In Scotland, in the islands and in Caithness and Sutherland, it was the Norwegians who predominated; in the eastern half of England it was the Danes; and both Norwegians and Danes in Ireland from where raids and settlement infiltrated into the western half of Scotland and the north-west of England. The influence of the Swedish Vikings on Britain was relatively minor. In 793 the monastery of Lindisfarne was sacked by the Danes; two years later it was the turn of Iona. So frequent and destructive were these raids to become that the monks of both communities were driven to seek refuge elsewhere. The monks of Lindisfarne in 875, under Eardulf, carring with them the precious and powerful relics of Saint Cuthbert fled to Chester-le-Street and their brothers of Iona went to Kells in Ireland some time after 807.

Scotland, with its physical similarities to their homelands, had an obvious appeal for the Vikings but they were active in expansion over a much wider area in Europe and beyond. They were to be found in Russia, at Kiev and Novgorod, where they installed themselves as rulers, and at Bolgar on the middle Volga, to which they were attracted by opportunities for trading. In France they gave their name to Normandy, the home of their descendants who, in the eleventh century conquered England, and afterwards moved into Scotland. They had contacts with the Greeks of Byzantium and even with the Islamic world. In the ninth century the Norwegian kingdom of Dublin was set up. There were other Viking bases in Ireland at Wexford, Waterford, and Limerick. The Viking settlements in Ireland for some time maintained a strong link with those in England, for example the Five Boroughs of the Midlands, and the kingdom of York, to which access may have been possible through Scotland along the waterways of the Clyde and Forth. Iceland was colonised after 870, Greenland, where the settlements were to last for 500 years from the end of the tenth century, and even Newfoundland was reached – although there is no evidence of settlement there comparable to that in Greenland.

As had been the case with the Germanic tribes in an earlier period, the motives behind the Viking expansion were varied. The need to find land for a growing and demanding population weighed heavily with invasion followed by settlement, possibly as early as 800 in Britain. Simple rapacity placed its part as with other pirates. The remoteness of Iona, which had attracted monks and hermits, made it an easy target, while its accumulation of wealth proved irresistible. In their attacks on defenceless communities such as Iona the Vikings excelled in cruelty. One example is the martyrdom of Blathmac, an Irish priest of Iona who refused to reveal the whereabouts of the shrine of Saint Columba, although offered his life and was torn apart. It was with some reason that Strabo, the monk who related the story of Blathmac's end, described his murderers as 'the violent, cursed host'. There was a more mundane side to the Viking migrations; commerce drew them into markets with wanted goods obtainable only in northern Europe. The Vikings were as adventurous and enthusiastic in their search for these as in the pursuit of gold and silver in the monasteries of western Europe. Skins, furs, and walrus tusks were greatly prized.

Political change in Scandinavia also led to migration. This appears to have been most true in Norway. Here, the attempt by Harald Fairhair to bring all of that country under his control produced a reaction. After the Battle of Hafrsfjördr in 872 had confirmed his kingship over the whole of Norway, his opponents chose to go overseas rather than accept a situation they thought intolerable. These disenchanted chiefs, men accustomed to exercising their own form of authority, were now free from the restrictions Harald might place on them. Together with former supporters of Harald like Ketil Flat-Nose in the Hebrides they were largely responsible for the Viking colonisation of Scotland. Ketil who, it was said, knew Scotland well because he 'had plundered there widely', had been made governor in the Hebrides by Harald but, as a token of his break with the king, he ceased the payment of taxes to him and set himself up as lord of the Hebrides. In Orkney, Caithness, Ross, Sutherland and the Shetlands, men of like mind created independent fiefs. They were, in a sense, building on foundations laid by Harald; he had himself conquered the Hebrides after taking punitive action against the pirates of the Northern and Western Isles.

THE VIKING SETTLEMENTS IN SCOTLAND

In their raids on Scotland the Vikings had used the 'langskip' or longship, unique to them, and ideally suited to their purpose. It was sturdy enough to transport between 70 or 80 men over considerable distances on the open sea, and at the same time shallow enough to permit penetration along inland waterways, or to be carried over obstacles, if necessary deep into hostile territory. The raiders were thus often able to attack before their presence was known.

When, however, colonisation replaced raid, the longboat could not have been adequate for the movement of families, possessions, provisions, and fighting men in the sort of migration which took place after the Battle of Hafrsfjördr. For this the Vikings must have had recourse to a larger boat than the longboat, the 'hafskip' or 'knorr', of deeper draught and broader beam. The new generation of Vikings, intent on obtaining, by conquest, fertile land which they would then hold by force, were formidable. But with the passage of time, they were inevitably open to the influence of the other peoples of Scotland, in the cultural as well as the military sense. This interaction may have been more common than suggested by the traditional picture of the wholesale destruction or enslavement of the native population. There is no reason to suppose that the later Vikings to arrive in Scotland were any less warlike than their predecessors. To their enemies they were as violent and as cruel as before

A Viking dragonship prow

but their later history is one of assimilation and of a willingness to adopt customs and practices which benefited them.

VIKING CULTURE

The civilisation which the Vikings introduced into Scotland was an advanced one, with a love of poetry and the arts, a superior place in society allocated to women and a well-established legal system, among its characteristics. Once settled in Scotland, the Vikings led an existence based on trade and farming mixed with raiding and piracy. Their graves naturally reflect this combination of lifestyles: in those of the men, at once warriors and cultivators, swords, spears, and shields are unearthed alongside sickles and ploughshares; in those of their womenfolk, we find brooches and beads, shears, needle-cases, ladles and bowls, the possessions of those who made and kept the home. Animals might be killed and buried with their owners. If human sacrifice was practised as part of their rituals by the Vikings who came to Scotland, it is impossible to prove from the evidence available to date.

The Vikings were devotees of the Germanic gods: Odin or Wodan, the patron of warriors and chief of the gods; Thor, perhaps the son of Odin, strongest among the gods and the bearer of the hammer together with Tyr, Loki and Balder – all with a vision of an after-life in Valhalla to which the bravest of warriors who have died in battle are called. However, the Vikings have not left in their graves objects relating to their worship. Nor, surprisingly in the light of their long supremacy in parts of Scotland, is there a great legacy of Viking building, least of all in Orkney, the centre of their Atlantic traffic. The cathedral of St Magnus at Kirkwall, the work of Rognvald in the twelfth century, is of this period but not uniquely Viking. At Jarlshof on Shetland ruins of homes give some indication of the rectangular dwelling-house which replaced the oval or Celtic house throughout the Scottish countryside. It is the house rather than the religious or military construction which survives from the Viking settlement.

External Pressures and Beginnings of Nationhood

The arrival of the Vikings, the 'Black Gentiles' of Denmark and the 'White Gentiles' of Norway who so exercised the imagination of the chroniclers, was an occasion for Christian lamentation and heathen saga. It was the last in that long series of mass migrations of peoples. These were undisciplined and largely unco-ordinated but dynamic in their effect, which, between the third and tenth centuries, was a potent force in the history of Scotland and of Europe as a whole. There was, of course, no sudden and complete end to the Viking settlement of Scotland for those causes which had first prompted it did not disappear of themselves. Nor, did the influence of the Vikings on Scotland change abruptly and permanently from the positive one of direct action and intervention in the affairs of the country, to the more negative but equally important one of assimilation into and of those four peoples of whom Bede was writing in 731. Not even Christianity, which the Vikings, pragmatic in matters of religion as in other ways, adopted in the tenth century, could radically alter their nature in the immediate future – the worship of Thor and Odin, with all that it meant, did not cease. The ability of the Vikings to impose their authority and culture on Scotland was, in the long term, shown to be no greater than any of the four peoples.

It is doubtful if the Vikings were temperamentally capable of a strategy for the conquest of Scotland and its unification into a single kingdom. The opposition which such a venture would have aroused was matched by their own disinclination to accept the strictures on their freedom of action, which an attempt at conquest and an eventual unification would have entailed. Orkney, it was true, was a great power in the context of Scotland in the aftermath of Viking settlement. Earl Thorfinn, for example, the contemporary of Macbeth the king of Scots from 1040 to 1057, held, as well as Orkney itself, Shetland, the Hebrides, Caithness and Sutherland, geographically a vast area. No king of Scotland could afford to ignore him or what his earldom represented. Indeed, Thorfinn was the grandson of one such king, Malcolm II (1005–1034) whose daughter married Sigurd the Stout. When Thorfinn, called 'the Mighty', died in or about 1065, another king, Malcolm III 'Canmore', married as his first wife, Ingibjord, who was either the widow or daughter of Thorfinn, with fateful results for Scotland. Such alliances between kings of Scotland and the Vikings who threatened their territories place Orkney in its proper perspective in the history of Scotland. But the internal dissensions of the Vikings in Scotland and in the parent-kingdom of Norway, and the often troubled relationship between the two, militated against the possibility of an extension of Viking authority from its secure base in Orkney to the whole of Scotland. The unification of Scotland into that single kingdom of which the Vikings were incapable lay in the future, to be achieved through a number of forces and trends present in the country in the tenth century, of which the Viking element was only one. To them was about to be added, as the century wore on, the critical factor of England, itself striving to deal with the Vikings.

THE SUCCESSORS OF KENNETH MacALPIN

Under Kenneth MacAlpin and his successors, the kingdom of Alba survived the intensity of the Viking onslaught. The external threat was aggravated by the system of succession in Alba which, unintentionally, but inevitably, encouraged violent and frequent changes in kingship. Its advantage was that it generally produced kings who had reached their maturity, but this was nullified by the opportunity it offered to contenders, with a legitimate claim under the system, to seize the crown. Because of the genius of Shakespeare, Macbeth is remembered as the murderer of Duncan I, whose place he took as king. Yet Macbeth was himself killed by his successor, Malcolm III, and in the tenth century, both Constantine III and Kenneth III had been killed by their successors. Kenneth III removed Constantine III in 995 and was, in his turn, killed by Malcolm II after a reign of eight years. Power had frequently been transferred between the death of Kenneth MacAlpin in 858 from, it is thought, a tumour, to 1034 when Duncan I became king, only to be murdered by Macbeth at a place not yet identified with certainty. Despite this tendency and the unremitting attacks of the Vikings on Dalriada, the homeland of the Scots, Alba survived. It gave Scotland a dynasty which ruled in the male line until 1034 and from which the present queen is descended in the female line.

The reign of Constantine II, sixth in line of succession from Kenneth MacAlpin, was an exception to the prevailing pattern by its remarkable length, 43 years. His own father, Aed, had ruled for only a year. We know more of Constantine than of Kenneth MacAlpin but he is, despite the stabilising effect his reign had on Alba, a somewhat shadowy figure. Such knowledge as we have of him makes the length of his reign a source of some wonder, for although he was undoubtedly an energetic and imaginative monarch, his miscalculations suggest incompetence. Yet he was able not only to retain his position for 43 years but to retire, by his own choice, to a monastery having ensured the integrity of his kingdom. The main Viking threat to Alba came, as before, from the kingdom of Dublin. Constantine was able to do little more than contain it but that was in itself no mean achievement. For Constantine, however, it was not enough to see to the defence of his kingdom. He undertook a southwards expansion which was at first successful, bringing Strathclyde under his dominion and making himself the first king of Alba known to have exercised authority south of the Forth–Clyde line. He was not satisfied

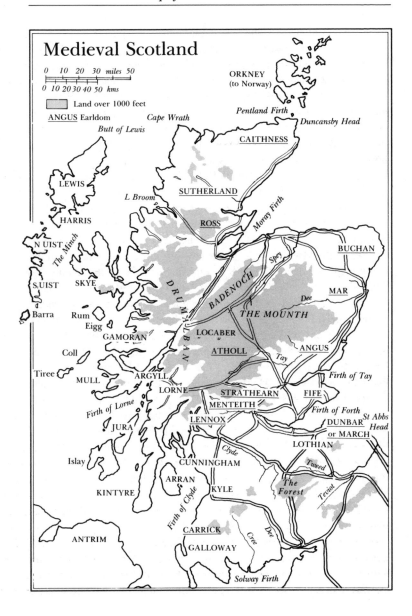

Medieval Scotland

0 10 20 30 miles 50

0 10 20 30 40 50 kms

Land over 1000 feet

ANGUS Earldom

ORKNEY
(to Norway)

Cape Wrath

Pentland Firth

Duncansby Head

Butt of Lewis

CAITHNESS

LEWIS

L Broom

SUTHERLAND

Moray Firth

HARRIS

ROSS

N UIST

The Minch

BUCHAN

Spey

S.UIST   SKYE

DRUMALBAN

BADENOCH

MAR

Dee

Barra   Rum

THE MOUNTH

Eigg

GAMORAN

LOCABER

Coll

ATHOLL

ANGUS

Tiree

Tay

Firth of Tay

MULL

ARGYLL

LORNE

STRATHEARN

FIFE

Firth of Lorne

MENTEITH

Firth of Forth   St Abbs

JURA

LENNOX

DUNBAR   Head

or MARCH

Islay

LOTHIAN

Clyde

CUNNINGHAM

Tweed

ARRAN

The

KINTYRE

KYLE

Forest

Teviot

Firth of Clyde

Dee

CARRICK

Cree

ANTRIM

GALLOWAY

Solway Firth

with this and appears to have assisted the people of Cumbria against the Vikings. He was not, however, strong enough to defy Edward the Elder, king of Wessex from 899 to 924. We read in the account of Florence of Worcester that Constantine, with the rulers of Strathclyde and Cumbria, acknowledged Edward as overlord. Florence of Worcester and other chroniclers reveal that Constantine again submitted to Edward in 921, as did others. Constantine was peculiarly unwilling to devote himself after these events to a more realistic policy. His aggressive stance brought him into conflict with Athelstan, successor to Edward the Elder as king of both Wessex and Mercia, annexed in 918. Athelstan was as ambitious as Constantine but more capable and was recognised in 925 as king of all England. After striking at the Welsh of the west and south-west, he invaded and ravaged much of the south of Scotland in 934, marching nearly to Stonehaven in an action which was imitated by Edward I in 1296. Constantine would not allow this slight to go unpunished. He entered into the alliance which, led in 937, to the Battle of Brunanburgh, to which reference has already been made. The defeat of Constantine and his allies was total. In the Irish accounts of the battle we learn that thousands died. The Anglo-Saxon chronicle mentions that among those left on the field was Constantine's son. Constantine fled north, his authority in his kingdom unimpaired by the disaster of Brunanburgh. That he remained king for six years after Brunanburgh must suggest that he had so established himself, both through his descent and his achievements, as to render himself immune to overthrow within his own kingdom. The picture we have of him must therefore be incomplete. If not a successful warrior, he was astute; although he had once fought the Vikings, he now saw the virtue of enrolling them in his struggle with Athelstan. It is reasonable, too, to argue that the agreement of 945 between Edmund I of England and Malcolm I, Constantine's immediate successor, owed something to the sense of identity and purpose which the latter had created in Alba. In that year, according to the Anglo-Saxon chronicle, Edmund ceded to Malcolm all of Cumbria provided that Malcolm should be 'his helper on land and sea'. The exact extent of Cumbria Edmund gave up is unclear; it is likely, however, to have meant the land south of the Solway as well as north into Strathclyde. Edmund probably saw in Malcolm a way to defend his northern possessions against Viking attack, thus limiting that coalition between Dublin and the Vikings of the eastern countries of England which constituted great danger for him. In the reign of Edgar, Edmund I's son, there was a further concession to the Scots. Kenneth II received the Lothians from Edgar who, we are told, treated him with great honour. We can no more be certain of what the Lothians were than of the meaning of Cumbria; it may be, however, that together they covered Scotland south of the Forth and Clyde with areas south of the present border on both the west and east of England. The kings of the Scots were thus masters of an extended kingdom which had come into their possession within 125 years of the death of Kenneth MacAlpin. They had, however, begun a relationship with their more powerful counterparts in England from which came much of the future pressure they would be subjected to. Both Edmund and Edgar of England, while making concessions to the Scots, were intent on using them as allies against external attack. They may also have seen them as 'clients' in the Roman sense, masters of buffer-states and therefore useful but, unquestionably, inferior. There is, in one account of events, an illuminating story of a pleasant scene on the River Dee in 973. The newly crowned Edgar, we find, was rowed on the Dee by eight under-kings, among them Kenneth II. Edgar was demonstrating their relationship to him; it was the precise nature of the relationship being created at this time which was to plague Scotland for centuries.

THE BATTLE OF CARHAM

It was not to be expected that the arrangements entered into in the middle and latter parts of the tenth century would go unchallenged. The unsettled earldom of Northumbria tempted the Scots. We cannot know whether Edgar, had he lived beyond 975, would have gone on to test the relationship with Scotland. His successor, Ethelred, to whom history has given the name of 'Unready' or devoid of counsel, was weak where Edgar had been strong. His inability to counter a renewal of the Danish attacks on England encouraged Malcolm II. In 1006 he mounted an invasion of Northumbria which like the rest of England was in a state of turmoil. Malcolm was repulsed by its earl and lost the Lothians. The reverse was temporary. Ethelred's position deteriorated and he was ousted by Sweyn I, 'Forkbeard', king of Denmark in his third invasion of England in 1013. When, a year later, he died suddenly, Ethelred was restored briefly until 1016. A further struggle for control of England ensued, culminating with the crowning of Cnut of Denmark as king of England. These continuing upheavals in England were not overlooked by Malcolm II. At the Battle of Carham which was fought on the Tweed either in 1016 or 1018, in alliance with Owen, titular king of Strathclyde, he destroyed the Northumbrian army and regained the Lothians. Owen of Strathclyde died about this time, either in the Battle of Carham or in its aftermath, and Malcolm made Duncan, his grandson, king of Strathclyde. Duncan came into an inheritance in 1034, as successor to Malcolm, of a kingdom which roughly covered modern Scotland with the exception of those areas still held by the Vikings. What had been the territory of the Scots, Pictland, the Lothians, Cumbria and Strathclyde were now united.

MALCOLM 'CANMORE'

If it is possible to speak of a degree of unity in 1034 within a large part of modern Scotland, the succession was, as before, a problem. Malcolm II, 'the honour of all the west of Europe' as he was described, had arranged that his grandson, Duncan, should succeed him. Malcolm had broken radically with tradition; the succession had hitherto passed from king to brother or cousin, never to son, let alone grandson. Moreover, Duncan had succeeded through his mother and with one exception, in 878 when Eochaid became king after Aed (Constantine II's father) such a situation had not existed since Fergus came to Argyll to create the kingdom of Alba. Malcolm was ruthless in his plan to guarantee Duncan's succession, not merely ignoring the custom of 'tanistry', that is, succession by cousinage, but killing anyone who might prevent the realisation of his plan. The descendant of one such victim, Gruoch, became the second wife of Macbeth, the mormaer, most easily if not entirely accurately rendered as earl, of Moray. Malcolm thus left to his grandson both a kingdom and the certainty of a feud with Macbeth and Gruoch.

Duncan was an ineffectual king. His failure to capture Durham in 1039 led to his return to Scotland, chastened and with his authority weakened. Macbeth killed him in 1040 and ruled for 17 years. He appears to have been a good king, active and conscientious, if not always able to hold on to the whole of the territory he had gained through the murder of Duncan. He lost Cumbria to Siward of Northumbria, with whom one of Duncan's sons, Malcolm 'Canmore', that is, Bighead or Great Chief, was able to find refuge. Macbeth had made an error, after killing Duncan, in sparing both Malcolm and his brother, Donald Bane. Malcolm in Shakepeare's play has the assistance of Siward in the defeat of Macbeth. Siward was, in reality, already dead when, in 1057, Malcolm defeated and killed Macbeth at Lumphanan in Aberdeen, between the Dee and the Don. Lumphanan was the second occasion on which Malcolm had defeated Macbeth. Three years before he had driven him out of the Lothians but Macbeth escaped to the north, to recoup his forces. Macbeth's step-son, Lulach, to whom he was devoted, appears to have reigned briefly after Lumphanan but he, too, was killed by Malcolm. In this bloody but traditional manner, Malcolm came into his inheritance. He was crowned king on 25 April 1058.

Malcolm III and The Normans

On 14 October 1066, William, duke of Normandy, defeated and killed Harold king of England at the Battle of Hastings. William made himself master of England with an amazing rapidity and in time brought his formidable talents to bear on Malcolm III. A more immediate consequence of the Norman Conquest for Scotland, however, was the appearance at Malcolm's court of a refugee from William, Edgar the Atheling or 'Prince'. He was the great-nephew of Edward the Confessor and thus the strongest hereditary claimant to the English throne when Edward died early in 1066, but was unable then to make himself king. With the Atheling was his sister, Margaret, whom Malcolm married in either 1069 or 1070. The marriage was happy and fruitful; they had six sons and two daughters. Of the sons, the fourth, Edgar, the fifth, Alexander, and the sixth, David, all became kings. A daughter, Matilda, married Henry I of England.

If the marriage of Malcolm and Margaret created a dynasty, it also embroiled Malcolm with William I of England. Malcolm saw in the unsettled state of England in the first years after the Battle of Hastings, an opening which might allow him to extend his territory southwards. He was not, however, to achieve lasting gains and on the five occasions he invaded the north of England he only brought retribution upon himself and his kingdom. His first invasion in 1070 was followed by a counter-invasion two years later by William. Malcolm offered little resistance to William who, supported by a fleet, moved easily northwards to Abernethy in Perthshire. There, Malcolm submitted to him and gave him Duncan, his son by his first marriage to Ingijbord, as a hostage. Duncan did not forget or forgive Malcolm's treatment of him and when he returned to Scotland in 1094 it was as the enemy of Malcolm's successor. Shortly afterwards, Edgar the Atheling was expelled from Malcolm's court and made his way to Flanders. The departure of Edgar, on whose behalf Malcolm may have claimed to act in invading England, did not stop the Scottish king from further, futile descents on the north of England. In 1091 he again submitted to an English king, this time William II. But he was prudent; he saw to it that his acknowledgement of overlordship did not prejudice the independence of Scotland. When Malcolm died, in 1093, he was once more engaged in an invasion of England during which he was killed outside Alnwick.

The reign of Malcolm III was not entirely given over to war. The influence upon him of his second wife, Margaret, was considerable. They acted together in many areas of government. Her biographer and former confessor, Turgot, prior of Durham and latterly bishop of St Andrews, himself an important figure in the Church in Scotland, tells us that at one council, Malcolm interpreted for his wife who knew no Gaelic. Margaret was vigorous in her attempts to reform and improve the Church in Scotland to bring it in line with general practice. By her invitation to members of the Benedictine order to found a priory at Dunfermline the queen helped to usher in an era of monastic foundations. The marriage of Malcolm and Margaret joined a king who sought territory and glory to a queen dedicated to the Church. Malcolm largely failed in his self-appointed task and the reaction of the Normans to his invasions was to push their own territory towards the Solway and the Tyne. The castles which they built at Carlisle and Newcastle marked limits beyond which Malcolm's successors could not realistically hope to penetrate for long. Margaret could not divert her husband from his dreams of conquest but sought instead to make of Scotland a kingdom not merely accepting current religious practices but linked with the modern world which England under the Normans represented. Margaret died within four days of her husband in November 1093.

The Old and The New

Malcolm III was succeeded not by any of his six sons but by his younger brother, Donald Bane who ruled twice as Donald III. Whether this return to the old practice meant a distaste in Scotland for the attitudes of the preceding years it is impossible to say, but it did not prevent trouble. Duncan, Malcolm III's son by his first marriage, had gone to England at the age of 12 as a hostage under the terms of the Treaty of Abernethy in 1072. He had been well and even honourably treated by both William I and William II who were no doubt looking to the day when they might find in him a king of Scotland sympathetic to them. Certainly, when in 1094 Duncan, now in his thirties, sought the throne of Scotland, he did so with the assistance of William II and with his responsibilities to that king understood. Duncan briefly ousted his uncle, Donald III, but ruled for only six months, as Duncan II, before being killed and replaced by his uncle. Donald managed to regain the throne which indicated that Scotland was not yet wholly prepared to embrace the new Norman influences to which Duncan, for so many years resident in England, was prone. It is interesting to note that some among the Scots who agreed to accept Duncan as their king did so on condition that he would not introduce any more Normans or Englishmen into Scotland. Already, between 1052 and 1054, Macbeth had used a small number of Norman knights, all of whom died in battle, a fitting end for descendants of those Vikings who hoped to find a home in Valhalla as worthy warriors. But Scotland had, in time, to adapt to the Normans. The reign of Malcolm III, in which the Saxon presence predominated at court, and that of his brother, Donald III, interrupted as it was by the claim of Duncan II, did not halt, other than temporarily, the spread into Scotland of Norman institutions.

On the death of Donald III in 1097, he was succeeded by the first of the sons of Malcolm III and Margaret to become king, Edgar. Like Duncan II he did so with help from England. In effect, Edgar was placed on the throne by William II having, as a condition, accepted him as his feudal superior. The willingness of Scottish kings and nobles to indulge in such agreements was to continue for several centuries. Edgar died without legitimate issue as did his brother and successor, Alexander I, who ruled from 1107 to 1124. Alexander, however, although he had spent time at the English court did not come to the throne as a vassal king. Indeed, he prevented the bishop of St Andrews from acknowledging English supremacy. His exact feudal relationship with Henry I is open to some question; he did serve with his army under Henry I in a campaign in Wales in 1114 – the act of a vassal. Alexander married Henry's natural daughter, Sybilla, and such marriages, whether of kings or nobles, were a major factor in the assimiliation of Scotland into what had now become the Anglo-Norman system.

THE REIGN OF DAVID I

It was under David I, king from 1124 to 1153, that Scotland moved more rapidly and positively into that system. David had spent his youth in England and through the marriage of Alexander I to Sybilla, was the brother-in-law of Henry I. David married Maud, daughter of Waltheof, earl of Northumbria, through whom he held the earldom of Huntingdon. Under his brother, Alexander, David had ruled the south of Scotland as earl, and therefore when he succeeded Alexander as king in 1124, he was already both an experienced administrator and aware of the virtues of the Anglo-Norman system of government. He was, however, careful to use it in such a way as to ensure that it was suitable to Scotland and not merely an imitation of what was found in England.

David brought into Scotland those families which were to increasingly dominate the history of Scotland. Thus we find a Bernard de Balliol, whose origins derive from Bailleul-en-Vimeu, and a Robert de Brus or Bruce from Brix, whose descendants took Scotland into war with England and into civil war in Scotland. Other names, which were to take their place alongside those of the leading figures, were Morville, Soules, Somerville, and Lindsay. If the Stewarts were Breton rather than Norman, deriving from Walter whose forebear had been seneschal of the bishopric of Dol in the eleventh century, it was during the reign of David I that they made their way to Scotland. What David wanted from these incomers was their expertise in war and government. In return he endowed them with extensive lands in his kingdom, in places where they would exercise under him the guardianship of the routes into Scotland along which invasion might be expected. In Annandale Bruce looked to the south, to England, but also, to the west, to Galloway, the route to and from Ireland and not yet under David's control. Soules was given Liddlesdale as protector of another traditional invasion path. Stewart was lord of Renfrew, his task to secure the coast from attack from the Western Isles.

It was these French-speaking newcomers who with David's encouragement implemented in Scotland the practices, customs, and legalities of what we know as the feudal system. They constituted an aristocracy and if it was natural that they should encounter hostility and opposition, they overcame these in much of Scotland, particularly perhaps in the south, where they dominated because of the status given them by David. Land now replaced the tribe or the family as the basic unit of society. It was held in return for service, usually military, and depended for its success upon strict adherence to the code which bound both the lord, who gave, and vassal, who accepted. The first recipient of land from a lord might in his turn choose to pass a part of what had been granted to him to another, again in return for some form of service. Above everyone was the king from whom the whole intricate pattern originated. Those who were most powerful in the new social fabric of Scotland built the physical representation of their authority, the castle. The motte and bailey castle, wooden, standing on a mound, and protected by a ditch and a palisade, looked over the land. It had a double purpose, acting as a defensive structure and an offensive gateway in time of war, and in peace as a meeting-place, a court and a home.

David's reign witnessed, in tandem with the building of castles, the building of churches and cathedrals. He established the Augustinians at St Andrews, Holyrood and Jedburgh, and the Cistercians at Melrose, Newbattle and Kinloss. David was no doubt religious in the accepted sense of the word, making his devotions in due form and carrying out the requirements of his faith. But the Church could not be allowed free rein in a system as ordered as that which David was giving to Scotland. Scotland was divided into ten dioceses; in each the bishop was chosen by the cathedral chapter or by local clergy but David, like his successors, was anxious to have his views known. It was in keeping with his determination to keep the Church in Scotland under his tutelage that, with his support, the bishop of Glasgow refused to acknowledge the supremacy of York.

DAVID I AND ENGLAND

The death of Henry I in 1135 transformed the relationship of David with England. Henry's last years had been disturbed by the question of the succession. His only legitimate son and heir, William, had been drowned off Barfleur on 25 November 1120 while crossing from Normandy to England. Henry was thereafter obsessed by the need to ensure the succession of his daughter, Matilda, known by virtue of her marriage to Henry V of Germany as empress. In 1127 her father obtained from the magnates an oath of allegiance to Matilda. David, as earl of Huntingdon, was among those who promised their support to Matilda. On Henry's death, however, Stephen of Blois, grandson of William I, disregarding the pledge of allegiance which he had given to Matilda, took the throne. Before the inevitable civil war had broken out between Stephen and Matilda, David had seized Carlisle and Newcastle, the strongholds built to overawe the Scots and discourage invasion from the north. David was reviving by his action the old Scottish claim to Cumbria and seeking to establish a new one to Northumbria which came through his wife, Maud, the daughter of Waltheof, earl of Northumbria. At Durham in 1136, Stephen, although supported by the presence of an army, did not force David from England but granted Cumbria to him and agreed that the question of the future of Northumbria should be given due consideration. There is evidence that David was not content with the concessions made at Durham; it is likely that he quickly extended his authority as far south as the River Ribble in Lancashire.

In 1138 Matilda's half-brother, Robert, earl of Gloucester, rebelled against Stephen and open civil war broke out in England. David invaded England on the east side, moving through Northumbria, to which he still maintained his claim, and into Yorkshire. The savagery of David's army appalled contemporaries; it does appear, however, that it was not condoned by David himself who dealt severely with those who had exceeded his intentions. Burning and looting, killing of inhabitants and devastation of the land, were already common in such invasions and would intensify after 1296. On the Scottish side William Wallace and Robert Bruce would use such methods, as would Edward I and his son, Edward II. The savagery of David's army aroused the English. On Cowton Moor, near Northallerton, on 22 August 1138, David was defeated by an English army under William, count of Aumale, in the 'Battle of the Standard', so called because the English carried into battle with them a cart with a mast to which were attached the banners – in Norman-French 'estandards' – of St Peter of York, St John of Beverley, and St Wilfrid of Ripon. The latter was the bishop who at Whitby in 664 had argued, successfully, the case for the Roman against the Celtic Church.

The defeat of David at Northallerton was not enforced by Stephen with a political and military settlement. Instead, in the year after the battle, again at Durham, David obtained that control of Northumbria

David I and Malcolm IV (from a charter of 1159 to Kelso Abbey)

which he sought. Stephen granted to Henry, David's son, the whole of Northumbria, although the English king retained the crucial castles of Bamburgh and Newcastle. David thus was in possession of Cumbria and, on the east of England, as far south as the River Tees. David, as he thought, was able to guard against future events when in 1149 he met Matilda's son, Henry of Anjou, whom he knighted at Carlisle in a ceremony on Whitsunday. Henry swore on oath that, if he became king of England, he would uphold the concessions made by Stephen. The kingdom of Scotland now extended over the present border to include the counties of Northumberland, Cumberland, and Westmorland. Henry of Anjou proved more cynical, even than David himself had been in betraying his oath to Henry's mother, Matilda. When he became king as Henry II in 1154, he took back those lands which he had promised should remain Scottish. David was predeceased by his son, Henry, in 1152 and when he himself died in 1153, he was succeeded by Malcolm IV, his grandson, known as 'the Maiden'. Malcolm was 11 years old and under him Scotland lacked the strength to resist Henry II. At Chester in 1157, appearing before Henry to do homage for his English lands, Malcolm recognised his military inferiority to Henry by restoring to him Cumberland, Westmorland, and Northumberland. The border between the two countries was back where it remained, largely undisturbed, on the line of the Solway and Tweed.

THE TREATY OF FALAISE

The reign of Malcolm's successor, William I, 'the Lion', involved a further and more important deterioration in the relationship of Scotland with England. Henry II had been unable to satisfy the ambitions of his sons and in 1173, one of them, another Henry, whom he had associated with him in the kingship, with his brothers Geoffrey and Richard, rebelled. William, securing from the rebels a promise of Northumbria as far south as the Tyne, invaded England in 1174. His army followed the destructive traditions of the past, while William detached a force which he led to the siege of Alnwick. However, he lost touch with his soldiers in a thick mist and fell into the hands of the English; was sent by Henry II to Normandy and imprisoned at Falaise. There, as the price for his freedom from Henry, who had been victorious against the rebels, he stated that he was 'the liegeman of the lord king Henry against every man in respect of Scotland and all his other lands'. He submitted publicly to Henry at York, having been brought there from Falaise, and turned over to the English king five of his castles, Edinburgh, Stirling, Roxburgh, Jedburgh and Berwick, so that the treaty might be safeguarded. The Treaty of Falaise bound Scotland to England in feudal subjection. A precedent had been set which the 'Quitclaim of Canterbury' of 5 December 1189 removed in law but the effects of which could not be so readily dismissed. Richard I, by the quitclaim, allowed William to purchase from him, for 10,000 silver merks which Richard intended to use to subsidise his crusade, the feudal relationship which he had surrendered in such humiliating fashion at Falaise.

CONCILIATION AND CRISES

After the Quitclaim of Canterbury, relations between Scotland and England continued free of tensions while Richard I ruled. William even helped in the provision of the ransom which freed Richard from his captivity under Henry VI, emperor of Germany. However, the mood of conciliation did not last. Richard's death in France in 1199 was followed by the accession of his brother, John. When William argued once more for the Scottish claim to the northern counties of England, John at first avoided a response but in 1209 he resorted to force. At Norham on the Tweed, where later Edward I would exert his authority against the Scots in a prelude to war, John so cowed William, now aged 66, that the Scottish king paid him 15,000 merks to avert an English invasion of Scotland. William further agreed to the marriage of his two daughters, Margaret and Isabella, to John's sons, Henry, later to be King Henry III, and Richard. It was an inglorious episode in a reign of almost 50 years which was of such moment in the history of Scotland. The meeting at Norham appears to contradict the name of 'the Lion' which has always been applied to William I.

Alexander II, William's son and in 1214, the new king of Scotland, used the difficulties which John experienced with the barons in the latter part of his reign, and then his death in 1216, to interfere in the affairs of England. Firstly, he supported the barons in the struggle which resulted in the granting of the Magna Carta by John. Then, with John embroiled in civil war and his baronial opponents offering the crown to Prince Louis, son of Philip Augustus king of France, Alexander marched south to join Prince Louis. He took and held briefly Carlisle, the symbolic importance of which had not lapsed. Alexander's objective was, as always, the restoration to Scotland of the northern counties of England and a military presence was an initial step towards the full implementation of that policy. But neither the people of Carlisle nor their king would tolerate the situation which Alexander was striving to create. Louis' invasion, after a promising start with the barons taking most of south-east England, was a failure. John's death at Newark in October 1216 and the accession of Henry III were followed by the defeat of the rebels and Louis at Lincoln on 20 May 1217. The Treaty of Kingston on Thames of 12 September 1217 ended the war. Alexander lost Carlisle, all that he had taken, in the settlement but regained Huntingdon which he had earlier surrendered to John.

Throughout the rest of the thirteenth century the relationship between Scotland and England depended on the relative strength and weakness of the two countries. The marriage of Alexander II to Joanna or Joan, the sister of Henry III, allied the royal families and softened their attitudes to one another. However, it did not entirely remove the cause of friction, for example, in 1233 and 1234 when the rebellion of Richard, earl of Pembroke, absorbed Henry's attention and energies. Alexander now renewed the Scottish claim to the northern counties and the marriage of his sister, Marjorie, to Gilbert, the new earl of Pembroke in 1234, placed the Scottish king firmly in the camp of the opposition to Henry. The very strong possibility of an Anglo-Scottish war was, however, avoided with the assistance of the papal legate, Otto, acting for Gregory IX. Alexander and Henry met twice at York, in 1236 and 1237, and on the second occasion the outcome was the Treaty of York. Alexander formally abandoned the old claim to the northern counties and the border between the two countries was fixed, where it has since remained, on the line of the Solway and Tweed.

Despite the apparently cordial relations between the two kings in their meetings at York and the treaty made there, Henry, like Alexander, was ready to profit from what he regarded as the weakness of Scotland. In 1244 war seemed likely with both kings leading armies to

Newcastle. There, perhaps aware of the consequences of the worsening relationship, they opted for a peaceful solution and confirmed the Treaty of York of 1237. The kings arranged for the marriage of Prince Alexander, heir to the Scottish throne, to Henry's daughter, Margaret. It was this marriage, celebrated in 1251 when Alexander was 10 years old and Margaret 11, that Henry used as an excuse to interfere in Scotland. In 1249 Alexander, still a minor, succeeded to the throne and Henry gradually began to exert pressure on the government of Scotland. The natural concern of a father for his daughter living in another country was a convenient cover for Henry's actions. In 1255 he forced a reorganisation of the Scottish government; among those ejected from office was Alexander Comyn, earl of Buchan, from a family whose enmity to the English did not diminish with time. A council of English nominees assumed authority; Alexander was to enjoy Henry's protection, and it was stated that Henry would act against anyone who refused to accept the new regime. The earl of Buchan, with colleagues from the patriotic faction, was returned to power in 1258, having seized the person of the king and armed themselves. Their alliance with the disaffected Welsh made war with Henry likelier still but, as before, it was avoided by compromise. A regency was established with representatives from both the patriotic and the English side, and it ruled the country until the majority of Alexander III in 1262. He, while giving homage to Edward I in 1278 for lands held in England, was careful to state publicly that he held the kingdom of Scotland 'of God alone'. The formula defined Alexander's position to his own satisfaction; it would not indefinitely bind the devious and far-sighted Edward I, nor did it remove the threat, now dormant, of those Scottish subjects willing to ally themselves with England when circumstances encouraged it.

CHAPTER FOUR

The Heroic Age,
1286–1328

The Death of Alexander III

On the night of 18–19 March 1286, Alexander III, riding from a meeting with his council in Edinburgh Castle to rejoin his young wife and second queen, Yolande of Dreux, at Kinghorn, fell to his death on the shores of the Forth. Before he set out, the king had been reminded by his councillors of the difficulties of the journey, made worse on this occasion by the darkness and the weather. It is said that he turned aside their concerns with a joke. He chose, also, to forget the belief, widespread among his superstitious subjects, that this year, ushered in by tempestuous storms, was to be one of exceptional events and that this day, in particular, would be a day of judgement. The desperate attempts to make him change his mind continued even as he travelled. At the ferry-crossing at Dalmeny and, again, on the far side of the Forth, he would not heed the pleas of his companions and those of the local guides whose services he had engaged. Perhaps the drink he had consumed in Edinburgh had encouraged him in what they took to be foolishness; perhaps he had grown weary of the repeated anxieties of those with him. He insisted that they proceed. They lost sight of him in the darkness and it was not until the following morning that his body was found at the bottom of the cliffs.

At the time of his death Alexander was 44 and had ruled for 36 years, accomplishing much. On 2 October 1263, his defeat of the Norwegians at Largs led to the removal of a long-standing threat to Scotland. The death of the broken Hakon IV at Kirkwall on 16 December of the same year led to the succession of his son, Magnus IV 'the Law-Mender', less warlike and more realistic in his ambitions. By the Treaty of Perth, three years after Largs, Alexander gained from Magnus the Western Isles and the Isle of Man in return for an initial payment and an annual rent. When in 1281, his daughter, Margaret, married the new king of Norway, Eric II, a closer and better relationship between Scotland and Norway seemed to be guaranteed. Meanwhile, what would emerge as the greatest and most durable threat of all to the security of Scotland, that from England, had not yet appeared. Alexander's first wife, Margaret, was the sister of Edward I of England and the two kings had an amiable, if at times wary, relationship. While prepared to do homage to Edward for his estates in England, Alexander would not concede that Edward had any claim to Scotland. For his part, Edward, while Alexander lived, tolerated the situation. It required a man of considerable years to recall the days of strife between the two countries and one of vision to imagine in Edward 'the scourge of Scotland'.

All that Alexander had done as king, however, was at risk of failure in one crucial respect. The king, upon whose sexual activity the English chronicle of Lanercost commented critically, had not left behind a legitimate male heir. From his marriage to Margaret of England he had three children. Of the two sons, the younger, David, died at the age of eight in 1281; the other, named after his father died in 1284, aged 20. It is a tribute to Alexander III's sense of duty that, despite his grief at the death of his elder son, he had arranged within a week of the latter's death, for the recognition by his subjects of his grand-daughter, Margaret, as his heir, in the event that he had no more children of his own. Margaret, 'the Maid of Norway', the child of his daughter Margaret and Eric II of Norway, was only three years old in 1286 and in poor health. She had never visited the country of which she was now queen but Alexander's wish to have her recognised does not seem to have been opposed. Unknown to the people of Scotland and perhaps to the king himself, Yolande of Dreux was pregnant at the time of his ill-fated journey from Edinburgh to Kinghorn. But she miscarried and in September 1290 'the Maid of Norway', on her way to her new realm, died in Orkney. Her body was carried back to her grieving father for burial in Norway. Scotland, which had learned of her death in early October, had had no opportunity to know its young queen.

THE GUARDIANS

At the funeral of Alexander III and at a parliament at Scone, plans were laid for the government of Scotland in the period up to the coronation of the queen. Six men were chosen as 'custodes', Guardians, of the country. Robert Wishart of Glasgow and William Fraser of St Andrews were bishops; Duncan of Fife and Alexander Comyn of Buchan were earls; and John Comyn of Badenoch and Robert 'the Stewart' represented the barons. The list contains names which were to figure prominently in the history of Scotland in the near future. Wishart, courageous if not always consistent in his defiance, suffered imprisonment and the threat of death at the hands of Edward I. The fate of the name of Comyn, like that of the family itself, was decided by the actions of Robert I and, in contrast to that of Stewart, is no longer given its deserved place in the popular version of the history of Scotland.

The authority of the Guardians was quickly challenged in the southwest by a member of another prominent family. Robert Bruce, known to his contemporaries either as 'the Noble' or 'the Competitor', grandfather of the future king, was lord of Annandale and an inveterate opponent of the Balliols. He saw them, quite rightly, as a challenge to his claim to the throne. In 1238 Bruce had been named heir to Alexander II, then childless. The decision of the magnates who, summoned by the king, had named Bruce as heir had been rendered irrelevant by the birth of Alexander's heir in 1241. Bruce, in 1286 and in 1290, showed that he did not consider his claim nullified. He seized the royal castles of Dumfries and Wigtown as well as that of Buittle, the possession of the Balliols. To consolidate his position, he entered on 20 September 1286, into a pact with the lord of the Isles, the earls of March and Menteith, and Robert Stewart, at his castle at Turnberry. What Stewart, himself one of the Guardians, was doing in this company is uncertain, but he was throughout his life a man of mixed loyalties. The energy of Robert Bruce, well into his seventies at this time, was amazing and his behaviour was an indication of the single-mindedness of the magnates of Scotland which was so harmful to Scotland. The opposition to the Guardians in the south-west faded without further complications and Bruce's moves, if anything, strengthened the position of the Guardians. The composition of the body of the Guardians itself, however, reflected something of the political condition of Scotland; Wishart, the young Duncan of Fife and Stewart supported the Bruce cause, while Bishop Fraser and the two Comyns were allies of the Balliols.

Scotland survived the Bruce threat in 1286 and the potential for civil war which existed in the conflict of that family with the equally ambitious and powerful Balloils. The fragile peace which the Guardians maintained was in the interests of the people as a whole – it was to remain untouched by either the Bruces or the Balliols after the events in the south-west in the autumn of 1286. When next these two families clashed openly, it was after the death of 'the Maid of Norway' in 1290 which had introduced into the balance between them a factor, in the face of which each was impotent.

Edward I

The reputation of Edward I of England as the 'Hammer of the Scots' is deserved. In the years between 1296 and his death at Burgh by Sands in 1307 he inflicted on the Scots a series of devastating blows. His pursuit of William Wallace whose influence had largely disappeared other than in the inspirational sense, is, quite properly, advanced as proof of his paranoia. The method of Wallace's execution was evidence of that streak of cruelty which, at the end of his reign, Edward himself had come to view as harmful to his own plans. He misjudged the opposition to him and in so doing alienated those like John Comyn and Robert Bruce whose adherence was essential to the political settlement he meant to impose on Scotland in the wake of the military one. It is, however, too readily forgotten that his direct intervention in the affairs of Scotland was sought by the magnates of that country, unable to resolve the problem of the succession to the throne.

Edward must have been tempted to intervene on his own initiative. He could not have watched unconcernedly the actions of the Bruces in the south-west, for Dumfries was too near his own territory. If there had been similar episodes, indicative of a breakdown of law and order, he could scarcely have resisted the temptation, ever-present in his mind, to renew the English claim to suzerainty over Scotland which went back some three centuries. His patience, not one of the characteristics usually associated with Edward, is noteworthy in the light of the opportunity presented to him by Scotland. It is true, of course, that he was not entirely free to turn to Scotland. Rebellion in Wales and war with France distracted him from what became, in later life, an obsession. Nor, as he was to learn, could he rely on the whole-hearted support of his own magnates in his plan to make Scotland part of his kingdom. Given the condition of Scotland between 1286 and 1290, Edward's restraint is as remarkable, with hindsight, as the decision of the Scots themselves to ask for his participation in their affairs. They could not plead ignorance of his character – some of the Scottish magnates had fought in the English civil war between Edward's father, Henry III, and Simon de Montfort, and Edward, then Prince Edward, had been distinguished for his severity. His deviousness, which caused the Scots much trouble, was no secret; the contemporary 'Song of the Battle of Lewes', which was fought in 1264, told of his 'inconstancy and changeableness', and warned that he did not hold 'steadily his word or his promise'. This was the man to whom the Scots entrusted the future of their country after the death of 'the Maid of Norway'. He had been kept informed of developments in Scotland as early as September of 1286 when a delegation reached him in France to apprise him of the dispositions for the government of the country until the arrival of the queen. Edward was not able to return to England until the late summer of 1289, when he gave his full attention to his northern neighbours.

His first action was statesmanlike. He proposed the marriage of his son, Edward of Caernarvon, with Margaret, queen of Scots. The Guardians saw the virtue of the proposal, which was included in the Treaty of Birgham of 18 July 1290 and confirmed by Edward at Northampton in August. They did not neglect, however, to insist that Scotland was to remain, after the marriage, free and independent of England. Edward professed to be content with this but, in his turn, had been careful to define, in the course of his negotiations with the representatives of the Scots, what he considered to be his true relationship with them. If the marriage had taken place, it is unlikely to have deflected Edward from his determination to make himself master of Scotland; it could only have postponed the inevitable.

THE COMPETITION FOR THE THRONE

Civil war in Scotland was near in late 1290; had it occurred, Edward
would have been able to intervene in a situation which, he could argue,
threatened the peace and security of his own kingdom. Robert Bruce,
although now 80, was as ready to argue his case as he had been in 1286.
John Balliol, lord of Galloway, was his most formidable opponent, but
there were others who were not deterred by the evident weakness of
their cases from pressing their claims. That same political maturity
which had made the Scots seek a peaceful solution to their problems after
the death of Alexander III, now prevented civil war in 1290. All the
pretenders to the throne, like the Guardians and the people of Scotland,
accepted the need to avoid confrontation. Whether their decision to call
upon Edward to judge between the claimants to the throne was as wise
is at best arguable. Edward's standing in Europe was high, as yet
undamaged by the criticism levied against him in his own kingdom. Had
the Scots sought the help of any other monarch, Edward would certainly
have taken possession of Scotland by force. Edward gave the Scots some
indication of his intentions when they appeared before him at Norham
on Tweed in May 1291. They could not have been unaware that he had
summoned his army for 3 June, an unsubtle ploy which must have been
present in their minds when they asked him to judge between the
claimants to the throne. As always, Edward was polite but announced
that he would do so only if he was acknowledged by all as overlord of
Scotland. The initial reaction of the Scottish representatives to this
statement was one of bitterness; the bishop of Glasgow, Robert Wishart,
told him bluntly that his treatment of the Scottish people, without a
leader and dependent on him for disinterested advice, was deplorable.
Edward responded by telling the Scots that he saw Scotland as a fief
without a true male heir. If that were indeed the case, he could justify
direct intervention and the seizure of the country, in his capacity as
overlord. The helplessness of the Scots, always conscious of the
possibility of civil war, and now faced by Edward's threat of
intervention, could not be disguised by words. Although Edward
graciously granted them a space of three weeks in which to consider the
answer, they had no alternative but to agree to the terms he had laid
down at Norham.

In all, 13 candidates presented themselves before Edward. Although some, those who claimed by descent through illegitimate children of William I 'the Lion' and Alexander II, could be quickly ruled out, Edward was as punctilious in his consideration of their arguments as he was in his treatment of those with a better case. Eric II of Norway, whose claim, uniquely, was by ascent through his daughter, 'the Maid', was eliminated. Florence, count of Holland, advanced a strong claim but when after a year's delay, the necessary supporting documentary evidence could not be produced, his claim fell through. In the end the decision rested, as was always likely despite Edward's painstaking examination of the material laid in front of him, between three candidates. These were John Hastings, John Balliol, lord of Galloway, and Robert Bruce 'the Competitor'. They were the three descendants of the three daughters of David earl of Huntingdon, the younger brother of two kings, Malcolm IV 'the Maiden' and William I 'the Lion'. There was much learned discussion of Hasting's argument that the realm of Scotland should be divided between the three surviving candidates, with Balliol, as the descendant of the eldest of the three daughters of David of Huntingdon, entitled to wear the crown. With Hastings' argument at length rebutted, only the claims of Bruce and Balliol remained in contention.

At Berwick, on 17 November 1292, Edward's decision was given. He had chosen John Balliol. On 19 November, the castles of Scotland, the keys to which had been surrendered to Edward in token of his authority, were given up to Balliol and he was enthroned at Scone on St Andrew's Day, 30 November, On 26 December, at Berwick on Tweed, he gave his oath of homage to Edward. Edward had, throughout the proceedings which culminated in the selection of Balliol, given the impression of being dedicated to the proper hearing of the various claims to the throne. His choice of Balliol was one which met with the general approval of contemporaries, although the Bruce family could not be expected to view it with equanimity. Robert Bruce 'the Competitor' died in 1295 and his claim to the throne of Scotland passed first to his son and then to someone more worthy, his grandson, Robert, who inherited both the character of the 'Competitor' and his devotion to the promotion of the Bruce family.

The Reign of John Balliol

With John Balliol installed as king, Edward, hitherto so patient, moved much more rapidly and his undermining of the position of the new king began within a week of St Andrew's Day. In an action quite probably inspired by Edward, one Roger Bartholomew of Berwick appealed to Edward against judgements entered against him in Scottish courts. Edward reversed one of the judgements. A reminder from the Scots that Edward had promised that the laws and customs of Scotland would be respected was met with the reply that the promise had been binding only so long as Scotland was without a monarch. Edward went further in the summer with his insistence that Balliol should appear in person to answer appeals against judgements in his courts. Balliol summoned up the courage to refuse to meet this insulting demand but he crumbled before the English parliament in October 1293 and renewed his oath of homage to Edward.

Edward's methods and Balliol's inability to deal with them naturally met with opposition within Scotland itself, and Balliol's weakness brought him scant sympathy. There was an increasing resentment against Edward but it was not until the English king exceeded the bounds of what was thought entirely reasonable that the Scots united against him. In 1295 Edward, about to cross to France to wage war against Philip IV, summoned his army to gather at Portsmouth. He made the mistake of calling upon Balliol and certain of his magnates, among them Robert Bruce 'the Competitor' now aged 84 and James 'the Stewart', to serve with him in the forthcoming campaign. Not only did Balliol and the magnates refuse, but while Edward was deflected from his French campaign by trouble in Wales, the Scots were planning an alliance with his enemy, Philip IV. An offensive and defensive alliance between the two countries was signed on 23 October 1295 in France and ratified in Scotland on 23 February 1296. Balliol's role in these events and his attitude to them remain unclear. In the words of one account, however, the king was 'a lamb among wolves'. Edward, like the Scots, was now bent on war. He postponed his campaign in France and, instead, summoned his army to assemble at Newcastle upon Tyne on 1 March 1296. The Scottish army, in keeping with tradition, was called to gather, on 11 March, at Caddonlee, four miles north of Selkirk. The Bruces were absent; hopeful of replacing Balliol, they preferred to hold to the oath given to Edward in 1292. The Scots, united since the death of Alexander III in their determination to preserve the independence of their country, were divided at the outbreak of a war which would almost destroy that independence.

THE DEFEAT OF BALLIOL

The war which began in 1296 was characterised, on both sides, by exceptional brutality. On Easter Monday, seven earls of Scotland led an army over the Solway; they burned and killed in a raid which, failing at the gates of Carlisle, achieved nothing of consequence. In April they were in Northumberland, where they surpassed the cruelty inflicted in Cumberland; they committed sacrilege by burning churches and monasteries and, according to one English account, burned alive 200 schoolboys at Corbridge. These raids created an atmosphere of horror but they did not interfere with Edward's plans; they were the action of a nation lacking a coherent strategy. Balliol had been less than enthusiastic about the war, but the magnates had not yet produced an outstanding leader to replace him in this, their first campaign.

Edward, meanwhile, was not yet to be outdone in cruelty. When Berwick refused to surrender to him, he stormed the town on 30 March and carried out an indiscriminate slaughter of its inhabitants. For two days he allowed his army free rein to kill, pillage and burn – Berwick never recovered its position as the most important of Scottish towns, despite Edward's own efforts to restore it. Whether the Scots were cowed by Edward's treatment of Berwick we cannot tell; their immediate reaction to news of the event was once again to descend on Northumbria. It was a practice to which they would return throughout the war, futile though it so often was in terms of advancing their cause.

As Edward's army moved slowly northwards from Berwick, the Scots compounded the error of their raids into England by meeting the English, for the first but not the last time, in a pitched battle which they lost through their own ineptitude. When Edward heard of the fall of Dunbar, which belonged to his ally, Earl Patrick, he detached a column under John de Warenne, earl of Surrey, to recapture it. Warenne was not a gifted soldier but he was competent enough to recognise the opportunity which the Scots promptly gave him. The Scots for their part, saw no virtue in avoiding what they thought was a challenge, but by breaking rank they abandoned the superior position they had occupied on a hill, and swept to an unnecessary defeat. The cavalry fled and there was a considerable slaughter of the infantry; among the prisoners were two names which would recur in more heroic circumstances. William Douglas, father of Robert I's most famous lieutenant, James 'the Good', and Andrew Murray fell into English hands. Douglas, guilty of having broken his word to Edward, later died in the Tower of London, while Murray escaped from imprisonment in Chester to lead Scottish resistance in the north of Scotland, and to be with William Wallace at the Battle of Stirling Bridge in 1297.

After the rout of Dunbar the hope of defying Edward faded. He now made a leisurely, unopposed progress through Scotland, receiving surrenders and protestations of loyalty. At Scone he ordered the Stone of Destiny, on which kings of Scotland were enthroned, to be removed and carried to London, to be placed in Westminster Abbey. The hapless Balliol, who after the fall of Berwick had sent to Edward a public renunciation of his homage, could find no way to defend what was left of his kingdom. He fled from one hiding-place to another until he had to accept that his position was untenable. He was brought before Edward fearing for his life, but instead, he was ceremonially stripped of the attributes of kingship – the crown, the sword, the sceptre. The royal arms were torn from his tabard (he was now and henceforth 'Toom' or empty 'Tabard'), and he was taken to London, escorted by the earl of Lancaster, never to return to Scotland.

Edward reached Elgin, but then went back to Berwick to hold a parliament at which he received further submissions from the Scots. The names of those who had thus become the English king's men were entered in what is known as the Ragman Roll. Robert Bruce, son of 'the Competitor', had already asked Edward to make him king of Scotland, but Edward cuttingly dismissed him. Scotland was in his eyes no longer a kingdom but merely 'the land of Scotland'. He left the country to be governed by an administration under the victor at Dunbar, the earl of Surrey, Hugh Cressingham, the treasurer, and William Ormsby, the justiciar.

William Wallace

Edward crossed the Tweed into England on 17 September 1296 leaving behind him a far from secure situation. It soon was evident that without his presence the English administration in Scotland would face with opposition. Surrey, aged 65, was no longer an energetic man and in any case preferred his estates in Yorkshire to life in Scotland where, we are told, he believed the air was harmful to his health. The treasurer, Cressingham, was an able administrator but he was forceful, arrogant and was mocked for his illegitimate birth and unprepossessing appearance. He found himself faced with insurrections over too wide an area to cover; there were reports of problems in the Western Highlands, in Aberdeenshire and in Galloway. The English became convinced that Robert Wishart, bishop of Glasgow, and Robert Stewart were behind these problems. The English were right to see in the Church in Scotland an impacable enemy but their belief that it was Wishart and Stewart who prompted William Wallace into rebellion does not stand up to close scrutiny. As a true son of the Church and a vassal of Stewart, Wallace would have listened to both Wishart and Stewart, but our knowledge of Wallace gives to believe that he was very much his own man.

Almost nothing is known about Wallace before 1297. All we know is that he was the second son of Sir Malcolm Wallace of Elderslie near Paisley in Renfrewshire and came from a family which arrived in Scotland in the second half of the twelfth century from the borders of Wales. Wallace was, for his time, well educated and, contrary to English propaganda, was not base-born but of respectable, landed background. He may well have drifted into crime and outlawry. He was not important enough to merit attention in the records of the time, for his name does not appear on the Ragman Roll. The traditional date given for his rebellion against the English is May 1297, when he murdered the English sheriff of Lanark, William Heselrig, in revenge, it is said, for Heselrig's murder of Marion Braidfute, Wallace's wife or mistress. The occasion may have been less romantic; perhaps the origins of the quarrel with Heselrig lay elsewhere. Like Robert Bruce, the future king in 1306, Wallace was forced into hiding from the English and then into rebellion against them, in circumstances not of his own choosing.

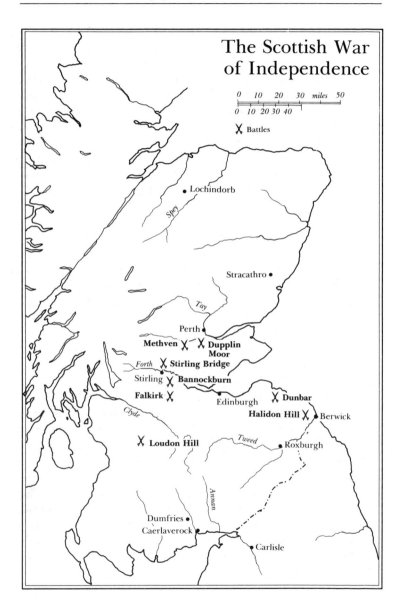

The Scottish War of Independence

0   10   20   30   *miles*   50

0   10 20 30 40

X Battles

• Lochindorb

Spey

Stracathro •

Tay

Perth •

Methven X — X **Dupplin Moor**

Forth X **Stirling Bridge**

Stirling X **Bannockburn**

Falkirk X   X **Dunbar**
                          Edinburgh •
                                      Halidon Hill X • Berwick

X **Loudon Hill**   *Tweed*   • Roxburgh

Clyde

Annan

Dumfries •
Caerlaverock •
                        • Carlisle

Without as far as we know any military training, Wallace proved himself an outstanding soldier in guerrilla warfare, and as at Stirling Bridge, on a greater scale. The natural leaders of the Scottish resistance, Robert Bruce, Stewart, and Wishart, had proved to be inept when faced with the English at Irvine, so Wallace carried out a raid on Scone, 80 miles from Lanark, in an audacious and almost successful plan to capture William Ormsby. Wallace already understood the value of speed and mobility and his sudden appearance at Scone surprised the English and encouraged rebellion against them in the land between the Forth and the Tay. Wallace returned to the forest of Selkirk, a natural habitat for him, after Scone, and continued to plague the English with his tactics so alien to those they were used to. Cressingham's reports on the situation tell us of its gravity from the English point of view. He could not, however, convince Surrey to abandon his idyllic retreat in England and take up his post again in Scotland. Inside their castles, the English were invulnerable but they could not restrain Wallace who rode across Scotland, through Perthshire and Fife, to Dundee and possibly as far north as Aberdeen. He did not seek a pitched battle but instead, sensibly, struck at the English unexpectedly, inflicting casualties and unsettling them, before moving on. It was a strategy impossible to counter.

The Battle of Stirling Bridge

Cressingham had written of an 'immense army' under Wallace's leadership. This is unlikely to have been an accurate assessment; Wallace, we may be sure, preferred the mobility which smaller numbers allowed and Cressingham may have employed exaggeration as a means of inducing the return of Surrey. Nevertheless, there can be no doubt that Wallace's success against the English was encouraging men to join him and the size of his army was radically increased when he was joined by forces under the leadership of Andrew Murray. Murray, after his escape from Chester, had made his way back to his homeland, in Morayshire, and led an intelligent resistance, based on principles similar to those of Wallace, against the English. Murray assaulted Castle Urquhart, took Inverness, Elgin and Banff. Like Wallace in the south he became the head of the resistance movement in the north. At some date unknown to us Wallace and Murray must have met, to plan a co-ordinated strategy. By the end of August, 1297, their armies had united and were advancing on Stirling. Surrey had finally left Yorkshire, unable any longer to avoid his responsibilities, and with Cressingham, the one lethargic, the other eager for glory in war, moved from Berwick towards Stirling. Although we do not know the exact numbers of either army, it is clear that the Scots were largely infantry, while the English infantry was supported by a considerable force of cavalry.

When Surrey and Cressingham reached Stirling in the first week of September, the Scots were already in position on the Abbey Craig, a mile to the north of the bridge over the Forth. Wallace had no intention of repeating the mistake of Dunbar and losing the advantage which the heights gave him. Surrey, having failed in prevarication and attempts to talk Wallace into surrender, sent his army across the bridge on 11 September. Wallace allowed the English vanguard onto the bridge and then, with the timing of a great commander, released his infantry against it. The momentum of the Scots carried them onto the bridge and drove the English into the river. Many were drowned, others killed before they could raise their weapons. It was impossible either to advance or retreat. Surrey with the rest of the English army could only watch the slaughter. Among the dead was Cressingham, and after the battle the Scots flayed his body, dispatching strips of his skin throughout Scotland to tell of the great victory. There were individual acts of bravery in the English army but Surrey himself was no hero. He fled to Berwick to take ship to England. It is believed that a hundred English knights and some 5,000 foot-soldiers were killed at Stirling. By any standards, it was a magnificent victory, achieved against the odds and by a man who had never before been involved in a battle of this kind.

WALLACE AS GUARDIAN OF SCOTLAND

Murray had been wounded at Stirling and although he lived for perhaps another two months, he was unable to assist Wallace in the war with England. Wallace was knighted and made Guardian, the first individual to hold the office. For one of his background it was a remarkable accomplishment – he had risen above his social class and led a successful rebellion against a king regarded as the foremost in the Christian world.

He acted throughout his Guardianship in Balliol's name and to the end of his life remained Balliol's man. As Guardian he involved himself in the routine of government, seeing to appointments such as that of William Lamberton as bishop of St Andrews, and seeking to restore trade with Lubeck and Hamburg in Germany. In the winter of 1297 he undertook an invasion of Northumberland, in the course of which he inflicted great damage and gained a reputation for cruelty. In his cruelty he was a man of his time, bent on retribution for ills done to Scotland by Edward. As a consequence he became the target of a campaign of hatred by English chroniclers. According to the same sources which attacked him, he was only driven out of northern England by the intervention of Saint Cuthbert. Despite his victory at Stirling and the ability he showed as Guardian, Wallace could never overcome the indifference, even hostility, of the magnates of Scotland without whose support he would soon have to meet Edward. The loyalty of these magnates to Edward had been, in the words of an English account, as liable to melt away 'as frost is in May'. They would not give to Wallace what they would not give to Edward.

The Battle of Falkirk

At the time when the Battle of Stirling Bridge was being fought, Edward was overseas engaged in a campaign in Flanders against Philip IV. He returned to England on 14 March 1298 and did not delay his preparations to deal with Wallace. The defeat at Stirling had united the English; even those magnates who were suspicious of Edward now accepted that it was necessary to destroy Wallace. Edward summoned his army to Roxburgh for 25 June and himself travelled north from London, calling at a number of shrines to seek divine help in his war in Scotland. He reached Roxburgh in early July by way of Newcastle and Alnwick and followed the east coast. Wallace, meanwhile, had retired before him, baffling Edward with this unfamiliar tactic. It is evident that Edward was uncertain what lay ahead; his army, drawn further into Scotland, was short of supplies. At Temple Liston the situation was so desperate that he allowed the plundering of nearby Kirkliston in order to alleviate his soldiers' hunger. The Welsh contingents, given wine, fought with the English and then threatened to change sides. Edward was rescued from his difficulties by a spy in the pay of Patrick, earl of Dunbar, who brought to Edward news of Wallace.

Wallace had placed his army in a strong defensive position at Falkirk. His spearmen were divided into four schiltroms, the classic infantry tactic later adopted by Robert I. The schiltroms, their spears bristling like hedgehogs, presented a fearsome appearance and obstacle. Each schiltrom was surrounded by a fence of stakes. Wallace had with him a small band of archers but lacked the cavalry which the magnates would have supplied. He was intent on a defensive battle; if, however, the expected English cavalry charges on the schiltroms were withstood, his infantry would advance. His position was protected in front by the Westquarter burn, in the rear by Callendar Wood. The battle was fought on 22 July. There was disarray among the English with Edward, perhaps appreciating the strength of Wallace's dispositions arguing against an immediate attack but being ignored by the earls of Norfolk, Hereford and Lincoln. They charged the Scots but were repulsed. Edward, seeing that the schiltroms could not be broken by cavalry charge alone, recalled the cavalry and brought forward his bowmen. The longbow was superior to that used by the Scots and Wallace had no means to protect the stationary schiltroms. Impotent, the schiltroms still retained their discipline as the arrows fell upon them. It was said by the English that the Scots infantry 'fell like blossoms in an orchard when the fruit has ripened'. When the schiltroms were breached, Edward sent the cavalry to complete the slaughter. With the battle lost, Wallace left the field, his reputation irretrievably damaged. He could not hope to remain as Guardian and resigned the office on the banks of the Forth.

THE END OF WALLACE

If Wallace was no longer Guardian, he still had a role to play in the affairs of Scotland. He became a kind of roving ambassador, travelling throughout Europe to seek help for Scotland. He may have gone as far north as the court of King Haakon V of Norway; he was certainly in France where Philip IV briefly imprisoned him before allowing him his freedom; and in Rome he was active in his country's cause. By 1303 he had returned to Scotland, where we find him with John Comyn and

William Wallace, Stirling

Simon Fraser fighting in the south-west of Scotland. Edward's loathing of Wallace denied him the opportunity to enter into Edward's peace in 1304 as so many of the Scots did. At the parliament of St Andrews Wallace was declared an outlaw by Edward and his Scottish supporters and the hunt for him was intensified. He could not survive for long under such circumstances and in August 1305 was taken in Glasgow, brought to London and put on trial in Westminster Hall on 23 August. The English law of treason under which he was tried allowed him no defence; he made only one recorded intervention in the proceedings when he denied that he could be guilty of treason against Edward since he had never been Edward's man. Found guilty of treason and other crimes including murder, arson, and destruction of property, he was condemned to be hanged, drawn and quartered. The sentence was carried out at once. Parts of his body were sent for public display at Newcastle, Berwick, Perth and Stirling. His head was hoisted on London Bridge.

THE MURDER OF JOHN COMYN

The death of Wallace did not produce a reaction against the English in Scotland. When rebellion finally occurred, the instigator was unusually ill prepared and the circumstances did him no credit. In the month after Wallace's execution, Edward issued an ordinance for a new administration. Among those who accepted Edward's intentions was the future king of Scotland, Robert Bruce, since the death of his father in 1304, earl of Carrick, and joint-Guardian after Wallace. Bruce's support for the patriotic cause had been inconsistent, determined by his ambition, and he submitted to Edward in 1302. In early 1304 he took part in an English raid into south-east Scotland which failed in its attempt to capture Wallace, whose loyalty to Balliol did not endear him to Bruce. Even as he worked on Edward's behalf, however, Bruce was plotting against him. On 11 June 1304, while with the English army besieging Stirling Castle, Bruce joined with William Lamberton, bishop of St Andrews, in a 'band' similar to that organised by Bruce's grandfather in 1286. It was a step to secure for Bruce the support of the Church. It is impossible that Edward could have been ignorant of Bruce's devious nature but he hesitated to act against him. The reason may lie in Edward's realisation that he could not impose a military settlement on Scotland; in the political settlement towards which he was now aiming he needed Bruce's participation.

Where Bruce had wavered in his adherence to the Scottish cause, John Comyn, 'the Red', lord of Badenoch, had held out until 1304 against Edward. His contemporary reputation was, with reason, greater than Bruce's, although like Bruce he cannot be absolved of the charge of having failed to support Wallace at Falkirk. Comyn was joint-Guardian with Bruce after Falkirk in an unhappy association and, later, sole Guardian. When he surrendered to Edward in 1304, it was on terms which prove the respect in which Edward held him. Comyn was, however, by reason of family ties, Balliol's man and as such hostile to Bruce. Without him Bruce's hopes of making himself king of Scotland could not succeed, and therefore, seeking an accommodation with Comyn, Bruce arranged to meet him in Dumfries on 10 February 1306. In front of the high altar of the Greyfriars' church, the two began their conversation. When Bruce proposed rebellion against Edward with the intention of restoring the Scottish monarchy, Comyn baulked. Either fearful of betrayal by Comyn or seeing in him the last obstacle to his plans, Bruce struck Comyn down and his friends dispatched the wounded man. Bruce was too astute to have intended Comyn's murder; he appears to have lost his nerve, thus committing not merely murder but sacrilege, and was left with no alternative to the rebellion he had suggested to Comyn. He seized Dumfries and other castles in the south-west from the English, mobilised his supporters there, and rode north to Glasgow. He obtained the enthusiastic backing of its bishop, Robert Wishart, for his enterprise before making for Scone. There, he was made king on 25 March 1306, six weeks after the murder of Comyn. The energy and speed with which Bruce acted are to his credit; the numbers who joined him suggest that already, before the murder, in the south-west and west of the country at least, he had prepared the population for the day which had now come. He had not, however, chosen that day and the weakness of his position was soon revealed.

BRUCE'S EARLY REVERSALS

Edward does not appear at first to have believed that Bruce had killed Comyn. Once convinced, however, he gave Scotland his undivided attention. Aymer de Valence was given wide powers to deal with the rebellion; he was, as John Barbour, Bruce's most celebrated biographer wrote, to 'burn and slay and raise dragon', that is, he was to show no mercy to Bruce and his followers. Valence acted quickly, capturing the bishops, Lamberton and Wishart, and moving on Perth. Bruce, foolishly ignoring the lessons taught by Wallace, offered the English battle. At Methven, on 19 June, he suffered the first of those defeats which almost cost him his throne and his life. In August, at Dalry near Tyndrum, he met with a second defeat this time at the hands of the Scots under John MacDougall of Argyll. Comyn's murder had meant that the Comyn--Balliol faction was Bruce's enemy, and thus the ally of Edward. Scotland was on the brink of a civil war.

Edward was himself as ruthless as he had instructed Aymer de Valence to be. William Wallace had been the first Scot to be executed under the English law of treason; now Edward proceeded to use that same law against those supporters of Bruce who were captured.

Christopher Seton, who had helped kill Comyn, was put to death at Dumfries; 14 Scots died in one day at Newcastle; Simon Fraser and the earl of Atholl met their fate in London; Bruce's brothers, Thomas and Alexander, perished at Carlisle, and his brother Neil was executed at Newcastle. Bruce's wife and his sister were imprisoned in England in relatively agreeable circumstances, but the countess of Buchan, Isabel, who had attended Bruce's coronation, and another of his sisters, were placed in cages suspended from the walls of castles. Bruce himself escaped the search for him but was forced into hiding, first on the mainland, then on the island of Rathlin.

THE TURN OF THE TIDE

In February 1307, Bruce returned to the mainland, to his earldom of Carrick. It is a tribute to his constitution that he had survived the search for him and the psychological blow of the treatment of his family and friends. He showed now that he had learned from his experiences for, having regrouped his forces, he used them in a series of guerrilla actions which brought him considerable success. When the English sought him out in Glen Trool, he ambushed them and drove them off with heavy losses. On 10 May he forced Aymer de Valence into battle on a narrow front which denied Valence scope for his calvalry and superior numbers, and defeated him. This victory at Loudon Hill, near Kilmarnock, avenged Methven. Enraged by news of Bruce's successes, Edward, 69 years of age, summoned up his last reserves of strength and set out to crush the rebellion. On 7 July, before he could cross the Solway, he died after a debilitating illness had deprived him of his strength but not of his indomitable will. His successor, Edward II, withdrew from Scotland on 25 August and did not return for three years.

The death of Edward I gave Bruce a release from constant pressure from England and allowed him to begin to consolidate his position in Scotland. To do so, he had to deal with his enemies, the Comyns and their allies. In October 1307 he marched north, to take his attack into the heart of Comyn territory. Despite the illness which struck him while he was at Inverurie in November, he fought off an assault by John Comyn, earl of Buchan, and conclusively defeated him. Comyn fled to England and died within a year. Bruce now devastated Buchan in a 'herschip' or harrying so severe that it was said that its effects were felt for 50 years. In the summer of 1308 Edward, Bruce's only surviving brother, attacked the Balliol territory of Galloway, causing great damage to the population but failing to evict the English from the castles they held. Bruce's conduct in Buchan and that of his brother in Galloway made it clear to their enemies that they could not escape retribution if they opposed Bruce. There remained Argyll, home of the Macdougalls, and Bruce moved against them in the spring of 1308. To deflect Bruce and to gain time, the Macdougalls asked for, and received, a truce which expired sometime in August. John Macdougall, John of Lorne, sought to ambush Bruce in the pass of Brander on or about 15 August but was defeated when James Douglas led a bold rush from the heights of the pass onto Macdougall's army. In Buchan, Galloway and Argyll, Bruce had broken Scottish resistance to him and the civil war was effectively ended.

THE BATTLE OF BANNOCKBURN

The success which Bruce enjoyed in 1308 continued in the following years. Beset by problems in England and indifferent to events in Scotland, Edward II allowed Bruce a freedom of action which would have been inconceivable under Edward I. Bruce pursued with vigour the conquest of Scotland, but to achieve his ends he had to take the castles held by the English. This was inevitably a slow process with such strategically important and widely separated castles as Perth and Dumfries holding out as late as 1313; even to Edward their value was clear and he had done his best to maintain and supply their garrisons. James Douglas took Roxburgh in February 1314 and Thomas Randolph with Douglas the most able of Bruce's lieutenants, took the prize of Edinburgh a month later. Berwick stayed English until 1318.

Stirling, however, perhaps the most important of all because of its dominant position overlooking the Forth, continued to defy Bruce. Between Lent and midsummer 1313, Edward Bruce lay siege to it but without success. The commander of Stirling, Sir Philip Mowbray, a Scot who had kept his faith with the English, asked for a year's truce at the end of which the castle would either be relieved or surrendered to Bruce. This Edward Bruce granted, and in so doing committed his

Robert the Bruce, Bannockburn

brother, the king, to what he had always hoped to avoid, a trial of strength with the English. Edward II could not refuse to bring relief to Mowbray; honour and the belief that in a pitched battle Bruce would be vulnerable as, traditionally, the Scots had always been, combined to ensure that the English would act.

The agreement between Mowbray and Edward Bruce meant that the battle would take place outside Stirling. If neither the battle itself nor the site were of Bruce's own choosing, he prepared meticulously for what was about to occur. Like Wallace at Falkirk, Bruce selected a position which would restrict the English cavalry. Unlike Wallace, however, Bruce had a force of cavalry whose presence was to prove crucial. It is likely that the English outnumbered the Scots by three to one but the morale of the Scots was high. Moreover, the English, after a long approach to the field of battle and led by a soldier inferior in ability if not in courage to Bruce, were already dispirited when the Battle of

Bannockburn entered its first stages on 23 June 1314. In a memorable encounter which preceded the main battle, Bruce killed in single combat Henry de Bohun, whose ambition had encouraged him to attack Bruce. The English army, in its turn, was no more successful than Bohun. Bruce's schiltroms were able to contain the repeated English cavalry charges but were threatened by Edward's bowmen who may have numbered as many as 5,000. Bruce, perhaps remembering Falkirk, had held in reserve some 500 light-horsemen under Sir Robert Keith and their intervention against the archers prevented the kind of disaster which had befallen the Scots at the earlier battle. Keith's horsemen drove the archers from the field and the schiltroms, whose discipline had sustained them in the face of the heavy English cavalry, were slowly turned into an offensive weapon, pushing with their 12-foot pikes against the English ranks and exercising what became an overwhelming pressure. The English were driven in upon themselves, unable to act in concert or even to wield their swords. Those English who tried to make their way from the battle were in danger of drowning, either in the Bannock burn which gave its name to the battle, or in the Forth. Edward II fought almost to the end but was taken from the field by his own men, conscious of the effect that his capture would have. The English losses at Bannockburn were severe over the two days on which the battle was fought and included the earl of Gloucester, Bruce's own cousin. The English baggage-train fell into Scottish hands as did Edward's shield, and considerable ransoms were obtained for those magnates taken in the battle. The earl of Hereford was later exchanged for Bruce's wife, his daughter Marjory, his sister and Robert Wishart. Of those English who fled, some were able to reach Carlisle under the leadership of Aymer de Valence, Bruce's old enemy. Edward was able to escape to Dunbar where he took a boat first to Bamburgh and then to Berwick.

Bruce's Invasions of England

Bannockburn offered Bruce the opportunity to end the war with England either by killing or capturing Edward II. He was able to do neither and Edward, though weak and incompetent, was too stubborn to surrender Scotland to Bruce. For his part, Bruce lacked the resources to hit at the true centres of Edward's power, which lay far to the south. It was not until 1328, 14 years after Bannockburn, by which time Edward was dead, murdered by his wife and her lover, Roger Mortimer, that Bruce was able to impose peace on England. During much of that time he held the northern counties of England in thrall, extorting blackmail, terrorising the inhabitants, and where blackmail was not forthcoming, ravaging the land and enslaving the inhabitants. The records of the period are full of the payments made to Bruce by the English; in 1318 Ripon, for example, bought the Scots off at a cost of 1,000 marks. The Scots, mounted on light ponies from which they took their name of 'hobelars', were extremely mobile and lived off the land. They proved invincible, and when Edward made his last expedition to Scotland in 1322 he was no more successful than before and was almost captured when the Scots pursued him back over the border into Yorkshire. One of the few Scottish failures was at the siege of Carlisle in 1315. The garrison then was commanded by Andrew de Harcla who in 1323 entered into a treaty with Bruce which might have ended the war. Edward, however, executed Harcla for treason and the best chance since Bannockburn to bring the war to a conclusion had passed. Edward was not to be persuaded to offer peace, not even by Bruce's continued forays into England with their damage to the economy of the north, the invasion of Ireland by Edward Bruce in 1315, which resulted in his death in 1318, or the opposition within England itself to the war.

THE END OF THE WAR

Edward II's unpopularity predated his defeat at Bannockburn. His fondness for his favourite, Piers Gaveston, was notorious and weakened Edward's position so that he was forced, after Gaveston's death in 1312, to relinquish some of his power. His struggle with the magnates prevented him from dealing with the increasing menace of Bruce and when he found a new favourite, Hugh Despenser 'the younger', he was drawn into a civil war with the magnates under Thomas of Lancaster. He defeated and executed Lancaster in 1322 but his wife, Isabella, who fell in love with Roger Mortimer, an enemy of Despenser, was a more formidable opponent. She and Mortimer deposed Edward, who was probably murdered on their orders. The accession of the young Edward

III under the tutelage of Isabella and Mortimer was to Bruce's advantage. The new regime accepted the reality of the situation and decided to sue for peace. Bruce from a position of strength insisted that no treaty of peace could be made until he was acknowledged as legitimate ruler of Scotland. What Edward II had refused, the English now granted. The Treaty of Edinburgh was signed on 17 March 1328 and ratified at Northampton on 4 May. Scotland was now Bruce's, its boundaries those of the time of Alexander III. It was, the English had acknowledged, independent of England for all time.

CHAPTER FIVE

Scotland after Bruce (to 1390)

1320: Year of Contrasts

Robert Bruce's sacrilegious murder of John Comyn in front of the high altar of the Greyfriars' church in Dumfries on 10 February 1306 aroused widespread horror and condemnation and led to his automatic excommunication by Pope Clement V. Following his coronation at Scone on 25 March 1306 the new King of the Scots, now known as Robert I, had two main objectives. Not least of these was the acknowledgement by the pope of the status which Robert had created for himself by his own efforts, and with it the removal of the sentence of excommunication which weighed so heavily on Robert to the end of his life. Neither was easily obtained; not until October 1328, when he had less than a year to live, was Robert freed of the ban of excommunication and it was even later, June 1329, that Pope John XXII was willing to authorise Robert and his successors to be crowned and anointed according to the rites of the Church. But by that time, as we shall see, Robert was already dead. In his long struggle with Clement V, who died in the year of the Battle of Bannockburn, and his successor, John XXII, who ruled until 1334, the king had the consistent support of the Scottish clergy under the leadership of Robert Wishart, bishop of Glasgow, and William Lamberton, bishop of St Andrews. One of Robert's first acts after the murder of Comyn had been to make his way to Glasgow to seek absolution from Wishart. The support of the clergy for Robert was in defiance of the pope who did not have scruples about offering practical help to Edward II. In 1318, for example, John XXII allowed Edward to divert to the prosecution of his war with Scotland some of the tithe originally collected for a crusade. The pope renewed the sentence of excommunication against the Scottish king in 1320 in order further to encourage Edward. Until late in Robert's reign the pope would not refer to him as 'king' but as 'the noble man who at present governs Scotland' or, more insultingly, as 'Robert Bruce, calling himself king'. The attitude of their spiritual leader, however, did not deter the Scottish clergy. In 1309, as Robert was slowly defeating his enemies within his kingdom and expelling the English garrisons from it, the clergy had written to the pope defining their relationship with and their allegiance to Robert who, they said, (Had) 'by the sword restored the kingdom'.

In 1320, with the sentence of excommunication renewed, the barons followed the example of the clergy in a letter, henceforth known as the 'Declaration of Arbroath', to Pope John XXII. The declaration, dated 6 April 1320, was quite probably the work of Bernard de Linton, abbot of Arbroath from 1311, and chancellor from 1308 to 1328, who had written the clergy's letter of 1309. It affirmed the determination of those who attached their seals to it to maintain Scottish independence and to support Robert in his endeavours. The barons stated that, as long as 100 remained alive, they would never agree to subject themselves to English rule. Robert was their king by consent, succession, and the will of God. The declaration, carried by Edward de Maubuisson and Adam Gordon, reached Rome by August. It did, however, contain a significant rider – if that same king whose virtues and achievements had inspired the letter, should betray those virtues and achievements by attempting to enter the allegiance of the king of England, he would be deposed and replaced by a king who would defend the independence of Scotland. It is ironic that shortly afterwards, Robert's position as king should be threatened by some of those who had, in the declaration, both praised and warned him. The Soules conspiracy failed in its objective but the mere fact of its existence demonstrates that, even as late as 1320, when it seemed all but Edward II and John XXII had accepted Robert as king, there lingered inside Scotland itself a residue of resistance to his rule.

Before the conspiracy of 1320 the reputation of the Soules family had stood high. The family had come to Scotland, like that of the king himself, in the time of David I, and Ranulph de Soules had been granted land in Liddlesdale and the hereditary office of butler in the royal household. Nicholas, the father of the intended beneficiary of the plot to kill Robert I and put William de Soules on the throne, was, by descent from Marjory, the illegitimate daughter of Alexander II, one of the 13 competitors for the throne of Scotland in 1291. William's great-uncle, John, was sole Guardian of Scotland in 1301, a colleague of William Wallace, and died in France in 1310, still devoted to the cause of Scottish freedom. The plot to replace Robert with William de Soules was betrayed in mysterious circumstances and Robert reacted with the utmost severity. Of the conspirators, Soules himself and Agnes, countess of Strathearn, were sentenced to perpetual imprisonment. Patrick Graham and Eustace Maxwell were acquitted, and David Brechin, Roger Mowbray, Richard Broun, Gilbert Malherbe and John Logie were given the death penalty. It is unlikely that the conspiracy could have succeeded but of the participants, Soules, Brechin, Mowbray, Graham and Maxwell were associated with the 'Declaration of Arbroath'. Futile though it was, Robert saw in it a real threat to him. The Scone parliament of 4 August was known as the 'Black Parliament' because of it judgements on the plotters, which were a reflection of the king's own attitudes. The conspiracy illustrated the refusal of the Comyn–Balliol faction to accept him as legitimate king. After all, Soules was the son of Margaret, daughter of Alexander, earl of Buchan, one of the guardians of 1286; and the countess of Strathearn was also a daughter of Alexander Comyn. In the remaining years of his rule Robert was not to be troubled by conspiracy inside Scotland but, as events would prove, he had not been able to protect his kingdom from outside intereference.

The Death of Robert I

In the last part of his life Robert was afflicted by a disease long thought to be leprosy but, if that were the case, he did not withdraw from society. This might have been expected for fear of infecting his immediate circle, and in particular his son and heir, David, born in 1324 to him and his second wife, Elizabeth de Burgh, daughter of Aymer, earl of Ulster. It is possible that the king had a wasting disease which affected the skin and it must not be forgotten that he had led a difficult, often dangerous life. He lived to the respectable age of 55, a testament to his constitution. He had built for himself a house at Cardross on the Clyde and there, with the war with England running strongly in his favour, he found the time to indulge in those pastimes which meant much to him, falconry, hunting, sailing, fishing and boat-building. In the late spring of 1329 he summoned the leading men of his kingdom to the house. It was apparent that he was gravely ill and he himself was aware of his deteriorating condition. He had earlier in the year undertaken a painful pilgrimage to the shrine of Saint Ninian at Whithorn to seek his intercession. Back at Cardross he prepared for his end. He had always wanted to go on crusade, perhaps in expiation of the murder of John Comyn, but that was to be denied him. Now, he asked that after his death, his heart should be taken from his body and carried on crusade so that in this way his wish could be met. The task fell to James Douglas 'the Good', the king's closest companion and the equal of Robert as a soldier. Robert died peacefully at Cardross on 7 June 1329. Papal permission had been received for the mutilation of the body necessary for the removal of the heart. His embalmed body was taken for burial to Dumfermline Abbey, where his wife Elizabeth, who had died two years previously, already lay. In the words of John Barbour, archdeacon of Aberdeen, writing his biography of the king almost 50 years after Robert's death, 'when the people knew that King Robert was dead, the sound of sorrow went from place to place'. There is no reason to doubt that this grief was genuine. Robert, certainly the most celebrated and arguably the most successful of Scottish kings, had rid the country of the English occupation and imposed on the government of Isabella and Mortimer, acting for the young Edward III, a treaty which seemed to guarantee Scotland's independence from England. No one could know that the optimism engendered by the Treaty of Edinburgh was ill founded and that within little more than three years of Robert I's death all that he had achieved would be put at risk.

The Accession of David II

David II succeeded his father at the age of five. At a parliament held at Scone on 3 December 1318, provision had been made for a guardian, or regent, should the king be succeeded by a minor, as was now the case with David II. The honour had been given to Robert I's nephew, Thomas Randolph, with James Douglas named as replacement should Randolph die. In 1318 the question of the succession was still a matter of great concern to king and country alike. By his first marriage, to Isabel of Mar, Robert had a daughter, Marjory, born in or about 1296. At the Ayr parliament of 27 April 1315, with her agreement and that of her father, she was passed over in favour of Robert's sole surviving brother, Edward, should Robert die without a male heir. Edward was then about to embark on the conquest of Ireland. He has been harshly judged as arrogant and ambitious but to his contemporaries he was 'a man of great prowess in warlike actions for the defence of the rights and liberties of the Scottish realm'. Edward's notorious over-confidence brought about his death on 14 October 1318 while fighting against an Anglo-Irish army at Dundalk. The question of the succession had once again to be addressed. Marjory Bruce had died two years previously, in March 1316, the result of a fall from her horse, but she had given birth to Robert, the son of her marriage to Walter Stewart. The Scone parliament which named Randolph as guardian also arranged for the succession of Marjory Bruce's son should the king die without a male heir. However, the birth of David, son and heir to Robert I, on 5 March 1324, made the arrangements of 1318 redundant. When he became king on the death of his father, David had already been married for almost a year to the youngest daughter of Edward II, Joan. Joan, aged seven in 1328, was three years older than the husband she had acquired under the terms of the Treaty of Edinburgh. She was later known as Joan of the Tower because of her visits to her husband, a prisoner in the Tower of London after his capture at the Battle of Neville's Cross in 1346.

THE LOSS OF DOUGLAS AND RANDOLPH

In addition to the problems caused to any country by the accession of a minor, in the case of Scotland there was also the loss of its two foremost defenders within three years of the death of Robert I. James Douglas, it will be remembered, had undertaken to carry the king's heart on crusade against the enemies of Christ. His preparations complete and with a safe-conduct from Edward III, Douglas sailed from either Montrose or Berwick on the east coast of Scotland in early 1330. The fall, in 1291, of

Acre, the last stronghold of the Christians in the Holy Land, meant that there was no hope of going there. Douglas and his companions therefore made their way to Spain, where Alfonso XI of Castile and Leon, cousin of Edward III, was engaged in a war with the Moors of Granada. Douglas' reputation as a soldier ensured that he would be welcomed by Alfonso who gave him a command in his army. When the Christian army moved on the town of Teba de Hardales, it met with considerable opposition from the Moors. In the battle which followed, Douglas was killed. Robert I's heart, which Douglas had carried in a casket about his neck, was returned to Scotland and placed in Melrose Abbey, while Douglas' bones were buried in the church of St. Bride in Douglasdale.

Douglas had died far from Scotland, in circumstances which gave rise to enduring legend. Randolph, by now earl of Moray, died less romantically but his death was as dangerous for the independence of Scotland as that of Douglas. Neither man had, at first, been an ally of Bruce. Douglas, angered by the refusal of Edward I to restore to him lands forfeited by William, Douglas' father, had thrown in his lot with Robert I in the hope of regaining his inheritance. Randolph, Robert's nephew, fell into the hands of the English after the defeat at Methven in June 1306 and thereafter co-operated with them against his uncle. Randolph was captured by Douglas in 1309, but did not immediately give his allegiance to Robert. Even when he did and quickly rose to prominence, there were still disagreements between them. The king does not appear to have spared his nephew when he thought him careless or incompetent; at Bannockburn he rebuked Randolph with the memorable phase 'Ane rose from thy chaplet hath fallen' when Randolph failed to halt an English advance. After Bannockburn Douglas and Randolph were Robert's principal agents in the war with England, leading the assault on the northern counties of England and retaking castles from their English garrisons. This was often accomplished by ruse and treachery, Douglas at Roxburgh, Randolph at Edinburgh, while the capture of Berwick in 1318 was a joint effort. Robert's reliance on Randolph prompted him to send him to Ireland with Edward Bruce but not even Randolph could control the headstrong Edward. With Douglas in Spain Randolph's task was to oversee the government of Scotland for the young David II. He arranged for the anointing and crowning of

David at Scone on 24 November 1331 but Scotland was already faced with the possibility of renewed English interference in its affairs.

The Treaty of Edinburgh was considered shameful in England where Edward III did not hide his feelings; he refused either to attend the wedding of his sister, Joan, to David or to give her a dowry. In London a mob prevented the return to Scotland of the Stone of Destiny, taken from Scone in 1296 by Edward I. When Edward III, aged 18, overthrew his mother, Isabella, and Robert Mortimer in 1330, in order to assume power, he combined his natural aggression with the wishes of the people of England to seek revenge for the treaty. Edward, 'grim as a leopard' to his contemporary enemies, moved slowly at first but his encouragement of Edward Balliol, son of that John, king of the Scots, whom Edward I had so contemptuously deposed in 1296, could not be ignored in Scotland. In 1324 Edward II had invited Edward Balliol to England from the family estates in Picardy, where he had been living since the death of his father in 1313, with the clear intention of embarrassing the Scots. Edward II's problems with the magnates, his subsequent murder, and the desire of Isabella and Mortimer to end the war with Scotland relegated Balliol to the background. All that had changed, however, by 1332 because Edward III had been defeated by the Scots in 1327, in his first campaign against them, and he saw no reason to deter Balliol in his plans for an invasion of Scotland. Randolph, without the advice and strength of his colleague, Douglas, was in the midst of preparations to meet the expected invasion when he died at Musselburgh on 20 July.

Edward Balliol and the Disinherited

Balliol's expedition sailed from the Humber on 31 July and reached Kinghorn six days later. At a parliament held at Cambuskenneth Abbey, on 6 November 1314, it had been decreed that there could be no place in Scotland for any unwilling to serve Robert I alone. Those who would not come into his peace on these terms or who hoped to hold lands under both Robert himself and the king of England would not be tolerated in Scotland. They were thus disinherited. Now, with Robert dead and his kingdom under a regency they were returning. With Balliol there came, among others, Henry Beaumont, David of Strathbogie and Gilbert

Umfraville, all claimants to earldoms. Their army was small, between 1,000 and 1,500 in total, mainly infantry and archers, but stiffened by, perhaps, 500 men-at-arms. Despite this numerical inferiority, Balliol's army prospered at first because the Scots were in some disarray after the death of Randolph and their choice of Donald of Mar, nephew of Robert I, was not universally popular. He was suspected of involvement with some among the Disinherited, but he did not allow this to interfere with his plans to face Balliol.

At Dupplin Moor, near Perth, the Scots, considerably outnumbering Balliol, were decisively routed. They had lost the advantage of a superior position, quarrelled among themselves with Mar accused of treachery by Robert I's natural son, Sir Robert Bruce, and been consequently decimated by the arrows of the English archers. Mar was among the dead, many of them trampled underfoot when the second Scottish battalion crashed into the first. It was a pattern all too often repeated in the future. Certain of the Scottish leaders had forgotten what the reign of Robert I had taught: the necessity of avoiding pitched battles. Their successors, after Dupplin Moor, would often, in their turn, be just as foolish.

The Return of the English

Edward Balliol was crowned at Scone on 24 September 1332. Among those who officiated at the ceremony was William Sinclair, bishop of Dunkeld. Sinclair had endeared himself to Robert I by his warlike conduct when he drove off English invaders who tried to land on the shores of Fife in either 1316 or 1317; to Robert, Sinclair was 'my own bishop'. Now, in the reign of Robert's son, the bishop had allied himself to Balliol. He was not alone for Balliol had received other submissions. Balliol was aware, however, that he could not survive without English help and, before his departure from the Humber, he had secretly given his homage to Edward III, who had preferred at that stage to pretend to ignorance of Balliol's venture. Without Edward III's complete commitment to him, Balliol knew he was in danger. His success in capturing Mar's successor as regent, Andrew Moray, son of Andrew who had fought with Wallace, was not enough to fend off Scottish attacks. On 23

November 1332, at Roxburgh, Balliol set down in writing his recognition that Edward III was sovereign lord of Scotland. He also gave to the English king lands in Scotland to the value of £2,000 per year; these lands, including Berwick, were of great strategic value to the English. Edward III, for his part, vowed to maintain Balliol and his heirs in Scotland. Before either Balliol or Edward III could enjoy the benefits of these arrangements, the Scots had acted, and to good effect. They had yet another regent, the bearer like his predecessor of an illustrious name. Andrew Moray may have been captured, but Archibald Douglas, youngest brother of James who had died in Spain on crusade, readily took his place. Together with Robert Stewart and the new earl of Moray, John Randolph, he acted with such vigour and cunning that they almost captured Balliol as he lay asleep at Annan, on 17 December 1332. Balliol took to his horse and fled over the border to Carlisle, with, it was scathingly reported, 'one leg booted, the other naked'. Edward III, although no doubt disappointed in his vassal, would not let matters rest and sent Balliol ahead of him into Scotland, in March 1333. Balliol had with him an army largely provided by the English king and with instructions to begin the siege of Berwick. Edward himself arrived in Scotland in May to join Balliol in the siege.

Archibald Douglas sought to draw Edward away from Berwick by threatening the safety of the English queen, Philippa, then at Bamburgh but in vain. At Berwick the Scots had agreed to a truce; if by 20 July, they were not relieved, they would surrender the town. Douglas recrossed the Tweed and marched towards Berwick. At Halidon Hill some three miles (five kilometres) to the north-west of the town his army was crushed and he himself killed. The English enjoyed a position of strength because of the hill on which they were posted and the marsh which lay between them and the Scots. As Douglas moved forward, the English archers, as at Dupplin Moor, subjected them to accurate fire. The survivors, trying to push up the hill, failed against Edward's three battalions of men-at-arms. It is said that some 10,000 Scots were killed, including Douglas himself and five earls. Balliol now ceded most of Scotland south of the Forth to Edward. Just as Balliol himself had refused to deny his claim to Scotland while Robert I reigned, those Scots who now found themselves once more under English dominion would not allow the situation to continue. Balliol's subservience to Edward III and its consequences ensured that a further century of warfare would ensue. Individual Scots fought, as had Balliol, to regain those lands from which they had been disinherited in a political settlement which was enforced on them and, as a nation they strove to take Scotland back from the English.

When Andrew Moray had been foolishly released from captivity by Edward III, and David II and his queen sent, in May 1334, to the safety of the court of Philip VI, Scottish resistance was reinvigorated. Balliol, more capable than his father but ultimately no luckier, was increasingly seen as an English puppet, and Edward was therefore forced each year to march back into Scotland to sustain his vassal in those parts of Scotland he still held. At the same time, the English king was now about to begin his greatest adventure, in France, and in 1338 he crossed to Flanders to pursue his 'just quarrel', his claim to the throne of France. Edward's obsession with that country was fortunate for Scotland; otherwise, as one account suggested, 'he would have gained possession of the whole land, without difficulty, as far as it is humanly possible to judge'.

THE IMPRISONMENT OF DAVID II

By 1341 David II had been brought back to Scotland from France. A significant victory had been won at Culblean, on Saint Andrew's Day 1335, when Andrew Moray, his forces augmented by those of William Douglas, the 'knight of Liddlesdale', defeated and killed David Strathbogie, earl of Atholl. He was Balliol's steward of Scotland and guardian for him of the land north of the Forth. After Halidon Hill the English had reckoned that there was no one in Scotland capable of raising and leading an army against them, but Moray and those with him were proving the belief wrong. Moray had rediscovered the values practised by Wallace and Robert I, and denied to Balliol and his English allies the opportunities which Dupplin Moor and Halidon Hill had given them. As David II was coming back to Scotland in 1341, Balliol was moving over the border into England. After 1346 he was never again seen in Scotland.

Once restored to Scotland, David II, now aged 17, was naturally anxious to exert his authority, and to this end took the war into England.

He raided the northern counties in 1342, ravaging in the familiar manner Northumberland as far south as the River Tyne. That same spring, within Scotland itself, Roxburgh and Stirling were taken from the English. The first year of David II's personal reign had thus been one of triumphs. Even now, however, there were signs of those old internal problems which still plagued the country. William Douglas, Moray's colleague at Culblean in 1335, kidnapped one of the obstacles to his ambition in southern Scotland, Alexander Ramsay, sheriff of Roxburgh, and starved him to death in Hermitage Castle. Such violence became common, threatening the stability of the government as subject fought subject and necessitating, on a growing scale, the intervention of the king against what came to be called 'overmighty subjects'.

For 50 years, since the outbreak of the war with Edward I, Scotland had more or less had the support of France in the attempt to remain independent of England. In 1346, however, it was France which had been invaded and now sought assistance. Philip VI, who had sheltered the young David II and his wife when they were sent to France in 1341, was beaten at Crecy on 26 August 1346 by Edward III, who then began the siege of Calais. Philip appealed to David to launch a diversion. David responded by repeating his attacks of 1342 and 1345 on the north of England. His army, which had mustered at Perth on 6 October, marched south into Cumberland and Westmorland. After a stay at Lanercost Priory, which the Scots raided and devasted, the invaders moved on to the priory of Hexham and, we are told, 'stripped it of everything'. By 16 October the Scots were on the outskirts of the city of Durham. The next day, William Douglas, at the head of a raiding party, was chased off by the vanguard of an English army which had almost caught the Scots by surprise. In the battle which followed this clash both armies took up defensive positions, but it was the Scottish formation which, under the English arrows, broke first. Both armies were commanded by men whose families were already dominanting affairs under their respective kings: Douglas and Robert Stewart on the Scottish side, Neville and Percy on the English. When the Scots advanced, they were forced to change direction because of a ravine and they became confused and wedged together. The English archers again inflicted severe casualties and a brief recovery by Stewart's men was halted by the English cavalry.

When the Scots fell back, Stewart fled and with him many of the army. David was wounded in the face and after leaving the field was captured by one John Coupland. The Scottish losses were heavy in the battle and in the pursuit – John Randolph, earl of Moray, was killed and William Douglas taken prisoner.

David II was carried off after the Battle of Neville's Cross, to be a prisoner in England for 11 years, in relative comfort although closely guarded. Negotiations for his release began within the first year of his captivity and he himself was allowed to visit his kingdom for a few months in 1352 to try to arrange matters. The Scots would not tolerate Edward III's terms, which David had brought with him, and he was back in the Tower of London in June. In his absence, Robert Stewart, whose flight with the earl of March from the field at Neville's Cross had been ridiculed by the English, was made regent with the title of 'the king's lieutenant'. It was not until October 1357, at Berwick, that a treaty was finally agreed for David's ransom, set at 100,000 merks, to be paid in ten annual instalments. During his time in captivity, the Scots, under the influence of the French who were still at war with England, had broken the truce of 1356. Edward III, in the course of his last expedition to Scotland, had ravaged the south of the country in the 'Burnt Candlemas' of the same year, and he had destroyed Scottish hope of continuing French help by his defeat and capture of John II at the Battle of Crecy on 19 September. Meanwhile, Edward Balliol, after a long and hopeless sojourn in the family homelands in Galloway, had, in return for an annuity and other financial considerations, surrendered to the English king the crown and kingdom of Scotland. There, the 'Black Death', the bubonic and pneumonic plague, had struck; the Scots, believing that they had been spared, referred to it as 'the foul death of the English'. The plague struck again in 1362 and in 1379, to exhaust further a population whose sufferings were already many.

THE PROBLEMS OF DAVID II

After his return from England, David II ruled for 14 years until his sudden death in Edinburgh on 22 February 1371. He faced not merely the burden of his own ransom, which at the time of his death had not been cleared, but problems which had arisen during his captivity in England.

The lax nature of the lieutenancy of Robert Stewart meant that the king would be welcomed back to Scotland as the man to restore order to the country. Under Robert there had been a considerable decentralisation of government, to the benefit of the magnates on whom power devolved, but to the detriment of the administration and its finances. It was inevitable that David, in his plans to improve the situation, would meet with opposition; in dealing with it he proved frequently to be resolute. Stewart himself was at the root of much of the trouble. Recognised as heir presumptive as far back as the Scone parliament of December 1318, he was, like Robert Bruce 'the Competitor' in an earlier age, prompt to resist any infringement of his rights. The king's infatuation with Margaret Drummond, widow of Sir John Logie, was viewed with concern by Stewart because David's queen, Joan, who had gone to England in 1357, had died there childless five years later. In 1363, Stewart, in defence of his own interests, rebelled with William, earl of Douglas since 1358. They claimed to be acting against the 'evil counsel' on which, they said, the king had come to rely, but there is little doubt that their motives were less altruistic. David hit hard at the rebels, Douglas narrowly escaping capture at Lanark. Stewart, no more constant that he had been at Neville's Cross, deserted the lofty cause to which he had lent his name, and the rebellion collapsed ignominiously. The joint venture of 1363 did not bind Douglas and Stewart; even in 1371 the former challenged the right of the notoriously weak Robert to be king. By then, Stewart, although confirmed as heir in 1364, had fallen foul of David's second queen, the much detested and feared Margaret Drummond, and been imprisoned, briefly, in the winter of 1368. Stewart survived even Margaret's hostility, however, for she in turn lost the favour of her husband and was divorced by him in 1370. Stewart was soon after to have his revenge, for before David could take as his third wife his newest love, Agnes Dunbar, he died in Edinburgh.

David attempted to balance the power of the greater nobles, against whom he had moved with such vigour in 1363, by placing his trust in others of lesser rank. We shall not be surprised to find that, in common with other monarchs of the period, he favoured relatives; thus, the names of John Logie and Malcolm Drummond, kin of his wife, are among those associated with him. But he was wise enough to use men of ability also, such as Robert Erskine, Hugh Eglington and Archibald Douglas 'the Grim', illegitimate son of James 'the Good'. They acted as his contacts with the magnates of whose loyalty he was less certain. Not all of the lesser figures promoted by the king would establish dynasties of their own. The Drummonds, however, remained at the forefront of Scottish politics for some considerable time.

Whatever his domestic problems, David, of course, could never forget the external threat posed by Edward III. There remained the question of the ransom with its damaging effect upon government finances. Whether, as has often been argued, David was squandering the monies collected for the ransom is unclear but he himself sought an answer to the ransom by a compact with Edward III. In November 1363, having crushed the rebellion of Stewart and Douglas, he went to London where, in return for the cancellation of arrears of the ransom, Edward or one of his sons would succeed to the throne of Scotland. Such an

David II and Edward III from an illuminated fourteenth century manuscript

arrangement had been mooted in 1350 but had failed. The parliament of Scone, on 4 March 1364, refused to countenance David's proposal; debt was preferable to English rule. Quite what motivated David, the son of that king who had, in 1328, imposed his own terms on the English, we cannot tell, but his proposal was naturally condemned by his people. It was a sign of weakness, or perhaps weariness, from one who, generally, had been marked by his toughness of character. Parliament, in 1364 and subsequently, was increasingly a factor which David had to take into account in his thinking; he was conscious of the role it might play in government through exercising restraint on expediture. That ability could never be ignored by David or his successors and his need for extra finance brough representatives of the burghs into parliament. Their wealth derived from trade and gave them an essential role in the calculations of any monarch. At the end of his reign, in 1370, David's financial manipulations met with a rebuff from the 'Three Estates', nobility, the clergy and the burgesses parliament meeting at Perth; parliament acted to prevent any officer of the king from acting contrary to established law and practice.

The First Stewart King

When he succeeded to the throne in 1371, Robert Stewart, now Robert II, was the same age as his illustrious predecessor and namesake had been at the time of his death in 1329. That apart, there is little to suggest their direct relationship; whereas the threat to the Scotland of the grandfather had been external, from England, now under the ageing grandson, the threat came from within the kingdom itself. By the time of Robert II's accession, Edward III, victor of Halidon Hill, Crecy and Poitiers, was a victim of increasing senility. He was dominated by his mistress Alice Perrers, and content to leave the government of England in the hands of his fourth son, John of Gaunt. Edward was only four years older than the new king of the Scots but, unlike Robert II, he had a glorious past on which, in his more lucid moments, he might reflect. Robert was not so fortunate. He was praised by his contemporaries for his humility, a characteristic which was admirable in a priest, but less desirable in a king when it was allied to indecision. His nerve had failed him in 1363 when he rebelled against David II, as it had in 1346 when he fled from Neville's Cross; it was not to be expected that at 55 he would replace one characteristic with the more necessary one of strength. He was intelligent enough, however, to know that the succession, so often the cause of difficulty, must be assured at once, the more so in the light of his advanced years. At Scone in March 1371, the month after Robert's accession, his eldest son by Elizabeth Mure, John, earl of Carrick, was declared rightful heir. It is believed that Robert had at least 21 children, both legitimate and illegitimate, and there was some doubt about John himself because his parents had been, under canon law, thought too closely related. John, in time, succeeded with the title of Robert III, a tribute to the statesmanlike approach his father had brought to the question of the succession. What had been decided in 1371 was affirmed two years later when parliament, as well as affirming John as heir, defined the succession in the event that he died without issue. Robert II, while thus ensuring the future of John of Carrick, did not neglect his many other children. Robert and Alexander, his sons by Elizabeth Mure, would be, respectively, duke of Albany and earl of Buchan. These and the other children of Robert II, whether from his first or second marriages, together with their illegitimate siblings, formed a layer of nobility always likely to come into conflict with the magnates, and not always loyal to their father. It was said of Robert's sons and with good cause that 'some were peaceable and benign, some insolent and malign'. It was the latter who troubled both the king himself and those families whose power in Scotland was now increasingly to challenge that of the monarchy.

RELATIONS WITH ENGLAND

However ineffectual Robert II might be in domestic affairs, he could not, any more than any other Scottish monarch, resist the temptation to profit from any period of English weakness. Scotland and France had this much in common: that part of each country was still in English hands. Robert renewed the alliance with France as a preliminary to his attempt to strike at the English, whose king was entering his last years. In 1376 the Scots crossed the border and in 1378 took Berwick only to lose it again. Robert grew bolder and when in 1377 Edward III died, to be succeeded by the ten-year-old Richard II, Robert stopped payment of David II's ransom. He even dared to criticise Charles V who, he considered, had not supported him adequately; all this suggested a confident king, certainly one ready to seize the initiative offered by a temporary English decline. But he could not drive the English finally out of Scotland. Scottish aggression was followed by English attack or invasion. The capture and destruction of the English castle of Lochmaben brought John of Gaunt to Edinburgh which he held to ransom with Robert unable to intervene. In 1383, Richard II, now aged 18, led a huge army over the border, inflicting much damage, but unable to advance beyond the Forth. The Scottish leaders, some with long experience of war with England, wisely refused, greatly to the distaste of their French allies, to be drawn into a pitched battle and Richard, like Edward II in 1322, had no alternative but to retire over the border.

Inevitably, fortune again favoured the Scots. In 1387, the Lords Appellant gained control of Richard's government, allowing Robert an opportunity to take the war into England in the following year. The invasion was ambitious and well planned and the Scots, their forces divided, ranged widely across the northern counties. It was not, however, Robert who gained a lasting reputation in the public mind from the invasion of 1388. At Otterburn, on 15 August 1388, James, second earl of Douglas, defeated an English force under Henry Percy, son of the earl of Northumberland. Douglas' death at the moment of victory in a battle itself of local rather than national significance earned him, in ballad and poetry, an immortality denied to his king.

A DISTURBING LEGACY

Robert II had not been a young man when he came to the throne in 1371. As his reign moved into its second decade he naturally lost his resilience and his physical condition, equally naturally, deteriorated. From the start of his reign he had been faced with opposition within Scotland when William, the first earl of Douglas, had put himself forward as a candidate for the throne. Douglas was bought off but a precedent had been set. The rule of an ageing king proved as damaging to internal order as would that of a minor. The delegation of authority to members of the nobility encouraged excesses and factional rivalry which only a strong king could contain. Robert was not that. By 1384 his incapacity was recognised; at a council held at Holyrood abbey in November it was admitted by the king that he could not 'attend himself personally to the execution of justice and the law of his kingdom'. Robert's admission did not lead to his deposition but his son, John of Carrick, was given the authority which Robert had been unable to exercise. It required a little less than four years to demonstrate John's own inadequacy for the task allocated to him. The occasion of his removal from the post he had held since 1384 was an accident; during a council held at Linlithgow he was kicked by a horse and severely injured. Thereafter he remained lame. The 'Three Estates' used his infirmity as an excuse to replace him with Robert Stewart, earl of Fife, Robert's second son. Before the end of the year the king had formally acknowledged what was in effect his demotion and that of his heir. A king and an heir who shared such an indifference to the maintenance of their status shared also a marked reluctance to govern with a firm hand. Robert II died, aged 74, on 19 April 1390, at Dundonald Castle. His successor, who was 53, assumed the name of Robert because his own, John, was thought to be redolent of that Balliol who had reigned so disastrously a century before. An age quick to note parallels and to draw disturbing conclusions from them did not overlook this one. That the Scots were correct in their foreboding was at once clear. Four months elapsed between the death of Robert II and the coronation of Robert III at Scone on 14 August. They were months in which Forres and Elgin were burned. Behind these outrages was the new king's brother, Alexander Stewart, earl of Buchan, whose greed had so alienated the bishop of Moray that the latter had censured him. The earl, the 'Wolf of Badenoch', as he was known, retaliated in memorable fashion. The earl's relationship with the king ensured that criticism was directed elsewhere and blame laid at the door of the Highlanders whom he had led. The new king, while still acting in place of Robert II, had been given the task of bringing the Highlanders under control. As Tacitus had created one stereotype of the Scot in writing of Agricola's campaigns, so at least one chronicler now labelled the Highlander as 'wild and untamed', inferior to the 'law abiding and peaceful' Scot to the south of the country. The Gaelic speaker thus suffered by comparison with the speaker of English. Time would not alter these perceptions, any more than John of Carrick's transformation into Robert III would guarantee him the strength he had once lacked in his dealings with the Highlanders and the other unruly elements in Scotland. Weak as earl, he was no different as king.

CHAPTER SIX

The Crown and its Overmighty Subjects, 1390–1550

Robert III, king from 1390 to 1406, a gentle and melancholy man, was remarkably self critical. He was unable even to carry himself with royal dignity because of the physical disability from which he had suffered since 1388 when he was kicked by a horse belonging to the bearer of a significant name of the period, Sir James Douglas of Dalkeith. He chose as his epitaph the sadly revealing words: 'The worst of kings and the most wretched of men'. It was quite in keeping with such thinking that he should be reported as having said that a suitable burial-place for him would be a deep midden. Instead, his subjects, perhaps not unnaturally preferring to remember the deeds of the illustrious family from which he was descended rather than the inglorious and brutal events of his reign, laid him to rest in the peace of Paisley Abbey, founded in about the year 1163, by his ancestor, Walter son of Alan, first of the hereditary stewards of Scotland.

Robert's accession, as has been seen, was prefaced by violence in the Highlands, a reminder of the violence of the reign of his predecessor. In 1390, there was further evidence of a link to that reign. In 1388, when Robert III, then earl of Carrick under his proper name of John, had been removed from his office of guardian of the realm, his brother Robert, earl of Fife and Menteith, had assumed the post. At the beginning of his reign in 1390, the new king, still judged incapable, had to allow his brother to continue in office as guardian at a salary of 1,000 marks per annum. The earl of Fife, created duke of Albany in 1398, was to be an important, if dangerous and divisive figure throughout the rest of the reign of Robert III and also well into that of the next king, James I.

The Battle of the Clans

It is perhaps indicative of the failure of Robert III to impose his rule on his kingdom and of his desperation at the disorder inside it that he should have lent his presence, and therefore his encouragement, to an event which took place at Perth on 28 September 1396, in which he apparently saw the prospect of bringing an end to the troubles in the Highlands. The situation involved two clans, Chattan and Kay, who were engaged in a feud the origins of which, as so often, are today obscure. They met before the king, some nobles, and a number of French and English knights, on the North Inch at Perth to put the merits of their respective cases to the test in judicial combat on a grand scale. An enclosure of wood and iron had been erected at a cost of £14.2s.11d. in which 60 men, 30 from each clan, joined in battle. It is recorded that when the king threw down his baton to end the affair, Clan Chattan had emerged victors. Twenty-eight of their opponents lay dead inside the enclosure with perhaps as many as 21 of Clan Chattan killed. We do not know whether as a result of this bloodthirsty encounter the feud between these two clans ceased but it is certain that this example of the king's justice did not bring about the return of peace to the Highlands he had hoped for. Contemporary accounts do not tell of any such peace but of 'great and horrible destruction' with 'justice, as if outlawed, in exile outside the boundaries of the realm'.

FAMILY RIVALRIES

Even with a king as compliant as Robert III had chosen to be, the earl of Fife was not to be allowed unimpeded licence to govern the kingdom as he might have wished. In 1393, in an action as bold as it was uncharacteristic, the king removed the earl from office and took the reins of government into his own hands. Quite what prompted Robert into such a vigorous move is unclear, but he must have felt sure of support. There was inevitable jealousy of the earl from those who thought themselves his peers, and his financial dealings were a matter of some comment. It is possible that behind the king in his coup were his queen, Annabella Drummond, mother of his seven children, and their son, David, earl of Carrick, now aged 15 and heir to the throne. Both the queen and her son could find reason to see an opponent, if not yet an enemy, in the earl of Fife; she because her brother-in-law appears rather unnecessarily to have interfered in her enjoyment of monies granted to her in 1391 as queen; David because of a natural antipathy towards an uncle whose power and wealth exceeded his own. David, too, probably resented the supervision which his uncle exercised over him at this time. It might have been better for Scotland had the king either resisted his own inclinations and external pressures to replace his brother or disposed of him entirely.

Restored as head of government, Robert III continued, as before, inept. He sought to reconcile his son and his brother by creating both dukes in imitation of the English fashion. On 28 April 1398, at Scone, his son became duke of Rothesay, his brother duke of Albany. In this attempt at bringing the two together he was as unsuccessful as he was in so much else during this period of personal rule. By January of 1399 the country had had enough of Robert and at a general council meeting at Perth, the king and his officers were bluntly blamed for the 'misgover-

The Great Seal of Robert III

nance of the realm'. Robert was given an opening to lay the responsibility for the unhappy state of affairs on others, particularly the new duke of Albany, but he ignored the opportunity to rid himself and the country of one whose malign influence brought misery to both. Abany escaped the fate which a more vindictive or less honourable monarch might have planned for him but had to look on while Rothesay was named the king's lieutenant for a period of three years, under a commission from his father to govern Scotland.

THE DEATH OF THE DUKE OF ROTHESAY

Rothesay surpassed his uncle in his ability to make enemies. Albany, of course, having lost office, was already to be numbered among these; despite the recent blows to his prestige, he was far from being without a voice in the councils of the realm. Rothesay did not delay in offering insults to the nobility. He had been betrothed to, and may even have married Elizabeth, daughter of George Dunbar, earl of March, who had paid Robert III a large sum of money for the arrangement. When, however, the third earl of Douglas, Archibald 'the Grim', offered the king a greater figure in order that his daughter, Marjory, should marry Rothesay, the contract with March was repudiated and instead Rothesay married into the Douglas family. March seems to have been at least as much angered by the loss of the payment he had made to the king as by the insult to his daughter, Elizabeth. As the king proved less than willing to see the force of his argument, March, early in 1400, asked for help from the new king of England, Henry IV, on grounds of their feudal relationship. March, perhaps to show his sincerity, joined in an English raid, led by the Percies, into Scotland. Henry, sensing that he might renew the ancient English claim to overlordship of Scotland, invaded Lothian but, despite Robert's unwarlike attitude in the face of invasion, he retreated back into England in September.

It was not enough that Rothesay had alienated March; he treated his Douglas bride with contempt, considering marriage no obstacle to his philandering. Archibald Douglas was no man to have as an enemy but, luckily for Rothesay, in this instance he restrained himself and loyally continued to back Rothesay in his work as the king's lieutenant. Rothesay appears to have acted on occasion with some energy but what he might have achieved was thwarted by his own foolishness. When, in turn, Douglas Walter Trail, the bishop of St Andrews and queen Annabella, all died within a year Rothesay was deprived of their advice and authority. It was perhaps inevitable that the king should find it impossible to protect his son against demands for his removal. Rothesay was arrested and handed over to Albany and the new earl, the fourth, of Douglas who took him to Falkland Castle. There he died, in March 1402, at the age of 24, in circumstances which led to the greatest suspicion. It was suggested that he had been starved to death; Albany and Douglas were closely questioned by a general council but exonerated, and the king himself publicly stated that they were innocent of any crime. Albany resumed office and Douglas, later in the same year, striving to emulate his ancestor, James, at the Battle of Otterburn, was captured by the Percies at Homildon Hill in Northumberland on 14 September when the war with England was resumed. In a remarkable change of mood, Douglas joined with the Percies in their rebellion against Henry IV which ended at Shrewsbury on 21 July 1403. There, he was captured once more and did not see Scotland again until 1409. It was not without reason, therefore, that he was known to his contemporaries as 'the Tyneman' or 'Loser'. With him was taken Albany's son, Murdoch, who remained a factor in Albany's thinking until Murdoch's release in 1416.

THE END OF ROBERT III

The king could not fail to see in Albany a threat to his surviving son, James, born at Dumfermline in 1394, and now, with the death of Rothesay, the heir to the throne, Robert decided to send James to France for safety. He made his plans with care and secrecy but omitted to seek a safe-conduct from England, perhaps because there was a truce between the two countries at this time. Due to a delay of a month while James waited on the Bass Rock for a ship, the secret could hardly be kept. On 14 March 1406, the Polish ship, the 'Maryenknyght' was boarded off Flamborough Head, 20 miles south of Scarborough, by English pirates, and James, the heir to the throne of Scotland, was made a prisoner. He was taken to London and lodged in the Tower of London. Not until 18 years later was he released.

When the king heard of James' capture he was in Rothesay Castle where he may have thought himself secure. Not surprisingly he began to languish; it is said that 'for grief thereafter he took not food'. He was already in his sixty-ninth year; one son had died in suspicious circumstances, another had now been taken from him. He was alone, physically weak and mentally drained, and died on Palm Sunday, which in that year fell on 4 April.

The Dukes of Albany

There was no alternative to Albany as regent of Scotland, upon the death of Robert III. The appointment was made at Perth in June 1406 when the 'three estates' met in general council. Albany was king in all but name; in a letter to Henry IV in 1410 he wrote of the people of Scotland as his 'subjects'. If Albany was at least as anxious to arrange for the release of his son, Murdoch, as for that of his sovereign, James, he had in his own mind at least good cause; Murdoch was back in Scotland in 1416, James not until 1424. Albany was careful to enlist the support of the Douglas family for whatever plans he had for the throne; in 1409 he entered into a 'band' for mutual defence with Archibald the Tyneman. One clause of the 'band' makes a direct and intriguing reference to the possibility of Albany becoming king. In London James, the rightful king, could not be unaware of such manoeuvres and, once back in Scotland, would move with ruthless purpose against both Albany's son and the Douglas family. Albany's reliance on the Douglases, of course, clearly indicates their growing power in Scotland and of this, too, James could not be ignorant. Hoping to maintain peace in the country, Albany, like both Robert II and Robert III, bought off the Douglases and others by gifts of land and by turning a blind eye to their excesses of violence and plundering of government revenues. It was uncommon for action to be taken against the lawless, although in 1411, Albany's nephew, Alexander earl of Mar, met and defeated Donald, lord of the Isles, at Harlaw in Aberdeenshire. This put an end to Donald's plan to seize by force the earldom of Ross. So great was the slaughter on that occasion that the battle was afterwards known as 'Red' Harlaw. Only a king, and a strong one at that, could improve matters. James was still a prisoner in England when, in 1420, Albany died, at the age of 81, to be succeeded as regent, quite naturally it seemed, by his son, Murdoch. The new regent had no more reason than his father to hurry to secure James's release, nor under him was there a significant decrease in lawlessness. Even Murdoch's own sons were notorious for their contempt for their father's rule.

The Return of James I

James I had been king for 18 years when, under the terms of the Treaty of London which was agreed in December 1423, he was able to return to Scotland the following year. He was crowned at Scone on 21 May 1424 and at once gave evidence of his intent. The first parliament of his reign, held within a week of his coronation, laid down the principles by which he meant to rule. His consistency in upholding these principles restored the royal finances, decimated the ranks of his enemies in the nobility, and brought about his own murder. He was no more punctilious in insisting

James I

that his ransom, in his case 60,000 merks be paid, than his predecessor, David II, had been in the previous century. James was a vigorous and cynical young man, no doubt embittered by the unwillingness of the dukes of Albany to arrange for his earlier release. But he was well educated and of a poetical bent, intelligent and not easily deterred. He was fortunate in his marriage to Joan, daughter of John Beaufort, earl of Somerset, and grand-daughter of John of Gaunt; she was to play an unforgettable if horrifying role in events at the end of his reign. He was fortunate, too, that he reigned at a time when England could mount no serious and prolonged attacks on Scotland; Henry V died in 1422, to be succeeded by an infant in whose name a council of regency ruled. Above all, it was James' own resolute behaviour which assured him of support among his own countrymen who were sick of strife and lawlessness.

JAMES AND HIS OVERMIGHTY SUBJECTS

It is said that, while still a prisoner in England, James had sworn that, if allowed to return to Scotland, he would make 'the key keep the castle and the bracken bush the cow'. He meant by this quaint expression that his law would reach all, irrespective of station. He kept his word. Within a year of his coronation, he had engineered the fall of Murdoch, duke of Albany. The duke was first imprisoned and then with his sons, Walter and Alexander, and his father-in-law, Duncan, earl of Lennox, he was executed on the Heading Hill at Stirling in May 1425. The charges which the king brought against this important group did not deceive his contemporaries. Financially, the king was able to benefit since the earldoms of Fife and Menteith and Lennox fell to him with their revenues; James had understood that a king without money was likely to be a king without authority. There was more to come. The ruthlessness which permitted James to disregard the fact that Lennox was in his eighties at the time of his execution led him to strike with great severity and cunning in the north of the country. He used the Inverness parliament in 1428 to seize and imprison some 50 Highland chiefs, three of whom he executed as an example before releasing the others, suitably chastened. The new lord of the Isles, Alexander Macdonald, son of the man defeated at Harlaw in 1411, held no terrors for James. Having bluffed Macdonald's army at Lochaber in June 1429, the king forced him to appear as a penitent during mass at Holyrood. The Douglases could not hope to be overlooked by James as he put his kingdom to rights. Nor were they. Archibald the Tyneman, the fourth earl, had been killed in 1424 at Verneuil, fighting with the French against the English. However, his son, also Archibald, presented an attractive target for James who in 1431 arrested Douglas and imprisoned him in Lochleven as a warning. Among the many arrested by James was Sir Robert Graham. Imprisoned in 1424 for some unknown reason, Graham was soon at large but when he upbraided James in parliament, he was banished. Graham would return from 'the cuntreis of the Wild Scottis' to end James' reign in dramatic and bloody fashion. James' people as a whole seem to have had mixed reactions to his methods. Their gratitude for the firmness of his rule was matched by a widespread recognition of his greed and acquisitiveness. In 1425, a year after his return, he found it necessary to enact that seditious talk would be punished by death. The luxury of his court did not go unnoticed by a people afflicted by plague and failed harvests. His ransom was used as an excuse to raise taxes, the proceeds from which did not reach England. He was slow to repay loans while enforcing debt on others. Often unpopular through his policies, he became, if at least one source is to be believed, unpleasant in his person.

Religion and Learning

As Scotland was passing through weak rule and disorder into a period of strong government and repression, it was being affected by events taking place in Europe. In 1378, Pope Urban VI in Rome found himself opposed by a nominee of those cardinals who wished to depose him. This was Clement VII who set himself up at Avignon, from which the papal court had just returned at the end of the long sojourn known as the 'Babylonish Captivity'. Until 1417, when the Council of Constance deposed the Avignon pope, Benedict XIII, and Martin V was elected in Rome, the Church was in the grip of the 'Great Schism', damaging to its unity and productive of heresy. In Bohemia, John Hus, born in 1369, rector of the university of Prague, preached religious reform and, although he himself was burned in 1415, the movement which he had started grew into one with a strong nationalist element. Paul Craw, a doctor, brought back from the continent to Scotland something of the teachings of Hus and, seized for his heresy, was burned for his faith at St Andrews in 1432. Craw was not, however, the first heretic to die at the stake in Scotland. As early as 1399, the ill-fated duke of Rothesay had been required, when made his father's lieutenant, to 'restrain cursit men and heretics'. It was not Rothesay but his uncle, Albany, who was praised as the defender of the Catholic faith, and under him Scotland had its first execution of a heretic, one John Resby, burned at Perth in 1407. Resby, sometimes thought of as the first Protestant martyr in Scottish history, was a follower of the Englishman, John Wycliffe, whose preaching had social as well as religious implications. As a Lollard, the name by which those who had accepted Wycliffe's doctrines were known, Resby received scant sympathy. There was no Lollard uprising as in England, where Sir John Oldcastle led an abortive coup in 1413–1414. The passions of religious debate and the violence of religious war lay far ahead.

With the beginnings of religious dissent, however easily crushed in Scotland, came that intellectual stirring which led to the foundation of the first of the Scottish universities. In the 'Great Schism', Scotland, with France, had sided with the pope, the so-called 'anti-pope', in Avignon. The tradition of Scottish students attending the university of Paris continued but when, in 1408, France switched its allegiance from Avignon to Rome, the popularity of Paris with Scottish students waned. It was soon realised that Scotland must provide its own university and two were created within 40 years. In 1412, under the bishop of St Andrews, Henry Wardlaw, and with the support of the absent king, James I, a university was established in the town. William Turnbull, bishop of Glasgow, a scholar of some repute, was not to be outdone and in 1451, obtained from pope Nicholas V a bull for the foundation of the university of Glasgow. Before the end of the century, in 1495, largely because of the endeavours of James IV, the university of Aberdeen had been created. Of the four premier Scottish universities, there remained only Edinburgh; that came into existence in 1583.

The Murder of James I

When Sir Robert Graham was brought to trial at Stirling in March 1437, for his part in the murder of James I, he believed that he would be seen as one who had rid the country of a tyrant. Graham had miscalculated. He was not praised but reviled in a contemporary verse which ran:

> Sir Robert Graham.
> That slew our king:
> God give him shame.

There was, beyond doubt, much dislike, even hatred, of the king but Graham and his fellow conspirators acted not from a desire to free Scotland but to replace James with their own government. They were all, in varying degrees, self interested. Graham himself, whatever illusions he may have had about his motives, was somewhat unbalanced, driven by a exceptional loathing for James which was personal in origin. The father of Robert Stewart had died in England, one of the hostages for James' ransom and cynically ignored by him. Walter, earl of Atholl, the surviving son of the second marriage of Robert II, to Euphemia of Ross, countess of Moray, was ambitious, hoping at least to be governor, if not king, being next in line to the throne after James' son, should the young prince die. The reaction of the people to the murder of the king, on 21 February 1437 in the Dominican friary in Perth, was a wise one in respect of the motives of the murderers. James I, as Graham would have had it, had already manifested some of the characteristics of a tyrant but regicide had been unknown in Scotland since the eleventh century and was viewed with horror. James' queen, Joan, herself wounded at Perth, had the murderers hunted down within a month and her vengeance was merciless. Graham and the others suffered three days of judicial torture before being allowed to die; in a mockery of his royal pretensions, Atholl had a red-hot crown placed on his brow before he was beheaded.

THE MINORITY OF JAMES II

James II, aged six, was crowned and anointed on 25 March 1437 at Holyrood Abbey, as he was a minor, a regency was necessary. James I's treatment of the upper nobility had resulted in its reconstruction; his policy of execution, seizure of land, and the subtle cultivation to his cause of certain of the nobility had transformed its ranks. Of the noble houses it was that of the earls of Douglas, descended from Robert I's 'Good' Sir James, and known as the 'Black' Douglases which now dominated Scotland. There would be an important role later in the century for the other branch of the family, the 'Red' Douglases, but at the time of the accession of James II, it was a 'Black' Douglas, Archibald, once imprisoned in the previous reign, who was the obvious choice for regent with the title of lieutenant-general. Douglas' existing titles were impressive: he was duke of Touraine by descent from his father who was killed at Verneuil in 1424, fifth earl of Douglas, count of Longueville and lord of Galloway and Annandale. Despite his credentials, Douglas was ineffective in dealing with a resurgence of lawlessness; he may well have felt himself, in fact if not in theory, the equal of the king and therefore unwilling to ease the coming of any authority other than his own. Scotland suffered not merely from lawlessness but from plague and famine in successive years. Douglas himself died in 1439, perhaps a victim of the former. He was not replaced as lieutenant-general and the years which followed his death saw the gradual build-up of that tension between his family and the king which was to have such dire consequences for the 'Black' Douglases.

THE 'BLACK DINNER'

The first assault on the Douglases came not from the king who was at the time only ten but from two men, ostensibly his servants and acting in his name. Sir Alexander Livingston, keeper of Stirling Castle, and Sir William Crichton, keeper of Edinburgh Castle, were originally enemies, each intent on gaining possession of James II as a means to power. Both understood, however, that a major stumbling-block to the fulfilment of their ambitions was the new earl of Douglas, a boy of 14 or 15. Despite his youth, Earl William might one day hope to achieve something of the standing of his father. Livingston and Crichton, temporarily allies, could not permit this. They lured William and his only brother, David, to Edinburgh Castle. At the end of dinner, Crichton placed a bull's head on the table as a signal that the two Douglases were to be seized. Tried on a trumped-up charge of treason, they were condemned to death and executed on Castle Hill. The murder, for such it was, gave rise to a rhyme:

Edinburgh Castle, toune and tower,
God grant thou sinke for sinne,
And that even for the black dinoir
Earl Douglas gat therein.

The death of Earl William did not, as might be thought inevitable, produce a vendetta by the Douglases against those who had killed him. This was an age of realpolitik. The main beneficiary of the removal of earl William was a Douglas, his great-uncle, James, earl of Avondale, known because of his bulk as 'the Gross'. There is little doubt that James connived in the events in Edinburgh on 24 November 1440, after which he gained possession of the earldom of Douglas. The alliance between Crichton and Livingston did not long survive the death in 1443 of James 'the Gross'. His successor, William, eighth earl of Douglas, joined with Livingston against Crichton. Throughout Scotland the violence spread as the main participants attacked each other's lands and the Church in the person of James Kennedy, bishop of St Andrews, took the side of the Crichton faction. Many of the most famous names in Scottish history were now engaged on one side or the other of the struggle, among them Home, Hepburn, Ogilvy, Lindsay, Hamilton and Crawford. With the reappearance of the common enemy, England, attention was briefly diverted to the international scene. Cross-border warfare had never really ceased despite truces between the two countries; families such as the Douglases and the Percies who had fought at Otterburn were unlikely to be at peace for long. In 1448 war on a larger scale broke out when an English army under the earl of Northumberland raided into Annandale. The Scots under Hugh Douglas, earl of Ormond and son of James 'the Gross', defeated it at Gretna on the Sark on 23 October. The English, however, were back in the summer of 1449, burning Dumfries and Dunbar. Alnwick and Warworth were the Scottish targets and were duly burned before another truce was concluded on 15 November.

A MURDEROUS KING

Before these events in the war with England, James II, now aged almost 19, had married. His wife was Mary of Guelders, niece of Philip 'the Good', duke of Burgundy. At much the same time, James took over the government, proving to be as ruthless as his father but, as would become clear, more vicious. Not yet ready to challenge the power of the Douglases, he first turned on the Livingston family. Apart from Alexander who was justiciar, members of the family held crucial appointments in government. James, desperate for money, had the Livingstons brought to trial in Edinburgh on 19 January 1450. Two were executed and others imprisoned and their lands forfeited. James' financial position had improved as a result, but not enough, so like his father before him, he saw in the possession of others the means to transform his unsatisfactory situation. We do not know when he decided that he could no longer avoid the use of force against the Douglases; certainly he was too intelligent to have intended murder by his own hand. When William the eighth earl went on pilgrimage to Rome in October 1450, the king made his move, overrunning and seizing William's lands in Galloway and Selkirk. Upon the return of the earl, the two were, strangely, reconciled, the earl's lands being given back to him. The king's recourse to force had failed to ensure lasting gains; he cannot have been other than humiliated and more conscious than ever of the threat posed by the Douglases. The earl, for his part, continued in his disregard of royal authority. James, learning that Douglas had entered into a bond with the earls of Crawford and Ross, now felt that the danger to him was greater than before. He demanded a meeting with Douglas to discuss the situation and gave him safe-conduct to come to Stirling Castle. On the evening of 22 February 1452, king and earl faced each other, each understandably suspicious and with his own concerns. The king could not allow Douglas and his allies to continue to encroach on his power; the earl feared that without the bond with Crawford and Ross, the king would deal with his subjects piecemeal. James appears to have ordered Douglas to break the bond, to which Douglas retorted that 'he mycht nocht, nor wald nocht'. James, like Bruce at Dumfries in 1306, lost his head and stabbed Douglas with his dagger. In one account, the earl's brains were dashed out by a courtier and others, with James, joined in the murder; 26 wounds were later found on the body.

THE RUIN OF THE 'BLACK' DOUGLASES

James, the ninth and the last earl, brother of the murdered man, rose quickly and forcefully against the king. At Stirling, at the head of 600 men, he dragged the king's safe-conduct through the streets and swore to be revenged on the king's 'Cruelle tyrannie'. The king, however, was no less intelligent than violent; he was able to defeat the Douglas reaction both in the field and in parliament. By August 1452, he had received the earl's submission, having already an assurance from his subjects in parliament that the eighth earl had brought about his own death at Stirling 'by resisting the king's gentle persuasion'. James appeared at this stage to be anxious to be conciliatory but he would not wait indefinitely to break the power of the Douglases. The ninth earl, now isolated in Scotland, where his previous allies were no longer enthusiastic for his cause, sought help from England, from Henry VI. Like his predecessors, Henry VI recognised in the earl someone through whom he might interfere in Scottish affairs. James II now had his excuse to attack Douglas who could be charged with treason. Douglas lost his nerve and fled to England, while his brothers, made of sterner stuff, stayed in Scotland to fight. At Arkinholme near Langholm, on 1 May 1455, in what the king described as 'a lethal combat', the Douglases were defeated by some 200 loyalist Borderers. Of the brothers, Archibald, earl of Moray, was killed, Hugh, earl of Ormond, was wounded and captured and later executed, and John, Lord Balvenie escaped to England. The king now no longer had need to be patient or conciliatory. In parliament in June 1455, the last earl was found guilty of treason and the Douglas lands were forfeited to the Crown.

Among the factors which contributed to James II's success against the most important and powerful family in his kingdom was his use of heavy artillery in his campaigns. With bombards, including the famous 'Mons Meg', he reduced castles such as Hatton and Abercorn. Perhaps the greatest prize of all was Threave in Galloway, which the earl of Douglas, still in England and now Henry VI's man, had hoped to relieve. James' victory over the 'Black' Douglases was achieved at considerable cost to Scotland which was ravaged by king and earl alike. The use of artillery deprived the king's enemies of strongholds and the physical signs of their hold over the countryside. It is somewhat ironic that James should himself fall victim to the weapon on which he relied. On Sunday 3 August 1460, as he conducted the siege of Roxburgh, which had been in English hands since the last century, he decided to honour the arrival of his queen by having a royal salute fired. James took up his position beside one of the guns, 'the Lion'. Unfortunately, it blew up and the king was killed by the fragments. Five days later the castle fell to the Scots and was dismantled. On 10 August, a week after his father's unnecessary death, James III was crowned in Kelso Abbey.

A SERIES OF MINORITIES

For almost a century after the death of James II one minor after another succeeded to the throne. If the process was in each case peaceful, it was also dangerous to the security of the kingdom. In 1460 the new king was nine years old. James IV was 15 when he became king in 1488, James V was a year old in 1513, and Mary was no more than a week old when her turn came to rule Scotland in 1542. Two of these kings died in violent circumstances. James III was murdered by an unknown assassin in the aftermath of the Battle of Sauchieburn, near Bannockburn, in 1488; James IV was killed fighting against the English at Flodden in 1513. The only woman among these monarchs, Mary, fared badly; she was forced to abdicate in 1567 in favour of her son, James, himself only a year old, and went to England from which she never returned.

The 'Red' Douglases

Each minority necessitated a regency with its attendant problems and opportunities for the unscrupulous and the ambitious. As early as 1462 that same James, last earl of Douglas, who had fled ignominiously from James II, was trying to re-establish himself in Scotland. He failed then, as he failed again in 1484, by which time the king was more than a match for him; but Douglas represented that ever-present threat from the nobility whenever there was either a minority or a hint of weakness in the monarch. Where one branch of the Douglas family had faded, another, the 'red' Douglases, descended from a natural son of William the first earl of Douglas, rose to prominence and power as earls of Angus. Archibald, known as 'Bell the Cat', the fifth earl of Angus, was a figure of great note in the reigns of James III and his successor, James IV. He led those who hanged James III's favourites at Lauder Bridge in

1482, fell under suspicion of treasonable correspondence with the English in the reign of James IV but, reconciled to the king, lost two sons at Flodden. The sixth earl of Angus, another Archibald, who married in 1514 Margaret, the widow of James IV, in time came to be virtual ruler of Scotland, when it was said that 'none durst strive against a Douglas, nor yet a Douglas man'.

The Threat from England

Somehow, Scotland, and with it the Stewart monarchy, survived the threat posed by members of the nobility. It survived, too, interference from England which, although distracted by its own civil disorders, was always ready to seek to profit from problems inside Scotland. Successive kings of England sought to impose their will on Scotland. This spanned from the time of Edwards IV's encouragement of the last earl of Douglas, through the support given by Richard of Gloucester to the duke of Albany, the rebellious and treacherous brother of James III, to the notorious campaigns of the Earl of Hereford who, acting under the orders of Henry VIII, burned his way through the Lowlands of Scotland in 1544 and 1545. The capacity of Scotland to regenerate itself even after defeat in battles such as Flodden in 1513, in which James IV was killed, and Solway Moss, after which James V is said to have died of a broken heart, demonstrates a continuance of that independent spirit nourished by Wallace and Bruce so long before. Not even the rout of the Scottish army at Pinkie in 1547 could bring the Scots to agree to that loss of freedom which Henry VIII's proposed marriage of his son, Edward, with the young queen Mary, would entail. As had happened before, Henry's 'Rough Wooing', the name by which his Scottish policy became known, ended as unsuccessfully as the attempts of his predecessors to make themselves masters of Scotland.

The Hard-Working Kings

Of those monarchs who had succeeded as minors, Scotland was well served by two when they assumed power, James IV and James V. Each in his own way helped to move Scotland forward into an age of great

The Renaissance façade of Falkland Palace

change without allowing its independence to be lost, or the self-destructive nature of its people to triumph over the national interest. James IV was not only a considerable scholar with a command of several languages and an enquiring mind allied to an uncritical acceptance of the teachings of the Church. He was also a strong and energetic monarch who moved restlessly about his kingdom to see its government and the upholding of the law. He was particularly active in the north and west, where he brought the lands of the lord of the Isles under the Crown in May 1493, and in the Borders, where he understood the need for firm rule where too often there had been disorder. Under James IV there ws a marked encouragement of learning; the university of Aberdeen was founded in 1495 and in the following year an education act was intended to ensure a grounding in Latin for those who would then proceed to a degree in law. In 1507 Scotland had its first printing-press, 'ane prent', set up by Walter Chapman and Andrew Millar. Not surprisingly, perhaps, in a period in which there was such a royal concern for the mind, there was also something of a golden age in Scottish literature. The poets Robert Henryson and William Dunbar are the best remembered figures and with reason. Henryson taught law at the university of Glasgow, and Dunbar was a priest in government service and probably accompanied the Scottish ambassadors to London in 1501 to discuss the matter of the king's marriage to Margaret Tudor. However, the career of Gavin Douglas, a more neglected writer, is more remarkable. He rose to be bishop of Dunkeld in 1515 but as the son of the fifth earl of Douglas he was to die of the plague in London, a proscribed rebel and traitor.

James V lacked his father's education and interest in literature but shared his commitment to strong government. He appeared unable, however, always to distinguish between the proper use of the law and his personal interpretation of it and was not averse to violence in the pursuit of his aims. No ruler hated the Douglases more than James who had been under the control of his stepfather, the sixth earl of Angus, until 1528. James broke the power of the earl of Angus but did not forgive or forget the family itself. In 1537 he trumped up a charge of conspiracy against Angus' brother-in-law, the master of Forbes, who was executed. More horrific still was the king's treatment of Angus's sister, Jane, wife of Lord Glamis. James accused her of witchcraft and of plotting to kill him and she was burned to death in Edinburgh on Castle Hill. When he marched into the Borders, where disorder had long been prevalent, he guaranteed himself a place in the literature of the district. At Caerlanrig, near Hawick, he hanged the notorious freebooter, Johnnie Armstrong of Gilnockie and some 40 of his followers. Armstrong, a menace to Scots as well as to English, guilty of any number of crimes, carried himself, according to tradition, with that arrogance and confidence which have always marked the folk-hero. He charged the king with being 'graceless', upon which James lost his temper and Armstrong died on his orders. What was a sordid episode in which a king hanged a rebellious subject without trial was transformed in ballads. Armstrong was not a villain but a hero and James treacherous and contemptible. We do not know what James thought of this transformation in the public mind but we do know that there was much admiration for him in the country at large. If the nobles, because of his strength, thought of him as 'the Ill-Beloved', the people knew him with some affection and admiration as the 'Commons' King' and 'the Goodman of Ballengeich', much given to roaming around the countryside in a variety of disguises. Like his father, James was keen to maintain ties with France as a means of counteracting the threat of Henry VIII of England. His first wife was Madeleine, daughter of Francis I, but she died not long after the wedding. His second wife was Mary of Lorraine, whose father was Claude, duke of Guise. Their daughter, Mary, the future queen of Scots, was born at Linlithgow on 8 December 1542. The Scotland which she inherited six days later on the death of her father had assumed its final form in 1472 with the annexation or Orkney and Shetland, formerly the property of Norway. The rule of James V has not always been seen as an unqualified success but he bequeathed to his infant daughter a country which had succeeded in remaining independent despite internal dissension and external pressure. Not even a country as strong as Scotland clearly was, however, could withstand without damage to its institutions and security, the events which lay in the immediate future.

CHAPTER SEVEN

Reformation and Reaction,
1550–1580

The King's Prophecy

James V, unable to be with his army because of illness, was at Lochmaben when he was told of the English victory at Solway Moss. He was informed that his favourite, Oliver Sinclair of Pitcairns, had been taken prisoner as he fled 'full manfully' from the field. It was Sinclair's sudden claim to the leadership of the Scottish army that had provoked bitter argument as the battle was about to begin. Robert, fifth Lord Maxwell, James' Warden of the West March and admiral of Scotland, the earls of Cassillis and Glencairn, and the Lords Gray, Fleming, Somervell, and Oliphant, also fell into the hands of the English in what was a rout and a disgrace. Despite a numerical supremacy of perhaps as many as six to one, the Scots had been out-thought and out-manoeuvred by Henry VIII's Warden of the West March, Sir Thomas Wharton, who had brought a force from Carlisle to meet the Scots. Wharton had no doubt that the principal cause of his success had been his 'prickers', light scouting horsemen, under William Musgrave. They, Wharton said, had 'gatt theyme (the Scots) in a shake all the waye'. There is no means of knowing the numbers of the Scottish dead; certainly many were drowned in the River Esk and some 1,200 were captured. Wharton claimed that he had lost only seven dead and one prisoner, but only a quarter of his force had actually been engaged in the battle.

It is tempting to believe that if James himself had been present, the outcome of Solway Moss would have been different. There would have been no dispute over leadership, of course, and those who found Sinclair's pretensions intolerable would have been united behind their king. Yet, not even James' presence at the head of the army could have removed one of the reasons for the loss of morale in its ranks, religious differences. James was unsympathetic to the new thinking which was already established in Scotland, and it was that thinking which would eventually drive his daughter, Mary, out of Scotland. Broken by the news from Solway Moss, James went first to Edinburgh, then on to Linlithgow, where his wife awaited the birth of the child who would so shortly inherit the crown. From there he went to his beloved Falkland Palace, the building of which he had completed. He was only 31 but tired and dispirited. Two of his sons had died in the previous year and when he was told of the birth of a daughter, 'a vereye weyke childe, and not like to live', he lost his own will to live. It is said that thereafter he 'spake but few wise words' before he died, but among those words was the prophecy by which he is perhaps best remembered. With his thoughts on

James V

Marjory Bruce, the daughter of Robert I, who died at about the time of the birth of the first of the Stewart kings, Robert II, James said: 'It came with a lass and it will go with a lass.' James was no doubt referring to his daughter but the prophecy did in fact come true when on the death of Queen Anne in 1714, the crown passed from the House of Stuart, the French spelling which had long since replaced that of Stewart, to the House of Hanover in the shape of George I.

The first heretics to be burned in Scotland for their religious beliefs were men such as James Resby in 1407, Quentin Folkhyrde in 1422 and Paul Craw in 1433. They were followers of the teachings of either John Wycliffe in England or John Hus in Bohemia. The heresies which Resby, Folkhyrde, Craw and others unknown to us preached so enthusiastically and widely throughout Scotland caused scandal and concern to Church and State alike; both thought themselves under attack and were therefore prompt to take action. When Bishop Henry Wardlaw was founding the country's first university at his own St Andrews, he was at pains to stress that it was through higher education that the Church would be provided with a supply of those scholars who would argue the case for the Church, and thus ensure that it would be able 'to withstand heresies and errors'. The two royal dukes, Rothesay and Albany, as we have seen, were alert to their roles in defence of their faith against heretics. Courageous and persistent as were the likes of Resby it is unclear quite how great was the effect of their teaching. Nor can it be shown that the manner of their deaths aroused sympathy or brought large numbers of converts to their beliefs. It may be that the swift and cruel treatment meted out to them had the desired effect of snuffing out unorthodoxy. The alliance of Church and State against heresy was cemented by the parliament of 1425 which decreed that the Church, with the help of the State, would seek out and deal with 'heretics and Lollardis'. The teachings of Wycliffe, it is true, lingered on in Scotland to the end of the fifteenth century, but apparently in such a form that heresy of whatever kind was no longer viewed as the threat it had once been considered.

SCOTLAND AND THE REFORMATION

Thirty years later the situation had changed. The Reformation, which began on the Continent, had both religious and political consequences in Scotland, as elsewhere. The doubts about the spiritual values, teachings and institutions of the Church which Wycliffe and Hus had raised now came to the surface once more, but with more force and more support from society at large. Heresy, as it were, had become fashionable and it was finding definition in forms which guaranteed that it would not be driven underground or destroyed. Martin Luther in Germany posted his 95 theses on the door of a church in Wittenberg and publicly burned the Papal Bull which excommunicated him. His condemnation as a heretic before the emperor, Charles V, at the Diet of Worms in 1521 was a gesture which, in his case, had lost its meaning and failed to halt him or the spread of his ideas. The Frenchman John Cauvin, or Calvin as he is better known, forced to move hurriedly from Paris to Geneva when his scholarly opinions brought him an unwelcome and dangerous notoriety, built a theocratic state in Switzerland. Through his teaching he influenced the most famous figure in the Scottish Reformation, John Knox. William Tyndale's translation of the New Testament into English found its way into Scotland, probably by the east-coast trade routes, as did the news of his martyrdom on the Continent in 1536. Henry VIII, while still maintaining that he was a true and faithful son of the Church, was introducing that series of measures which was, in time, to result in the Church of England breaking with Rome. It is unlikely that either Luther or Calvin would have envisaged the outcome of their desire for reform. While representing and articulating a deep-rooted unease about the Church, each was still a man of his times. They were not liberals as the word is understood today; Luther was an anti-Semite and Calvin condoned the burning of his opponent, Servetus. They questioned doctrine but were drawn into the world of politics as they did so.

In Scotland the Church itself recognised its problems. In 1549, at the instigation of John Hamilton, formerly bishop of Dunkeld, but by now archbishop of St Andrews after murder had removed his predecessor, a provincial council was called. This was the legislative body of the Church and acknowledged that it presented an unattractive image, one conducive to disaffection and heresy; there was 'a corruption of morals and profane lewdness' and 'crass ignorance of literature and all the liberal arts'. The clergy passed a number of statutes to counteract these and other faults, but the need to call provincial councils on similar matters in 1552 and 1559 is evidence that these statutes, in general, were not enforced. The catechism produced in 1552 with its directions to priests reveals how poor were the teaching skills then to be found in the Church; they were to read 'clearly, articulately, and with attention to the stops' when preaching to their flocks. Too often the lower clergy remained ignorant and unpaid, the prelates wealthy, corrupt, and disreputable. The Church in Scotland offered a target for those who had genuine religious concerns as well as those who saw, in its riches and lands, an irresistible temptation. Printing made it easier to circulate attacks on the Church; some were in the nature of lampoons, humorous or scurrilous, but others were more contemplative in style. Either at the end of 1558 or on the first day of 1559 there appeared, nailed to the doors of friaries, the 'Beggars' Summons'. The friars were called upon to leave their homes so that they might be returned to the poor for whom they were originally planned. It was a time in which questions were being asked and a bewildering variety of answers advanced.

'The Reek of Master Patrick Hamilton'

The Church, of course, had always had one answer to questions which challenged its authority and, unwisely, continued to use it when open and genuine debate, with the possibility of accommodation and reconciliation, might have been more effective. In 1528 Patrick Hamilton was burned at the gate of St Salvator's College for propounding 'divers heresies' of Martin Luther and his followers. Hamilton, of royal descent through his mother, the daughter of Alexander Stewart, duke of Albany and brother of James III, had been abbot of Fearn in Ross-shire. While a student on the Continent he had been exposed to the teachings of Luther. He appears to have been a gentle man but resolute, with the fervour of a convert. Arrested and offered the chance to recant, he replied: 'I will rather be content that my body burn in this fire for confessing my faith in Christ, than it burn in the fire of Hell for denying the same.' He was 24 when he died, after six hours at the stake. Hamilton was not the last Scot to be burned for the new faith; the octogenarian, Walter Mylne, was executed in 1558 despite public hostility to the sentence and the provost of St Andrews refusing to associate himself with the burning. But Hamilton's death caused particular outrage and his courage won many admirers. His agony was watched by Cardinal James Beaton, then archbishop of St Andrews, who had been responsible for his arrest and condemnation. Beaton suffered no remorse for Hamilton's death but one of his servants reported to Beaton that if he were to burn more heretics he should do so in a deep cellar 'for the reek of Maister Patrick Hammyltoun has infected as many as it blew upon'. There were, indeed, many so infected but the Church had yet to learn the lesson suggested to Beaton in 1528. If the penalty for questioning the Church was death by burning, those committed to the new faith would prove themselves ready to fight for it.

The Murder of an Archbishop

On 29 May 1546, Cardinal David Beaton, successor to his uncle, James, who had died in 1539, as archbishop of St Andrews, was stabbed to death in his castle and his body suspended by a rope from a window. John Knox tells us in his *History of the Reformation* that the archbishop had been murdered because he had put to death 'that notable instrument of God, Master George Wishart'. Knox further claimed that Beaton had always been 'an obstinate enemy against Christ Jesus'. In the forthcoming struggle for religious and political supremacy between, on the one hand the adherents of the old faith, and on the other those who espoused the doctrines of Luther and Calvin, such extreme language and the ready justification of violence became depressingly familiar. Like Hamilton, Wishart, who was strangled and burned at St Andrews on 1 March 1546, is remembered for his courage and composed demeanour on the day of his death; he is said to have given his executioner the kiss of peace. But, unlike Hamilton, Wishart was almost certainly no political innocent. He had fled Scotland in 1538 when suspected of heresy and gone first to Germany and Switzerland, then to England, where in Cambridge he studied for some time before returning to Scotland in 1543. Wishart cannot be entirely cleared of complicity in a plot, to which Henry VIII of England was in some degree party, to remove Beaton who was then strongly anti-English, from his place at the centre of Scottish politics.

The plotters were indifferent as to whether Beaton should be killed or simply kidnapped.

Wishart, in his writings, emphasised preaching and faith in the Church to the detriment of traditional institutions; such thinking could not be tolerated by the Church. Whether Wishart was an agitator acting for the English government and thus intent on the destruction of the pro-French party, to which the archbishop belonged, cannot be determined, but Wishart's death and the murder of Beaton revealed that there was now a combativeness about those who had embraced the new faith. The murderers, led by Sir William Kirkcaldy of Grange, no doubt loathed Beaton for the execution of Wishart but they were equally opposed to his politics. Having found that the murder caused horror rather than sympathy, they garrisoned the castle with the help of friends and refugees from persecution, and held out until the summer of 1547. They hoped for English help but Henry VIII died in that year and they had instead to surrender to an attack by French ships. The 'Castilians' as the murderers were now known were sentenced either to prison or to row in the French galleys. Among those who were carried off to the galleys was John Knox.

The Political Situation

On the accession of the infant Mary in 1542 a regent had been appointed. James, the second earl of Arran, was the great-grandson of James II and now heir-presumptive. He had to defend the integrity of a Scotland shattered by events at Solway Moss and open to the enticements and bullying of Henry VIII, who had already fought France twice and was about to embark on a third war with the French. Henry needed to be certain that at the very least Scotland would adopt a negative attitude to the war and not interfere on the side of the French. As was his custom, Henry could see the value of moderation but preferred a blunter approach. He was able, in the atmosphere of religious change in Scotland, to convince its leaders and its regent, some of whom were already inclined to be both anglophile and in favour of the new faith, of the advantages of a marriage treaty between the two countries. By the Treaty of Greenwich of 1 July 1543, Mary was to go to England at the age of ten to be married to Henry's heir, Prince Edward. The treaty, however, was repudiated within the year. The pro-French and Catholic party, headed by the queen mother, Mary, and Cardinal David Beaton, was too strong for Arran and rejected the treaty. It was this overthrowing of the agreement, so dear to Henry's heart, that was followed by his enraged instructions to the earl of Hertford to carry out the 'Rough Wooing' of 1544 and 1545. Henry, and after his death Hertford, as lord protector in the minority of Edward VI, succeeded by their brutality in strengthening opposition in Scotland to English policies. The Scots, naturally, turned to France for help. This was given on condition that the infant queen was sent to France for safe-keeping and eventual marriage to the dauphin. Mary was taken from Inchmahome Priory to France in 1548, to remain abroad for 12 years. The Scots received the promised French assistance and in 1550 the English withdrew from their strongholds in the Lowlands. They had been, it was said, 'clean dung out of Scotland'. A price had been paid, of course; Henri II of France, we are informed, had 'leaped for blitheness, and was so blithe that it seemed incredible' when he learned of the Treaty of Haddington by which the marriage of Mary Queen of Scots to the dauphin was arranged. His emotion is understandable; he had an ally against England and a grip on Scotland. That grip was soon to be tightened.

The adherence of the vacillating Arran to the pro-French policy was settled by Henri's bestowal on him in 1548 of the dukedom of Chatelherault in Poitou. Arran remained in charge of the government until 1554 when the queen mother replaced him. Mary of Guise was both able and intelligent with a great deal of political skill. She needed these attributes if she was to rule a country in which a religion, alien and hostile to her own, was by this time well established. The year before she replaced Arran, Edward VI had died and was succeeded by his sister, Mary. A devout Catholic and the wife of Philip of Spain, the son and heir of the emperor, Charles V, Mary almost at once began her attempt to reverse the progress of the Reformation in England, undeterred by rebellions against her. Under her some 300 Protestants were burned, and even before the first executions in 1555, some Protestants had already fled from England. Some went to the Continent, others to Scotland, where they reinforced the opposition to the Catholic faith and the French policy of the queen mother. In December 1557, the earls of Glencairn, Argyll and Morton, among others, issued a manifesto which, by its wording, made plain their intention to rid Scotland of the Church of Rome. They pledged their 'power, substance, and . . . (their) very lives to maintain, set forward, and establish the most blessed word of God'. With great purpose the movement to replace the Catholic Church in Scotland with a Protestant Church intensified its actions. Some of the Protestant leaders had already approached Knox, who was now in Geneva, to return to Scotland where, he was assured, there were many 'ready to jeopard lives and goods in the forward setting of the glory of God'. Knox took up the challenge but, on reaching Dieppe, was advised to delay his departure for Scotland. He did not, in fact, come back to Scotland until 1559. Mary of Guise had shown a remarkable toleration towards those who professed themselves about to overthrow the Church of which she was a member. The marriage of her daughter, the queen, to the dauphin, Francis, in May 1558, and the death in November of the same year of Mary Tudor, produced a reaction in her. Scotland was not tied more closely to France by the marriage, and the accession of Elizabeth I to the English throne meant that the Scottish Protestants could once again hope for aid from England. According to Knox, no doubt a less than disinterested critic, it was now that the queen mother was 'to spew forth and disclose the latent venom of her double heart'. Knox himself was to play an equally important, and perhaps as discreditable a role, in the events which followed.

John Knox

Knox had been released from his imprisonment in the French galleys in 1549. He went to England where, under Edward VI, he received advancement, being appointed in 1551 as one of the six royal chaplains. The accession of Mary Tudor, however, drove him out of England to the Continent and, in 1555, he made a visit to Scotland where he was able to benefit from the tolerant government of the queen mother and could preach without hindrance. Having acted as minister to the English congregation in Geneva, where he came under the influence of Calvin, he returned to Scotland, arriving at Leith on 2 May 1559, at a time when the queen mother and the Protestant reformers had reached something of an impasse. Knox's militancy and his forceful style of preaching supplied a new drive to the Protestant cause. He preached at St John's Kirk in Perth on Thursday 11 May, the day set by the 'Beggars' Summons' for the abandonment by the friars of their houses. Knox, fiery as he was, could scarcely have wanted the violence of the next days. His sermon against idolatry inspired the destruction of holy images in Perth, an example repeated throughout Scotland. It was not in the interests of the Protestants that there should be such destruction and the despoiling of religious houses. No government could permit lawlessness of this kind and on this scale, and Mary of Guise had every reason to act against those who could justifiably be considered rebels. The preaching of Knox and his colleagues, the riots in Perth and the burning down of houses of the Black Friars and the Grey Friars were ill timed from the point of view of the Protestants. Their military strength was not the equal of that enjoyed by Mary of Guise, who had some 4,000 professional French soldiers available to her in Scotland. For them, however, as for Mary, the time for temporising had passed. A war fought in the name of religion broke out in Scotland.

The Triumph of Protestantism

Mary was initially successful in the war with the Protestants. They proved no real match for her French soldiers who strongly fortified themselves in Leith before marching out and driving their opponents out of Edinburgh. The Protestants retired to Stirling where, on Christmas Day, their army was once again forced into retreat. However, the appearance of an English fleet in the Forth threatened French communications and allowed the Protestants to regroup. The intervention of the English was dictated by Queen Elizabeth's self-interest; a strong French presence in Scotland was unacceptable to her as she struggled to maintain her own position in England. She next sent an army, commanded by Lord Grey, to join with the Scots, and together they besieged the French in Leith, depriving them of food. Mary of Guise, already ill and no longer able to exercise influence over events, took refuge in Edinburgh, and died there during the night of 10–11 June 1560. In July, by the Treaty of Edinburgh, the French were to withdraw and Elizabeth gained crucial acceptance of her right to rule England. The Auld Alliance, which had come into existence in 1295 because Scotland and France shared a common enemy in England, had come to an end when Scotland and England now found a common threat to their new religion in France.

With military and political victory achieved and the alliance with France replaced by that with the England of Elizabeth, Knox and his colleagues were anxious to ensure an urgent settlement of religious problems. At the time of the Treaty of Edinburgh it had been decided that the 'Three Estates' should meet in parliament in August. A Confession of Faith, in essence a full statement of Protestant doctrine, was presented and accepted on 17 August. A week later, by three acts, the Church of Rome in Scotland was formally abolished. The authority of the pope was denied and the celebration of Mass was made illegal with death the penalty for a third offence. For Knox and others of his thinking the victory of Protestantism in Scotland had proved 'how wondrously the light of Christ Jesus had prevailed'. Their joy was understandable but Scotland still had a queen who was not only Catholic but still in France, the wife of its king, Francis II. Mary of Guise was not replaced as regent; the question of how the country should be governed after the triumph of Protestantism had not yet been finally settled. When, however, Francis II died in December 1560, Mary was no longer queen of France. The internal politics of France helped Mary to a decision to which she was perhaps already half-inclined when her husband died. Her mother-in-law, Catherine de Medici, who became regent, was jealous of her and of the House of Guise, to which Mary was attached because of her mother. Mary left Calais for Scotland and landed at Leith on 19 August 1561.

The Personal Rule of Mary Queen of Scots

A Catholic queen in a country newly Protestant could not expect an enthusiastic welcome. To Knox, her arrival meant 'sorrow, dolour, darkness and all impiety'. Yet if she was treated with some reserve, there was not at first overt hostility. She could not hope for, nor did she find,

Mary Queen of Scots

the kind of freedom and pleasures she had enjoyed in France as wife of the dauphin. She was in a different country with different and harsher standards and this she was not allowed to forget. Her wish to hear Mass in her chapel was met with rioting at Holyrood but she managed to persuade many that her wishes were reasonable; it was said by one who witnessed her at work that there was some 'enchantment whereby men are bewitched'. Knox, however, she could not win to her side. In an interview with him, she accused him of rousing her subjects against her, and his reply, as always, was severe; her survival as queen depended on her good behaviour. He told her that he would be 'as well content to live under Your Grace as Paul was under Nero'. He never appears to have changed his opinion of her and Mary, although she did not do anything to damage the new Church in Scotland, could never come to terms with the likes of Knox. When, eventually, Mary was driven out of Scotland, the cause was less religious than political.

She was sensible enough not to alienate her people at the beginning of her reign. Her first journey through Scotland, shortly after her arrival, took her to Stirling, Perth, Dundee, St Andrews and Falkland Palace. Everywhere she was met with enthusiasm and kindness but she was left in no doubt that her people, in general, were strongly in favour of the Protestant religion. She accepted the situation for the time being and appointed as her advisers two men who were Protestant but not extreme. They were William Maitland of Lethington, as her secretary of state, and her half-brother, the Lord James Stewart, the natural son of James V by Margaret Erskine. To Maitland she entrusted the delicate negotiations with Elizabeth which she hoped might end with Elizabeth's acknowledging her as rightful heir to the English throne; to her half-brother she gave the task of quelling the rebellion by George Gordon, fourth earl of Huntly, head of the most powerful Catholic family in Scotland. Huntly it was who, before her departure from France, had promised her that if she would but let him, he would make her a Catholic queen of Scots. When, however, Mary found the Gordons exhibiting 'manifest tokens of disobedience' towards her, she used Stewart against them. At Corrichie, some 15 miles from Aberdeen, the Gordons were routed on 28 October 1562. Huntly himself died in the battle, possibly from a stroke, and his son, Sir John, was executed a week later and the Gordon lands were forfeited. Mary had been strong enough to crush a rebellion against her and astute enough not to let her religion interefere with her decision. Her standing was inevitably improved with the news of Corrichie. Not all were convinced, however, that she could be trusted. Knox continued to have his doubts and in a sermon in 1563 warned of the dangers that might await Scotland and the Protestant faith in the event of her making an unsuitable marriage, that is, one with a Catholic prince. To consent to such a marriage with what Knox called, in his unforgiving language, an 'infidel', would bring 'God's vengeance upon the country . . . and perhaps small comfort' to the queen herself. Mary angrily attacked Knox when he appeared before her for what was their fourth and final meeting but he defended himself, as always, with vigour. She argued that any marriage of hers was no concern of his but Knox's fears were not ill founded. The Counter-Reformation had begun with the Council of Trent. In France, after a massacre of Protestant Huguenots at Vassy, religious war broke out. At the same time there were revolts against Spanish rule in the Netherlands, where Calvinism had gained ground. Elizabeth of England had given her support to the Huguenots and occupied the port of Le Havre, although the French regained it in 1563. Elizabeth would view with concern, like Knox, any proposed marriage with a Catholic, and hinted that a suitable match for Mary would be Robert Dudley, first earl of Leicester and Elizabeth's own favourite. Mary refused to take the suggestion seriously.

MARY'S MARRIAGES

Ultimately Mary married twice, although neither marriage was wise and neither lasted. It has been argued that the appearance in Scotland in early 1565 of Henry Stewart, Lord Darnley, son of Matthew, the fourth earl of Lennox, was part of a subtle scheme by Elizabeth to ensure that Mary would marry a 'safe' Catholic rather than one from the Continent. Quite how Elizabeth could have forecast Mary's reaction to Darnley has never been explained but the fact is that she fell in love with him and married him by Catholic ceremony on 29 July 1565. Mary would not wait for the necessary papal dispensation for the marriage; both she and Darnley were grandchildren of Margaret Tudor, the wife of James IV, and within the forbidden degrees of consanguinity. Mary had already proclaimed that Darnley was to be 'named and styled' king. That decision, like the marriage itself, was a mistake. Mary could now no longer be seen as likely to be 'allured into sweet reasonableness'. She had married a Catholic, made him king, and was clearly about to establish a government free of the advice she had so resented. There was a sudden and brief resistance in arms by Lord James Stewart, earl of Moray since 1563; in what was known as the 'Chase-About-Raid', Mary pursued Moray and his allies and forced them into exile in England. Mary exhibited on this occasion the courage and stamina which so amazed contemporaries throughout her life; it was reported that, in the hunt for the rebels, 'the Queen's courage increased man-like, so much, that she was ever with the foremost'.

Fortunate in her victory over Moray, she was less so in her marriage to Darnley. He was vain and headstrong, unfitted for the 'crown matrimonial' for which he so often asked; at her refusals his anger grew. At the same time as she was dismissing, almost contemptuously, her husband's requests for what he believed was rightfully his, she was advancing the career of David Riccio, a Piedmontese musician, whom she made her secretary for French affairs. Her favoured treatment of Riccio was, in the circumstances, another example of that lack of judgement which had led her to marry Darnley. To Mary, Riccio was a 'trusty servant', but Knox looked on him as 'that poltroon and vile knave Davie'. The nobility saw in him a man of 'base degree' and Protestants in general believed him to be an agent of the pope. Darnley, jealous of the man who it was said, was always 'speaking with Her Majesty', connived with Moray and the other lords who had been driven out of Scotland by Mary in the 'Chase-About-Raid'. They were to be allowed to return to Scotland, the Protestant faith was to be protected, and Darnley was to be given the 'crown matrimonial' which he so desired. Also, if Mary died without issue, he was to succeed to the throne. Before all of that, however, Riccio was to be murdered. On the night of 9 March 1566, as the pregnant Mary watched, Riccio was dragged from her presence. A number of men led by Patrick, third Lord Ruthven, and James Douglas, fourth earl of Morton, stabbed him repeatedly, and Darnley's own dagger was left sticking in the corpse, although he had been careful not to strike a blow. Mary behaved with remarkable composure and political skill after the murder. She appeared to forgive Darnley for the murder, met Moray and his associates and, with that done, persuaded Darnley to abandon them. Together, they escaped from Edinburgh three days after the murder and made their way to Dunbar, to the castle of James Hepburn, the fourth earl of Bothwell. In Bothwell Mary found the strong man she lacked in her husband. With Bothwell's help she quickly raised an army and marched on Edinburgh. Neither Moray, who had taken no actual part in Riccio's murder, nor those who, like Morton and Ruthven, had committed it, had the stomach for a fight. Moray retreated from Edinburgh but was recalled and pardoned by the queen; Morton, Ruthven and their associates sought refuge in England. On Monday 18 March, nine days after Riccio's murder, Mary re-entered Edinburgh, apparently with her power restored.

Darnley was left without friends. He had betrayed not only Mary, who could not feel safe because of his ambitions for the crown, but also Moray who was back in Mary's favour, and the murderers who were exiled in England. With the birth of their son, the future James VI, in Edinburgh on 19 June 1566, Mary could readily disregard Darnley. She feared, however, to divorce him in case her son's legitimacy was prejudiced; she complained to companions that she could find 'no outgait' to her problem. We do not know whether she was playing the part of Henry II of England in his dealings with Thomas à Becket; on the one hand hinting at the removal of Darnley, while on the other, remaining ready to claim that she had intended no such thing. It was noticeable, too, that in the last days of 1566, she was attentive to the Protestant Church with financial help to its ministers and, at the same time, pardoning the murderers of Riccio who were allowed to return to Scotland. If this was a means of attracting public sympathy before Darnley was to die, it cannot be proved, any more than her part in his murder. On the night of 9–10 February 1567, a little less than a year since the brutal death of David Riccio, Darnley was murdered at the house of Kirk O'Field on the Flodden Wall in Edinburgh. The house in which the king, stricken either with syphilis or smallpox, was resting, was 'blown up wi' pouder'. His body was discovered in the adjoining garden; he had been strangled. Today there is no certainty about what had happened; Mary may have colluded with the murderers who included Bothwell among them. Bothwell was held accountable by the public for the murder of Darnley and Mary herself was not free of suspicion.

Mary's subsequent conduct did little to allay that suspicion. It had been noticed that she displayed some familiarity towards Bothwell and now she went further. She had done virtually nothing to hunt down the murderers of her husband, although a few unimportant people had been charged and put to death after torture. This satisfied no one. Bothwell was acquitted after a trial made farcical by the armed presence of his men, and then he persuaded some of the Scottish lords to agree that he was a fitting replacement for the dead Darnley. As Mary was travelling from Edinburgh to Linlithgow, Bothwell .with some 800 men, intercepted and abducted her, taking her to Dunbar. She appears to have offered little resistance but it would be claimed later that, at Dunbar, he raped her. On 6 May, he brought her back to Edinburgh, 'leading the Queen's Majesty by the bridle as captive'. Twelve days before he had divorced his wife, Lady Jean Gordon, on the grounds of his adultery, and on 15 May Mary and Bothwell were married at Holyrood by the bishop of Orkney. The marriage was celebrated according to Protestant rites.

Mary met with universal condemnation. The pope would have nothing to do with her until 'he shall see some better sign of her life and religion'. The earl of Morton took command of the opposition to her and Bothwell, and then on 15 June 1567 at Carberry, near Musselburgh, Bothwell abandoned her. She surrendered to Morton and was imprisoned in Lochleven Castle. She abdicated on 24 July, and on 29 July, her son James, one year old, was crowned. Moray, absent in France, was to be regent. Bothwell, meanwhile, travelled to Orkney and Shetland and died in 1578, a deranged prisoner, in Dragsholm Castle in Denmark. Mary escaped from Lochleven on 2 May 1568 with the help of one of her guards, a youth of 18, George Douglas, who, it was said, was 'lost in a fantasy of love' for her. She raised an army of 6,000 but at Langside, without the advice of an able general, was defeated by Moray. The battle lasted 'one long quarter of an hour' and at the end of it Mary fled with 16 companions. As was so often the case, she ignored the sensible option and went to England instead of France. There she remained for 20 years until her execution at Fotheringhay Castle on the morning of 8 February 1587. Her courage had never deserted her and she died with the dignity expected of her. Her son, then 20, intent on the succession to the English throne, displayed no emotion of the expected kind on learning of his mother's death. He had not, in truth, known her and his opinions had been coloured by men to whom she was a whore, a murderess and a threat to the Protestant Church. Even in her exile Mary had been dangerous; she never abandoned hope of restoration and did not actively discourage those who she knew were plotting on her behalf. Two regents of Scotland, Moray and Lennox, were killed, Moray on 22 January 1570, murdered by James Hamilton, Lennox shot at Stirling on 4 September 1571 by some of Mary's supporters. Civil war, between the 'King's men' and the 'Queen's men', resulted in the intervention of Elizabeth. Her artillery breached the walls of Edinburgh, held in the name of Mary by Sir William Kirkcaldy of Grange, whose part in the murder of David Beaton, cardinal-archbishop of St Andrews, has already been mentioned. Kirkcaldy, said to be 'one of the most valiant men' of the time, who had given his allegiance to Mary because he did not approve of her deposition, was hanged. Kirkcaldy's companion in the French galleys, John Knox, had died in the previous year on 24 November 1572, on the same day that Morton succeeded John Erskine, earl of Mar, as regent. Morton described Knox as 'one who neither feared nor flattered any flesh'. Morton, another of Mary's enemies, had predeceased her and by the same means, decapitation. Morton was accused of the murder of Darnley and executed in June 1581. Through all of these events, James under a succession of regents and tutors, watched; it would have been difficult for him not to have held his mother in some measure responsible for the disturbances in the kingdom of which he was king, at least in name. If his reaction to her death was unnatural, it was understandable. Had she succeeded in her plans for returning to Scotland, she would have replaced him as ruler.

CHAPTER EIGHT

Union and Civil Strife, 1580–1688

The Education of a King

The unfortunate circumstances of the last years of the life of Mary Queen of Scots and her composed demeanour on the scaffold at Fotheringhay Castle in February 1587 have tended, perhaps understandably, to colour the popular perception of her and to disguise the harsh truth of her legacy to her son, James VI. She is most often thought of as a tragic figure and even, like her grandson, Charles I, who also died by the axe, as a victim and martyr. James, for his part, is remembered, in the cynical words of a French contemporary, either Henri IV or his minister, the duc de Sully, as 'the wisest fool in Christendom'. An impartial assessment of mother and son, however, might be less flattering to Mary and find that this passionate and wilful woman, destructive of her own not inconsiderable talents, was misguided rather than tragic. It may well be that James, with a genuine claim to be considered the most scholarly of all monarchs of Scotland, was the real victim, both of his mother's neglect and the inadequacies of his upbringing. When Mary, a widow, returned from France to Scotland in 1561 to begin her personal rule, she was better received than she might have dared to hope, in a nation recently and fervently turned Protestant. Six years later, having alienated her people by the rashness of her actions, she was forced to abdicate and after a desperate rally was driven out of Scotland. James was left at the age of one, effectively an orphan, in a country where his mother had contributed to the internal divisions, and in the hands of men intent on raising him according to an unsympathetic and intolerant regime. James was the first monarch of Scotland to be educated under the auspices of the reformed religion and his mentors sought to ensure that, from the outset, he would appreciate the unique nature of his role. Andrew Melville, after ten years in exile on the Continent, came to Scotland to be principal of Glasgow University and would not hesitate to inform James that 'there are two kings and two kingdoms in Scotland. There is Christ Jesus the King and his Kingdom the Kirk, whose subject King James the Sixth is, and of whose kingdom (he is) not a king, nor a lord, nor a head, but a member.' Surrounded by men of such positive opinions, forcefully and fearlessly expressed, and constantly reminded of the shortcomings of his absent mother, James appears to have taken naturally to learning. The most significant of his tutors was George Buchanan, a native of Killearn in Stirlingshire, who, like Melville, had fled to Europe to escape religious persecution. In this he was not entirely successful for he was imprisoned by the Inquisition in Portugal. Later he spent five years in Paris before taking up the post of principal of St Leonard's College in St Andrews. Buchanan was a latin poet, dramatist, historian and the author of pamphlets attacking James' mother, who had once shown him favour. His most celebrated work, a history of Scotland, was influential but disfigured by his attitude to Mary. Stern, unbending and a believer in physical punishment for the careless or incompetent pupil, he introduced James to classical and modern languages, history and politics, but was never deflected from the need to mould his young charge into a ruler acceptable to the Church. James became a scholar in his own right, an author and a patron of the arts, but he rebelled against the thinking of Melville, Buchanan and those others who during the regencies of his early years had striven in the Lord's name to dominate his mind. When, as he grew to maturity, he took upon himself the responsibility for government, he brought to his work as a king a highly trained and analytical mind. As his erstwhile tutors were to learn, he was capable of reaching his own conclusions about the nature of monarchy. James did not embrace the Catholicism of his mother, although he was accused of a sympathy for certain of its practitioners; nor did he adopt the more extreme beliefs of those who had overseen his minority. Instead, he looked to England where, he had come to imagine, the relationship between the ruler and the Church was more to his liking. It was now clear to him that, unless he could exercise some authority over the Church, he would be prevented from governing Scotland as he would wish.

John Knox had seen a place in the reformed church for bishops. That view had become unfashionable but James revived it as a means of establishing his control over the Church through the nomination and appointment of bishops. Inevitably, he came into conflict with the redoubtable and outspoken Andrew Melville, the scourge of bishops and the man who called James to his face 'God's sillie (weak) vassal'. James could not tolerate Melville's repeated assertions that the Church enjoyed a privileged position, separate and above the authority of the State. In his turn, he bluntly stated: 'No bishop, no king', words which left his opponents in no doubt as to his meaning. The struggle between the two theories was long and, in an age where violence lay close to the surface of society, at times dangerous for the king; indeed, in 1583, Melville acted so outrageously as to be accused of treason and had to take refuge in England. Melville had a strong following in Scotland for his ideas and James' triumph, which would result in the supremacy of the Crown with a consequent reduction in the independence of the Church, was often uncertain. James was, however, helped by the vehemence of Melville and the ministers of the Church who sided with Melville against him. This allowed the king to pose as a moderate, despite his determination to achieve his ends, and thus brought him support. It was a situation in which James showed himself to be more subtle and cunning than Melville, if no less resolute. He was not to achieve final victory in the matter of bishops until after he had succeeded Elizabeth on the English throne but by then he had already broken the resistance if not the spirit of Melville. In his later treatment of Melville James proved to be unforgiving. In 1606 he summoned him to London, had him imprisoned for more than three years in the Tower, and only agreed to his release at the entreaty of the duc de Bouillon. He would not, however, allow Melville back to his native Scotland. Melville died in 1622 in France, in the town of Sedan, where he had taught at the university after leaving England.

Melville may well have represented for James that period in his life when he was in thrall to an odious and unappealing philosophy. He also represented the opposition to the principles of kingship, which James laid out in his *Basilikon Doron*, the book of advice which he produced for his son, Prince Henry, in 1598 or 1599. James told Henry that 'the office of a King is a mixed office between the civil and ecclesiastical estate', an opinion which neither Melville nor his colleagues among the ministers of the Church could be expected to welcome. No less significant was James' guidance to his son on the question of a king's relationship with his subjects. 'When ye have by the severities of justice once settled your countries', James wrote, 'and made them know that ye can strike, then ye may mix justice with mercy.' We may be sure that James, in keeping with his painstaking nature, laboured long over his choice of words, which were a reflection of his experience as king. That experience, although by the time of the publication of the *Basilikon Doron* he had almost defeated the opposition to his plans for the Church, had not been a happy one.

Threats to the King

If James' treatment of Melville does him little credit, it should be remembered that Melville had himself not eschewed the use of violence against the king. When Melville had fled to England in 1583, accused of treason, it was in the aftermath of what was known as the Raid of Ruthven, of August 1582. James, by then aged 15, had come under the influence of his cousin, Esme Stewart, lord of Aubigny in France, who returned to Scotland from the Continent in 1579. Stewart, handsome and gallant, became the king's companion and was created first earl, and then duke, of Lennox. With another adventurer, Captain James Stewart, who subsequently became earl of Arran, Lennox overthrew the regent, Morton. Lennox's religion, however, led to suspicion that he was an agent of the pope and to an attempt by the earls of Gowrie and Mar to capture James and end Lennox's ascendancy over him. For some ten months the king was held a prisoner in Ruthven Castle, Gowrie's home in Perthshire, and Lennox was compelled to leave Scotland, escaping to France, where he died in May 1583. James escaped from his captors in June 1583 and was able to exact his revenge against Gowrie, who attempted a second coup, again with Mar. Gowrie was executed but Mar, like Melville, had fled to England. Melville's attitude to the Raid of Ruthven, like that of the General Assembly of the Church, had been one of approval, disregarding the violence behind it and the implicit threat to the king's person. The raid, the assembly ruled, had delivered 'the true religion . . . from evident and certain dangers' and had protected James himself from 'no less evil'. To what extent James' life was in danger cannot now be known, but there can be no doubting the fear which he must have felt. James, not without reason, has been accused of lack of judgement in his choice of friends, such as those he acquired in England, for example Robert Carr and George Villiers. Neither Lennox nor the less attractive Arran, however, was without ability. The appeal of the former to the young James, for so long under the control of older and humourless men, can readily be appreciated. James was prone to extreme reactions to persons and events and never forgave Melville for his support of the raid. Nor could he accept with equanimity the Ruthven Raiders, with the strength of Elizabeth of England behind them, when they returned to Scotland in 1585. Mindful as always of his hope of succeeding Elizabeth, James, however, chose not to oppose their return.

The Raid of Ruthven had been the work of Protestant extremists. James was not, however, immune to intrigues against him by Catholic subjects. The leading figure in a series of plots was George Gordon, earl of Huntly, who, with Francis Hay, earl of Errol, in the north and Lord John Maxwell in the south, was suspected over a number of years of conspiring to restore the Roman Catholic religion to Scotland. James was curiously unwilling to act against them. Most scandalous in the eyes of his subjects was his refusal to deal with Huntly for the murder of James Stewart, earl of Moray, at Donibristle in Fife on 7 February 1592. On several occasions James was presented with convincing evidence of the treasonable activities and correspondence of Catholic plotters but they continued to conduct their intrigues with apparent impunity. Even when spurred on by the outraged Elizabeth who, in 1589, had already exclaimed that 'no king a week would bear this', he would not destroy the threat which these men represented both to himself and to the reformed religion in his kingdom. It was their own lack of courage and the death of Maxwell in a bloody feud with another border family, the Johnstones, which ultimately defeated the intentions which the Catholic faction so openly and carelessly proclaimed. The Catholic threat to James faded, although the king, despite his marriage in 1589 to the Protestant princess, Anne, daughter of Frederick II of Denmark, was never to be free of the charge of Catholic sympathies while he remained in Scotland.

If, however, James' own version of events is to be believed, the most serious threat to him came from an episode about which there is still considerable doubt. On 5 August 1600 James rode with Alexander, the master of Ruthven, brother of John, earl of Gowrie, to Gowrie House in Perth. The king, ever gullible, as his obsession with, and cruelty to women accused of witchcraft demonstrate, was to speak to a man said to have in his possession a pot full of gold. Once there, as he claimed afterwards, he felt that he was about to be murdered. He summoned help and the earl and his brother were killed. James' account was not widely believed in Scotland. Some thought him jealous of the brothers because of their close friendship with Queen Anne; certainly, the king's relations with his wife were somewhat strained afterwards. Others, suspicious of his conduct towards the Catholics, thought he was motivated by a desire to remove the Gowries, an ultra-Protestant family. James may have been concerned by the arrival at Gowrie House of the sons of the first earl of Gowrie, one of the leading participants in the Ruthven Raid of 1582 which had imprisoned James and separated him from his friend, Esme Stewart, duke of Lennox. James was not renowned for his courage and their presence may have caused an excessive reaction in him and his cry of 'Treason' which brought about the death of the Gowries. The Gowrie Conspiracy, whatever its origins, was the last attempt on the king's person before he left for England. It may have been aimed only at restraining him but opinion today tends to the view that there was indeed, on that day in 1600, a plot of some kind against him.

The Succession to the English Throne

Early on the morning of Thursday 24 March 1603, Queen Elizabeth died. The task of informing James of Elizabeth's end fell to Sir Robert Carey, who covered the distance from London to Edinburgh, a distance of some 400 miles, in 60 hours, an impressive achievement for the time. Carey handed to James Elizabeth's coronation ring, taken from her finger and, in Carey's own words, his new master told him: 'It is enough; I know by this that you are a true messenger.' The news of his succession to the English throne was the happiest moment in James' life. He had worked towards it for years, accepting Elizabeth's execution of his mother, adapting his policies to suit her requirements and cultivating his friendship with her chief minister, Sir Robert Cecil. His trust in Cecil was repaid for without him there was no guarantee that Elizabeth, capricious and suspicious, would have agreed to his succession. James' sympathy for Robert Devereux, earl of Essex, executed for treason in 1601, was known to Elizabeth and to the end of her life she refused openly to acknowledge James as her successor. At the moment of her death she was too weak to do so; those at her bedside, among them Carey, noted that she could signify her agreement to his succession only by a gesture. There was no question, however, despite her public behaviour, that she knew James' claim was the only valid one; descended through his mother and father from Margaret Tudor, he had no real rival to the English throne. He was anxious to go to England, confident that

James VI of Scotland and James I of England

a new and better life awaited him there. He was careful, however, to reassure his Scottish subjects that he would not forget them; before he left Edinburgh for the south on 5 April, less than two weeks after Elizabeth's death, he told them that he would visit them 'every three years at the least, or oftener'. He failed to keep his promise, however, and only once, in 1617, did he return to Scotland. Instead, he ruled Scotland from England through its own privy council. This method appeared to satisfy James' absolutist inclinations: 'I write, and it is done', was how he defined his government. These were different sentiments from those expressed before leaving Edinburgh, when, in his speech in St Giles, he had proclaimed: 'Think not of me as a king going from one part to another, but of one king lawfully called going from one part of the isle to another so that your comfort may be the greater.'

THE FAILURE OF UNION

We do not know whether James, not averse to the occasional lie in pursuit of his aims, had truly meant what he said to his Scottish subjects, many of whom were reported to be deeply moved. He did, however, consider them as an important part of the true union he was determined to achieve between Scotland and England. To the first parliament of his new reign, meeting in London in March 1604, he announced his plan for closer union. The Commons was not enthusiastic, maintaining that the Scots rather than the English would benefit, and did not give a warm welcome to the numbers of 'needy' Scots James had brought with him. In Scotland itself there was no greater commitment to the king's plan but there, as in England, in deference to his wishes, commissioners were appointed to meet with their English counterparts. James, attracted at first by the title of emperor, settled for that of 'King of Great Britain, France, and England'. But almost two years after he had first proposed a closer union he was still faced with the apathy, if not the outright hostility, of his subjects, both Scottish and English. The former feared that the king was using the matter of union as a means of imposing Anglicanism on them; the latter had by now grown to know James well enough to distrust him on a number of issues. James, vain and convinced of the rightness of his cause, cannot have been other then surprised by the opposition to his plan. However, in this he must have been unique, since even the French ambassador knew the truth of the situation for he had already said: 'The little sympathy between the two nations, the differences of their laws, the jealousy of their privileges, the regard of the succession, are the reasons they will never join with one another, as the king wishes.' Elizabeth's recent interventions in the affairs of Scotland, the centuries of warfare between the two nations, the contempt of the English for the Scots and the respective merits of Presbyterianism and Anglicanism, were all matters of which James was not ignorant, yet he discounted them and it was to his cost. Two things he did achieve, the principle of dual nationality for those born after his accession in 1603 to the English throne and the abrogation of the Leges Marchiarum or laws of the Borders, that unique system, over 400 years old, by which the lands between the two countries were governed. Although James was absent from Scotland, he had not forgotten the crucial need to keep it firmly under control. The Borders, the Highlands and the Islands, the source of much trouble for him as for his predecessors, were dealt with harshly by his ministers, in whose selection he showed much common sense. In the Borders, from the beginning of James' time in England, the choice offered was a cruel one: those who escaped execution were either embarked to Ireland by Sir William Cranston or employed abroad as mercenaries by Walter Scott of Buccleuch, himself once a formidable troublemaker. The Highlands witnessed a purge, not undeserved, of the Macgregors, who had, as James was about to leave for England, carried out a raid down Loch Lomond; their chief was arrested and hanged in Edinburgh, a safe-conduct from James notwithstanding. In Orkney the earl, Patrick Stewart, convicted of treasonable negotiations with the king of Denmark, was executed and James exercised his authority there through the bishop, James Law. The king was never able to look upon areas such as these as other than sources of disaffection and civil unrest; he thought of them as not merely remote but alien. One consequence of his education, which linked him to his tutors, was his intolerance; he had no sympathy for the culture of the Highlands any more than for that of the Borders. He was therefore precluded from adopting a more humane and long-term policy towards them. In his treatment of them he was cunning and ruthless but he gave to Scotland, both before and after the death of

Elizabeth, a greater degree of order than it had enjoyed for many years. He tried to establish a Scottish presence overseas. Both by choice and by coercion, Scots settled in Ulster in increasing numbers and, by the middle of the seventeenth century, may have numbered as many as 50,000. An attempt by Sir William Alexander to found Nova Scotia, a New Scotland in North America, foundered despite James' personal interest and encouragement, and in 1632 Charles I turned all the Scottish settlements in North America over to the French. The great age of the Scots abroad was yet to come.

New King, Old Divisions

James VI of Scotland (James I of England), king of Great Britain, as he was so anxious to be known, was a monarch of very considerable achievements. He outlasted and outwitted those who, throughout his reign in Scotland, had tried, by persuasion or by force, to govern and use him for their own ends. He came to understand the value of strength, even severity, in the treatment of recalcitrant subjects. But he was keenly aware, while in Scotland, of the paramount need for the conciliation of the various groupings, political and religious, which might otherwise have torn the country apart. His successes in Scotland, which saw during his reign a growth of respect for the law, greater peace and some measure of prosperity, are too readily overlooked. Once he had moved to England, however, that natural inclination to absolutism which so distinguished his family, asserted itself in a climate which he believed, mistakenly as events were to show, was more congenial to it. James claimed that he 'knew the stomach' of the people of Scotland and there is some truth in the claim. However, the man who had so skilfully managed the disparate elements in his northern kingdom had, by the end of his reign, gone a long way towards creating the circumstances in which the survival of the monarchy was at risk. Under a new king, James' son and successor, Charles I, Scotland was to suffer for James' errors and, perhaps inevitably, it was not a new problem but an old one, that of religion, which was responsible.

James died on Sunday 27 March 1625, in the home of the Cecils, now earls of Salisbury, one of whom had eased his accession to the English throne. Already in Scotland there had been opposition to his plan to mould the Scottish Church in the image of the English. In 1610 the general assembly, dominated by James' supporters, had accepted bishops. The king's return visit to Scotland in 1617 was marred for many by further evidence of his intentions when he wanted the assembly to accept five changes covering baptism, the observance of Holy Days, confirmation by bishops, kneeling for communion and the private administration of sacraments. The assembly resisted and refused. James was not to be defeated and, in the following year, the Five Articles of Perth were accepted by the assembly meeting in the town. If James was satisfied, his people were not; in his later years he could no longer ignore their feelings. It was not, however, James but his son who had to face the consequences of James' determination to enforce his views on Scotland.

The Accession of Charles I

Charles, born at Dunfermline in 1600, had become heir apparent at the age of 12 on the death from typhoid of his elder brother, Prince Henry. It was for Henry that James' book, the *Basilikon Doron*, was intended, but its principles were passed on to and absorbed by Charles. He had inherited his father's strong addiction to the doctrine of the divine right of kings to rule because they were appointed by God. The doctrine was not new, having first appeared in England during the reign of Elizabeth in the *Homily against Wilful Rebellion* of 1569, but it fell to Charles to make it notorious. The doctrine did not at first arouse hostility in Scotland; it was the king's decision to restore to the Church some of the property which had been given to the nobles at the time of the Reformation which, not unnaturally, provoked the anger of those who would lose what they considered to be theirs. He had previously indicated his insensitivity to Scottish feelings by his treatment of Archbishop John Spottiswoode at the time of James' funeral in 1625. Spottiswoode, archbishop first of Glasgow, then of St Andrews, had been close to James, whom he had accompanied to London in 1603, and was highly regarded in Scotland. Charles' attempt to make the archbishop wear English vestments for the funeral was clumsy and a slight in the eyes of a people ready to find offence.

Nevertheless, when Charles made his first visit to Scotland, in 1633, he was made welcome. He had by this time broken with parliament in England and begun the years of his rule without it; a wiser man might have seen the visit to Scotland as an opportunity to strengthen his position there. Charles, however, was neither a wise man nor one able to produce the gesture or action guaranteed to bind his Scottish subjects to him. With him he brought William Laud, archbishop of Canterbury, the agent of the policy of 'thorough' or authoritarianism which characterised Charles' rule without parliament. Laud's presence in Edinburgh and the nature of Charles' coronation at Holyrood seemed to indicate to the Scots that Charles' religious inclinations were rather to the Catholic than to the reformed faith. At the parliament, which he held during his visit, he was no more ready to compromise. His father's plans for the future of the Scottish Church were endorsed; three years later, Charles issued a rule book which confirmed the detested Five Articles of Perth. He could find no place in his thinking for the assembly and to the nobles, who had prepared a list of their grievances, he turned a deaf ear. He went so far, in the following year, as to prosecute one of them, John Elphinstone, Lord Balmerino, for what was known as 'leasing treason', that is, spoken treason, because a copy of the grievances was found in his hands. The trial of Lord Balmerino made it unlikely that anyone would risk bringing to Charles' attention the true state of affairs in Scotland; it took a more direct and famous event to do that.

Riot and Covenant

The name of Jennie Geddes, an Edinburgh greengrocer, became known throughout Scotland by an act attributed to her, perhaps incorrectly, on Sunday 23 July 1637. In St Giles, John Hanna, dean of Edinburgh, was reading the new Book of Common Prayer, which people had taken to calling 'Laud's Liturgy', when he was struck by a stool flung by a woman in the congregation. Whether this was Jennie Geddes or not we cannot tell, but the throwing of the stool lead to a riot in St Giles. The riot did not last long but it precipitated an event of greater and more durable significance. Opposition to Charles was now overt and by the end of February 1638 there had occurred, in the words of Archibald Johnston of

Wariston, 'that glorious marriage day of the Kingdom with God'. He was referring to the National Covenant, in the framing of which he himself played a large and formative part. On Wednesday 28 February, and on several successive days, the Covenant was signed in the kirk of the Greyfriars. Those who signed the historic document stated their opposition to Rome and their support for the Protestant faith. They rejected the king's innovations in religion but at the same time professed their loyalty to their 'dread Sovereign, the King's Majesty, his person and Authority', and were ready to stand with him 'in the defence and preservation of the aforesaid true religion, liberties, and laws of the kingdom'. However stirring its words, however honest the sentiments of those who put their names to it, the Covenant of 1638 signalled a return to the divisions which had so plagued Scotland in the days of John Knox and Queen Mary. War between the king and his rebellious Scottish subjects was now likely. The Covenanters summoned their own general assembly at Glasgow in November 1638 and under the leadership of Alexander Henderson, Johnston's associate in the framing of the covenant, proceeded to abolish bishops, the Five Articles of Perth and books of prayer. Charles retaliated by declaring their actions illegal and he made ready to march against them. The forces which he raised in the north of England were no match for the Scots, whose general, Alexander Leslie, had served under Gustavus Adolphus, king of Sweden, in the Thirty Years' War. In the Bishops' Wars of 1639–1640 the Scots established and maintained what was to be a fateful superiority over Charles. In time they crossed the border and seized Newcastle and, having found that Charles could not be trusted, insisted that they would negotiate only with the English Parliament for a treaty of peace. With the Scots in control of the whole of Northumberland and Durham, Charles had no alternative but to recall Parliament, whose advice he had dispensed with for 11 years, if he were to buy the Scots off. By the Treaty of Ripon the Scots agreed to retire from England in return for payments of their expenses at the rate of £840 per day, a total in all of some £300,000. The Treaty of Ripon, signed on 16 October 1641, was ratified by the English parliament in the following month and then began to sweep away all that Charles had done during the past 11 years. Civil war would soon break out in England; in it Charles would lose his life and, a young Scot, James Graham, marquis of Montrose, one of the covenanting army under Alexander Leslie, would change sides and make his reputation before also losing his life in the defence of a doomed cause.

Scotland and the English Civil War

Faced by the hostility of parliament in London, Charles visited Edinburgh in the summer of 1641 hoping to enlist support against his English enemies. In Scotland, as in the south, there was discord. The Covenanters, having gained a victory against the king, had split. The power of Archibald Campbell, first marquis of Argyll, was a source of concern. The covenanters were now compelling people to sign the covenant which appalled Montrose, who was once in their army, and he briefly suffered imprisonment for his stance against compulsion. He became a Royalist but Charles' visit to Scotland was not a success. Charles was suspected, perhaps unfairly, of complicity in 'The Incident', a plot to capture and murder Argyll and James, duke of Hamilton; in this case, Charles' friends in Scotland served only to discredit him. Charles, the rupture with parliament now complete, raised his standard at Nottingham on 22 August 1642 and the English Civil War began. Edgehill, the first major battle of the war, was fought on 23 October and was indecisive; it brought home to each side its own incompetence and, before the end of the year, king and parliament alike had turned to the Scots for help. It was parliament which the Scots chose to support but only on condition that the English, in the Solemn League and Covenant of 1643 which bound both parties, would guarantee the reformed religion 'according to the Word of God and the example of the best-reformed Churches'. The Scots, that is, were trying to set up a version of their own Presbyterian Church in England. At the Battle of Marston Moor, on 2 July 1644, the Scottish contingent under Alexander Leven, created earl of Leven by Charles himself in an effort to ensure his loyalty, made a significant contribution to the decisive victory of the parliamentary army under Oliver Cromwell and Sir Thomas Fairfax. The Scottish cavalry, captained by David Leslie, and its infantry counterparts, with William Baillie at their head, had helped to rally the Parliamentarians in what was an ill-managed battle. The English, however, refused to give what the Scots believed was their due credit; already the allies were disagreeing and the Scots withdrew to Newcastle.

MONTROSE'S CAMPAIGNS

Montrose began his work as lieutenant-general of Charles' forces in Scotland without an army. He had ridden north from Oxford in March 1644, after meeting the king. Then he had been refused troops by Charles' nephew, Prince Rupert, and entered Scotland in disguise, with two companions. He succeeded in enlisting a number of Highlanders, whose quarrel was with Argyll and the Campbells rather than with the Covenanters, but his biggest source of support came from a force of some 1,000 Irishmen led by Alasdair MacDonald. Into this small army Montrose instilled the necessary discipline which, added to his own genius for guerilla warfare, brought him some astounding achievements. At Tippermuir, on 1 September 1644, he defeated 7,000 covenanters and took Perth. Twelve days later he was at Aberdeen, which he sacked before he took to the hills. Unlike his opponents, Montrose did not allow the weather to force him into winter quarters. In December he was ravaging the Campbell territories and, pursued by Argyll, turned and defeated him in a bloody battle at Inverlochy in February 1645. In the spring he took Dundee, won a victory at Auldearn, and in July defeated William Baillie, hero of Marston Moor, at Alford on the River Don. He again defeated Baillie, this time on 15 August, at Kilsyth, between Glasgow and Stirling. Whatever may be said of Argyll himself, not all of Montrose's opponents were incompetent; Baillie, for example, had served with distinction not only at Marston Moor but, like Alexander Leslie, under Gustavus Adolphus. Montrose's victories could not, however, help the king whose cause he had so remarkably defended; far to the south, at Naseby, on 14 June 1645, Charles and Prince Rupert were crushed by Cromwell and Fairfax in what was the first great success of the New Model Army. The battle marked the end of the first stage of the English Civil War. Although effectively master of Scotland, Montrose, too, was in difficulties. In numerical terms support for him had never been large; the Highlanders, incapable of sustaining a long campaign, were beginning to drift away and the Irish soldiers were more concerned with booty than with the king's cause. The Lowlands of Scotland offered little chance of gathering an army to supplement the meagre force of some 600 which was all that remained to him. Nevertheless, whether because of misplaced optimism or a sense of duty, Montrose pushed south. At Philiphaugh, near Selkirk, on 13 September 1645, Montrose's small army was destroyed by David Leslie's cavalry. Montrose was led from the field by friends. There was a sickening slaughter of the remnants of Montrose's army by the Covenanters who did not even spare the camp-followers. Montrose's great days were behind him. In the future he was to return from the Continent in support of Charles II, only to be defeated and captured at Carbisdale on 27 April 1650 and executed in Edinburgh on 21 May. Among those who were present in Edinburgh on the day of Montrose's execution was Argyll, whom he had earlier defeated. Montrose's bearing contrasted vividly with that of Argyll when, 11 years later, with a king again on the throne, the latter went to his death for his conduct during the supremacy of Cromwell. Montrose, betrayed to the government after Carbisdale for £25,000, met his end with courage and dignity, silencing the citizens of Edinburgh who had come to jeer at him. He repeated his belief in the National Covenant in terms which explain the difficulties which men were faced with in a time of strained and changing loyalties:

'The Covenant which I took, I own it and adhere to it. Bishops, I care not for them. I never intended to advance their interests. But when the King granted you all your desires and you were every one sitting under his vine and fig tree, that then you should have taken a party in England by the hand and entered into a league with them against the King, was the thing I judged my duty to oppose you to the yondmost.'

THE EXECUTION OF CHARLES I

Charles I, his armies defeated and his cause broken, chose to surrender to the Covenanters, camped outside Newark, on 5 May 1646. He may have thought that the Scots would prove more willing than the English to support him in his hope of reversing the military, and with it the political situation. The Scots, however, were not unanimously enthusiastic about Charles and when he refused to take the Covenant, because he would be undertaking to set up Presbyterianism in his kingdom, they had no wish to keep him. It was not enough that Charles agreed that he would 'be instructed concerning the Presbyterian government'. Neither he nor the Scots could truly believe that the outcome of such instruction would be that he would finally take the Covenant. In January 1647, the Scots handed the king over to the English parliament, receiving part-payment of monies due to them for their work on behalf of Parliament and a promise that Charles would not be harmed.

The seizure of the king by the English army in June seemed to threaten that promise, and certain of the more moderate Scots, the earls of Loudoun and Lauderdale among them, were sufficiently concerned to enter into negotiations with Charles. By the 'Engagement' of December 1647, made at Carisbrooke, the Scots were to invade England on behalf of Charles who, while still adamant in his refusal to take the Covenant, agreed to accept Presbyterianism as the religion of Scotland and to give it a three-year trial in England. The Scottish army, without the expertise of the Leslies, Alexander and David, who would not join it, descended on England with the earl of Middleton and the duke of Hamilton at its head. The Scots were crushed by Cromwell in Lancashire in August 1648; Middleton and Hamilton were both captured but, while the former was able to make his escape, Hamilton was executed. With the defeat of the 'Engagers', power within Scotland shifted back to the more extreme covenanters. In the Whiggamore Raid, the Covenanters of the south-west marched on Edinburgh and Argyll, not missing the opportunity, took office. He saw, realistically, that the future of Scotland depended, at least in part, on an accommodation with Cromwell. When Cromwell came to Edinburgh in October 1648, he and Argyll understood the mutual benefits arising from agreement: they would teach the 'malignancy' of the royalist cause. How long Argyll and Cromwell could maintain their co-operation is doubtful. The Act of Classes, passed in January 1649, debarred from office in Scotland any who could not prove beyond question their devotion to the covenant. This earnest of Argyll's intention to purge the government of Scotland of unworthy elements came in the same month as the execution in Whitehall of the king. Cromwell had used the arrangement with the Scots to free England of the fear of invasion from the north and to press on with Charles' trial. Scottish opinion was outraged by the execution and disturbed by the relationship between Scotland and the Commonwealth in the south. Argyll broke with Cromwell; within a week of Charles I's death, his son, Charles II, who was then in Holland where he was safe from Cromwell's agents, was proclaimed king of the Scots and of Great Britain, France and Ireland. No one could mistake the challenge to Cromwell and the Commonwealth which the proclamation posed.

Charles II and the Scots

Charles II was 19 years old when proclaimed king in Edinburgh. He was wary of the Scots; it was they who had handed over his father to the English Parliament and he did not share their views on religion. At first he rejected the suggestion that he should take the Covenant and cast about for some ally more to his liking. He sent Montrose back to Scotland before callously disowning him. A month after Montrose's execution, on 23 June, Charles, ready now to sign the Covenant for his own good reasons, landed in Scotland. His arrival brought Cromwell north to persuade the Scots to see the error of their ways; to the general assembly he addressed his famous plea, 'I beseech you in the bowels of Christ, think it possible you may be mistaken'. The Scots would have nothing of this, despite Cromwell's Old Testament language. He had anticipated this and, with a well-trained and experienced army, he routed the Scots at Dunbar on 3 September 1650. Superior in numbers, the Scots were led by David Leslie. He had the skill to offer a real threat to Cromwell, whose troops were decimated by sickness, but he allowed the ministers of the Church who were with him to dictate his tactics. Over 3,000 of Leslie's army were killed and 10,000 captured.

Scotland under Cromwell

Scotland was exhausted, its economy ruined. Warfare meant devastation, often employed as a matter of policy. There was no resistance to the occupation which Cromwell instituted and which existed for nine years. Scotland was conquered as it had not been since the time of Edward I and the English did not lightly give up a plan to treat Scotland as a conquered province. Instead, the idea of a union between the Commonwealth and

Scotland gained favour, with Scotland, it is said, allowed 'all the privileges of a free people'. Lieutenant-General George Monck, so recently responsible for the destruction of much of the area round Stirling, was named governor of a country which, according to Cromwell himself, was 'a very ruined nation'. The union with England did not greatly profit Scotland. Taxation was heavy and trade did not readily recover as it had in England. Scottish representation in what, in theory ought to have been a joint parliament, was limited; something of the English attitude to the Scots can be gathered from the contemporary remark that 'Scottish members are like a wooden leg tied to the natural body'. The Scots themselves were, as ever, distrustful of the English, even when the army of occupation gave that peace which had been so long missing. There was one serious rebellion, in 1654, when the earl of Middleton who had escaped both from Preston and Worcester, returned from France with a commission from his king. Monck dealt effectively with the rebellion and the forts erected at strategic sites such as Ayr, Inverness and Inverlochy, served as a reminder of English power. Argyll, who had at first held out against association with the English, came to terms with the new order, although his precise position, as always, was not easy to define; his compliance, however, would later bring about his downfall and death. Like the majority of his fellow-countrymen, he had accepted what he could not change.

The Restoration

The death of Cromwell on 3 September 1658 led to the realisation of the dependence of the government of England, and therefore that of Scotland, on him. Richard, his son, stayed in power for only six months and there was a general awareness that alone the restoration of the king could resolve the deteriorating political situation. In May 1660 Charles entered London in triumph and on 19 June, when news of his return reached Edinburgh, there was great celebration that Scotland again had a king, 'Charles Stuart, a long dark man, above two yards high', who had been chased out of the country by his enemies. Scotland was rid of the English but it never saw its new king; not once in the 25 years of his reign did Charles II visit Scotland. He ruled from London by decree, as his grandfather, James VI of Scotland (James I of England), had sought to do. Whatever distaste he felt for the Scots, Charles did not show himself revengeful towards a nation which had thwarted the royalist cause as often as it had supported it. Like Argyll, Archibald Johnston, instrumental in the creation of the National Covenant, was executed but there was less of a bloodletting than in England. Charles acted as if the past years had never been. He sent the earl of Middleton as his commissioner in Scotland and, in 1661, the Act Rescissory annulled all acts passed since 1633. The bishops were brought back but the king, too astute to attempt to enforce Anglican practices did not repeat his father's misguided determination to enforce a prayer book on Scotland. He could not, however, avoid all of the problems which matters of religion invariably meant in Scotland and one decision cost the country dearly. Congregations, which since 1649 had the right to elect their own ministers, reacted violently when that right was taken away from them and given instead to local landowners. Three hundred ministers, the majority in the south-west, refused to accept the new order and left their livings, preaching in the open-air, in the fields and hills. These Coventicles, as they were called, could not be tolerated by the government; those who did not attend church were faced with fines and violence if they did not pay the fines. The coventicles were declared illegal and those who participated in them were hunted down by government troops. There was a natural desire on the part of the Convenanters to defend themselves and their coventicles. In November 1666 the discontent with the harsh government policy, enforced by the earl of Rothes, Middleton's replacement, boiled over and open revolt broke out in the south-west. The Pentland Rising, a protest march which started at Dumfries and went through Ayrshire and Lanarkshire towards Edinburgh, posed, in reality, no great threat to the government, but the opportunity for conciliation was ignored in favour of brutality. At Rullion Green, near Penicuik, the marchers, lacking military skill if not courage, were crushed by the dragoons of Sir Thomas Dalziel of the Binns. Of the prisoners taken by Dalziel, some were hanged, others sent into slavery.

THE TRIUMPH OF THE EXTREMISTS

It is unlikely that Charles, a man of exceptional tolerance, approved of

Charles II

the methods employed to suppress the Pentland Rising; indeed, he is said to have sent a letter counselling leniency. The king had never gone as far in imposing his government on Scotland as he might have; if bishops had been reintroduced, the Five Articles of Perth had not been enforced. He understood the damage which Rullion Green and Rothes' repressive methods caused and Rothes was recalled, his place as commissioner taken by the earl of Lauderdale. Under him there was a softening of policy which was not entirely successful. When the evicted or 'outed' ministers were given the chance to return to their livings if they would agree to be loyal to the king, not all accepted. Charles' attempt to restore episcopacy, however moderate, was not forgotten or forgiven by their kind. In their own way, they, and their congregations, were as extreme as their opponents who persecuted them. They would allow only Presbyterianism and any concession to them was seen as weakness. The successive Letters of Indulgence which Lauderdale issued did not produce the desired effect and, like his predecessor, he had recourse to restraint. The Non-Conformists were now subject to severe penalties, from fines for continued absences from church to death for preaching at an open-air coventicle. Fines were imposed, too, on masters whose servants would not attend church. To ensure compliance with these regulations in the south-west, the government in 1678 installed the 'Highland Host', a body of some 9,000 troops. Their depredations added to the discontent already present. But the Covenanters themselves were far from above reproach. On 3 May 1679, some of them murdered James Sharp, archbishop of St Andrews, at Magus Muir outside the town. A previous attempt to kill Sharp had failed; on this occasion he was unfortunate enough to arrive on the scene when the Covenanters were waiting to waylay the sheriff. Unpopular as he was with some sections of the population, Sharp did not deserve to be hacked to death. The murderers rode to the west and joined up with a large and, as became clear, well-armed and trained Coventicle at Drumclog, between Kilmarnock and Strathaven. Drumclog was near to Loudon Hill, where Robert Bruce had won his first victory against the English. On 1 June 1679 at Drumclog the Covenanters defeated a government cavalry force under John Graham of Claverhouse, later to win immortality in another battle.

No government could disregard such a challenge to its authority; the Covenanters had shown that they possessed a capacity for war which had to be eliminated. After Drumclog, moreover, they had been as guilty of savagery towards their prisoners as had the government after the Pentland Rising. Glasgow fell to the Covenanters when Graham of Claverhouse could not defend it and action against the rebels could no longer be delayed. At Bothwell Brig Charles' natural son, James, duke of Monmouth, defeated the Covenanters who were once again the prey to division. But Monmouth was careful to release those who submitted to the king; there were a few executions and some deportations but Monmouth, no doubt in keeping with his father's wishes, acted with restraint. Monmouth's humane treatment of his prisoners might have led in time to a general pacification of Scotland but extremism was not yet dead in Scotland. The year after Bothwell Brig, the fanatical Richard Cameron, 'the Lion of the Covenant', publicly disowned the king's authority at Sanquhar in Dumfriesshire on 22 June. Although he was killed not long afterwards at Aird's Moss, his followers, the 'Cameronians', desperate and vicious, fought on with Donald Carghill and James Renwick at their head. Their violence was met by greater force from Charles' brother, James, duke of York, sent north in place of Monmouth, and harder and less conciliatory. With the help of Graham of Claverhouse in the field and Sir George Mackenzie in the courts York brought his own kind of justice against the Cameronians. Graham became 'Bluidy Clavers' and the lord advocate was named 'Bluidy Mackenzie' but, in reality, they were no worse than those they fought.

James VII of Scotland (James II of England)

Charles II, in a manner worthy of his grandfather, had trodden the difficult path of a seventeenth-century king for 25 years when he died on 6 February 1685. It was no mean achievement to survive the plots and politics of his reign in England and if he preferred to leave Scottish affairs in the hands of others, it was to the benefit of his own reputation. He had not created the circumstances in which disorder flourished in Scotland and, despite his inability to resolve the problems which religious differences caused, he has not been pilloried like his brother and successor, James. Whereas Charles did not parade his inclination towards Catholicism, James made no attempt to disguise the fact that he was a Catholic. The exclusion bills of 1679 to 1681, framed to prevent James from succeeding his brother, failed, and in Scotland, as in England, opposition to his becoming king was relatively muted. He was proclaimed king in Edinburgh on Tuesday 10 February. James moved swiftly against the Covenanters; in April, an act was passed making support for the Covenant treasonable and attendance at a coventicle punishable by death. He had not studied the lessons of his brother's reign and knew no middle way. He was soon faced with rebellion.

Monmouth, Charles II's son by Lucy Walters, had been an energetic and capable commander for his father in Scotland. Ambitious and popular, he was denied legitimacy and plotted against his father, only to be exiled. Not unnaturally he resented the succession of his uncle in 1685, but in his rebellion in the same year he lost at Sedgemoor and was executed. The earl of Argyll, son of Montrose's enemy, aimed to support

Monmouth with a rising in the west of Scotland but was as ineffectual as Monmouth and, like his father 24 years before, he went to the scaffold. James' severity against the rebels in England and Scotland was ill judged but in character. The ease with which Monmouth and Argyll were routed deceived him into thinking that he could force through religious change. When the Scottish parliament warned him against abrupt moves, he declared that a king had 'no dependency on parliaments'. When his commissioner, the duke of Queensberry, would not become a Catholic in order to please him, James dismissed him and chose in his place the earl of Perth, who had no such religious scruples. Others followed Perth's lead and James was able to obtain the support which he required if he were to carry out his intention to give his fellow-religionists freedom of worship. An ambition laudable today, the achievement of religious freedom was not viewed as such in an age when James' cousin, Louis XIV of France, was persecuting the Huguenots. It was easy for Scots to believe that freedom of worship for Catholics was a first step towards the introduction of Catholicism instead of Presbyterianism. James did not extend freedom to the more extreme Protestants; those Cameronians who had escaped his justice, joined with the more peaceful Presbyterians in opposition to the king. That opposition was not limited to any one class, nor was it without an element of self-interest. High office had been lost by men who would not convert to Catholicism; if less honourable in their objection to James than those moved by religion, they were more powerful. The birth of a son, James Francis Edward Stuart, to the king and his wife, Mary of Modena, on Sunday 10 June 1688, meant that a Catholic succession was guaranteed. From England an urgent message was sent to William of Orange, husband of James' daughter, Mary, inviting him to invade England and overthrow James. The Scots looked on, unwilling as yet to engage themselves on either side. On 5 November, William landed with his army at Torbay in Devon. James fled, his courage gone with the defection of his leading ministers. He was captured but, sensibly, his captors allowed him to escape to France on 23 December. His wife and son were already there.

CHAPTER NINE

A New Age,
1688–1820

The Beginnings of Jacobitism

On 13 February 1689 parliament offered the crown of England to William of Orange and his wife Mary as joint sovereigns on condition that they were willing to accept the Declaration of Rights. In Scotland events moved more slowly. James VII had called the troops in Scotland south before he chose flight rather than resistance to William of Orange. The status of the government in Scotland with James on his way to France and William awaiting the verdict of the Scottish people was uncertain. With a wisdom born of experience, its leading figures had made their way to London, where all decisions would ultimately be made. The volatile nature of the situation in Scotland had been made clear before the end of 1688. Support for William, the Protestant, had manifested itself both in the capital and in the south-west of the country, where the Covenanter element had carried out the 'rabbling of the curates', dispossessing and driving out James' nominees in the height of winter. The Stuart dynasty, however, more than 300 years old, could not be so easily removed; loyalty to it was strong, particularly in the Highlands, and whatever its flaws, it would continue to find a romantic response in Scotland.

The first struggle between the Williamites and the Jacobites was settled not on the field of battle but in the Convention of Estates which William, approached by leading Scots for his help, called after he had accepted the offer of the English crown. The Convention, the name by which parliament was known when there was no king on the throne, met in Edinburgh on 14 March 1689. It heard letters from both William and

James stating their respective claims to the throne of Scotland. James' letter was undiplomatic, alienating those to whom it was addressed and losing him the sympathy of others inclined to his cause. On Friday 11 April, the convention published the Claim of Right declaring that James had 'forefaulted' or forfeited the crown of Scotland and offered it to William and Mary. The Claim of Right, although modelled on the English Declaration of Rights, was more radical; the Scots were intent on replacing James with monarchs more conscious of what was expected of them. Catholics were barred from the throne and from offices of State and there would be no more bishops for, as was said 'Prelacy . . . is, and has been a great and insupportable grievance and trouble to this Nation'. William, more tolerant than his Scottish subjects, needed Scotland as he needed England in his opposition to Louis XIV of France. Therefore, any distaste he felt for the terms put before him in London by Scottish representatives had to be ignored now. King of Scotland William might be in name but the settlement of April 1689 was opposed in a variety of ways. At the time of the meeting of the convention, Edinburgh had been overlooked by a Jacobite garrison in the castle and it was not until June that that threat was removed. The former king himself was not slow to go to Ireland to raise his standard in the first stages of a campaign to regain what had been his; Ireland was too close to Scotland for developments there to be disregarded. In religious circles, the Episcopalian interest resented the Presbyterian ascendancy while the Cameronians, still extreme, were angered that the Covenant no longer had pride of place. It was in the Highlands, so often a centre of disaffection to government, that trouble began. At the head of this first of the Jacobite rebellions, was one of those charismatic figures which the Stuarts, the now common French spelling of the older Scots form, always seemed able to conjure up in their periods of greatest trial.

'BONNIE DUNDEE'

James Graham of Claverhouse had been a persecutor of the Covenanters, almost fanatical if not always successful, as his ignominious defeat at Drumclog in 1679 had illustrated. He was one of those summoned to the south by James after the landing by William of Orange at Torbay and had been made Viscount Dundee by James. Dundee's somewhat undistinguished military career might have consigned him to oblivion but for the action of the Convention of 1689 in declaring him a fugitive and a rebel. Dundee was thus set on the path which led, in his case, to glory and an early death at the age of 41. Like Montrose, Dundee looked to the Highlands for an army to use against the new government. He showed a genius for uniting the clans against William; he disposed of considerable funds and knew how to work on the fear the clans felt for the Campbells, led by yet another Argyll. Dundee secured the adherence of Cameron of Lochiel, who joined him in person, and set off to seize Blair Atholl, the key to the route between the Highlands and the Lowlands. Against Dundee the government sent General Hugh Mackay, who had fought on the Continent. Like many after him, Mackay could not understand the attitude of the Highlanders; the people there, he stated, lacked a 'true sense of the deliverance which God had sent them'. Mackay's army was badly trained and with Mackay no match for Dundee, it was routed at Killiecrankie on 27 July 1689. The ferocious assault of the Highlanders, who struck the government lines before the soldiers could receive them with the bayonet, won the day and set an exhilarating example which would be fatal in later engagements involving Jacobite forces. Dundee, struck by a musket ball fired from the ranks of Mackay's own regiment, was killed, like Douglas at Otterburn, at the moment of victory. As had happened with Douglas, Dundee's death brought him greater reputation than he had known in life but it effectively ended the rebellion. The Highlanders started to drift away and, in Dundee's place, Colonel Cannon, who had brought reinforcements from Ireland, had neither Dundee's leadership qualities nor his tact in keeping the clans loyal to James. At Dunkeld on 21 August the Jacobites failed to overcome their opponents, in whose ranks served the Cameronians, as fearless in war as they had been in their religious beliefs, and the defeat at Cromdale in the following May ended the rebellion for which 'Bonnie Dundee' had been responsible.

William could not afford to forget the Highlands even with Dundee dead. An attempt was made to buy loyalty; in all some £12,000 was made available. When bribery was not altogether successful, recourse was had to another tactic. In August 1691 the clans were ordered to swear an oath of loyalty to William before the following New Year's Day. The consequences of the failure of Alasdair, chief of the MacIan MacDonalds of Glencoe, to take the oath within the time allowed are notorious. The Massacre of Glencoe, on 13 February 1692, was carried out by soldiers under the command of Captain Robert Campbell of Clenlyon. The Highlanders were no strangers to treachery but the massacre was perpetrated by a force acting on government orders; the fact that Campbell's men had been billeted on the MacDonalds for almost a fortnight before the deed was done only added to the horror with which the news was received. William himself could not escape censure, although it was his secretary of state, John Dalrymple, the Master of Stair, who suffered most from public opinion. William defended the unpopular Stair but by 1695, when the government was roundly condemned by a commission of investigation for having 'barbarously killed men under trust', he could no longer retain Stair in office. The condemnation in itself demonstrates that higher standards were now expected of the government even in its dealings with the much detested Highlanders. However, the clans had been cowed, at least for the immediate future, by the massacre and Dundee's death and the events in Glencoe meant that for some time Jacobitism was dormant.

THE DARIEN AFFAIR

Scottish distrust of English intentions was further fuelled by the collapse of a trading venture which started promisingly. In 1695, by act of parliament, the Company of Scotland was set up to establish colonies abroad, in Africa and the West Indies. The Scots, excluded by the Navigation Acts and by monopolies from the benefits of foreign trade which the English themselves enjoyed, saw the opportunity to benefit from the Company of Scotland. There was therefore much enthusiasm for a plan advanced by William Paterson, an economist born at Tynwald in Dumfriesshire. Paterson, a founder of the Bank of England which was incorporated by act of parliament in 1694, proposed a settlement on the isthmus of Darien in Panama, where the distance between the Atlantic and the Pacific Oceans is only 40 miles. A company was formed with the endorsement of the Scottish parliament and with great public invest-ment. Paterson accompanied the first expedition to Darien but the high hopes of the early days could not be sustained. Initial English interest

Parliament House, Edinburgh

wavered and a second and third expedition could not rescue the settlement. The climate, of course, was a factor, as was the overt hostility of the Spanish, in whose area of influence Darien lay. It was widely believed in Scotland that the government in London, anxious to placate Spain because of the war with France, and jealous of its own trading, had refused to help. Its assistance might have reduced the odds against the settlers. As would so often be the case, the Scots blamed their southern neighbours, deservedly or not, for a reversal. The suffering of the settlers had been immense; only 300 returned to Scotland in 1700 out of some 2,500 who had sought a new life and prosperity in the Darien scheme. William could not persuade the Scots of his support even when, in October of that year, he promised in a letter to parliament that he would promote Scottish trade. The bitterness in Scotland would not disappear and his death, on 8 March 1702, was not the occasion of great distress. It was not the Jacobites alone who felt gratitude to the mole, the 'little gentleman in velvet' which brought about William's unexpected death when his horse threw him; for neither the Massacre of Glencoe nor the Darien affair had caused the Scots to trust him. His successor, Anne, the last of the Stuart monarchs, would very quickly learn the extent of the anti-English feeling in Scotland.

The Act of Union

William and his wife, Mary, who died in 1694, had had no children; the obvious successor was therefore Mary's sister, Anne. Unlike her sister, Anne, married to Prince George of Denmark, was extremely fertile, although of her 17 children most died in infancy. The death of her heir, William, duke of Gloucester, in 1700 at the age of 11, provoked a crisis about the eventual succession. Without reference to Scotland, the English parliament, by the Act of Settlement of 1701, decided that if Anne was predeceased by all of her children, as was indeed to be the case, the crown should be offered to Sophia, Electress of Hanover, grand-daughter of James VI of Scotland (James I of England) and 'the heirs of her body being Protestant'. The Scots in their turn made their own decision on the succession; the Act of Security of 1703 provided for them to make their own choice of a successor to Anne under certain circumstances. Not until the queen agreed to accept this would the Scots grant her supplies. If there was a loathing for the English in Scotland, in the south there were stronger emotions still, accentuated after the death of James VII in September 1701. For when Louis XIV of France, who was at war with England over the Spanish succession, recognised James VII's son, Prince James Edward, as James VIII of Scotland (James III of England), it was viewed as a threat to England, where the thought of the Scots welcoming a Catholic restoration could not be tolerated. There was now the possibility of war between Scotland and England. Matters worsened with the Aliens Act of 1705 by which the English threatened to treat the Scots as aliens unless they agreed to the succession of Sophia and her heirs, and with the hanging in Scotland of three English merchant sailors on a trumped-up charge of piracy.

It became clear, however, that war would benefit neither country. Scotland needed trade with England and the English, in the war with France which would continue until 1713, knew that their northern boundary must be secure. Both William and Anne had realised that peace between Scotland and England was imperative and that it would best be found through union. Even as he lay dying, William had warned the English parliament that 'nothing can contribute more to the present and future peace, security and happiness of England and Scotland than a firm and entire union'. Anne followed William's lead with a plea that parliament look at means of achieving union. Despite anger and opposition in Scotland, where it was argued that the people would be 'utterly ruined should these laws take effect', 31 Scottish commissioners and a similar number of English commissioners were working on proposals for union by April 1706. It was inevitable that there would be a violent reaction to the terms for union when these were presented to the Scottish parliament on 12 October 1706. There were riots in Edinburgh, Glasgow and Dumfries, and such was the atmosphere that English troops took up station on the border, ready to intervene in Scotland. In parliament, John Hamilton, second Lord Belhaven cried that the union meant the murder of Scotland and spoke, as so many did, of surrender. Against such a background and with prolonged debate the terms were confirmed, in contrast to the smooth passage the terms enjoyed in the English parliament at Westminster. In the end, the language of Belhaven counted for less than that of William Seton of Pitmedden who saw union more realistically: 'This nation, being poor, and without force to protect its commerce, cannot reap great advantage by it, till it partake of the trade and protection of some powerful neighbour nation.'

Scotland, after 400 years of independence from England, poor, beset by famine, and with the disaster of Darien still fresh in the memory, accepted what it could no longer refuse. On Tuesday 25 March 1707, Queen Anne's commissioner to the Scottish parliament, James Douglas, second duke of Queensberry, and henceforth the 'Union Duke', pronounced the sentence, 'My Lords and Gentlemen, the Public Business of this session being now over, it is full time to put an end to it'. The Scottish parliament would never meet again. The Act of Union passed into law on 1 May 1707. Scotland sent members to the Commons and peers to the Lords, received that equality of trade with England which was held to be so important, accepted the succession of the Electress Sophie, agreed to a common system of coinage, but retained its own system of law. But just as the Act of Union did not bring an immediate prosperity to Scotland, so it did not remove the Jacobite threat. The year after the Act of Union was passed, the French attempted to land the young James Francis Edward, son of James VII of Scotland, on the Scottish coast at Burntisland. Admiral Forbin was driven off by bad weather and the proximity of George Byng, Viscount Torrington, with 26 ships – but it was a warning. The union continued unpopular in Scotland, where Belhaven's view that it meant 'entire surrender' had seemed accurate in the light of what was seen as English arrogance. The financial advantages of the union to the Scots were not accruing and the inability of their representatives in parliament to affect policy was much resented. As late as 1713, when Earl Findlater argued against the union in the House of Lords, he was defeated in the subsequent vote by a margin of only four. In such an atmosphere, the Jacobites thought that they had good cause to hope for a restoration of the Stuart dynasty.

The Pretenders

The last of the Stuart monarchs, Anne, died on Sunday 1 August 1714, to be succeeded by George, son of Sophie, the Electress of Hanover. The arrival of George I did not lead to immediate trouble. However, it was his insensitive treatment of one of those who had facilitated the passage of the Act of Union which led to a Jacobite rebellion in the north. John Erskine, eleventh earl of Mar, 'Bobbing John' because of the ease with which he changed sides, had supported William III and worked in government under Anne. When George I let it be known that Mar would not continue in royal favour, Mar left England and sailed north, landing at Elie in Fife. Mar, now a Jacobite, proclaimed James Francis, 'the Old Pretender' as he is more usually known, king as James VIII on 6 September 1715, and soon had an army of 6,000, drawn largely from Mackintoshes and MacDonalds. Whether 'the Old Pretender' had authorised Mar's action is unclear but his name was enough to swell the ranks of Mar's army. The Jacobites outnumbered the government troops in Scotland but Mar was no Montrose. He captured Perth and Inverness but without help from France lost his nerve. While he remained in the Highlands, he sent a force of 2,000 men, under the leadership of William Mackintosh of Borlum, south into the north-west of England, where

A detail from the Stuart monument, St Peter's, Rome

there was sympathy for the Jacobite cause. At Preston, Mackintosh, no more competent than Mar, had to surrender to government forces.

The detachment of Mackintosh's troops had not succeeded in deflecting George's commander in Scotland, John, second duke of Argyll, from his strategy of containing Mar in the Highlands. Argyll, who had served under Marlborough on the Continent, was a soldier of some ability. He had occupied Stirling to prevent Mar from entering the Lowlands; a wiser man than 'Bobbing John' would have seen the sense in an outflanking movement. Such a manoeuvre was beyond Mar and he now had to fight and, more importantly, defeat Argyll. The Battle of Sheriffmuir, which took place on Sunday 13 November 1715, the same day as the surrender at Preston, was inconclusive. As the Jacobites themselves put it:

> There's some say that we wan,
> Some say that they wan,
> Some say that nane wan at a' man.

It was not enough that the government losses were higher than those of the Jacobites; Argyll's army was still in place. 'The Old Pretender' himself came to Scotland soon after, landing at Peterhead just before Christmas, but Sheriffmuir and Preston had lost him the campaign.

George I was intelligent enough to realise that repression after the rebellion of 1715 would be counter-productive. That he was correct in this belief was demonstrated by the lack of support for a Jacobite rising in 1719. Any support there was petered out after the Jacobites, this time with a Spanish contingent in their army, were broken at Glenshiel. One consequence of the abortive rebellions of 1715 and 1719 was the appointment of General George Wade to build roads and bridges which would allow the government to make a swifter and more effective response to any rebellion. For ten years Wade carried out a massive programme of opening up communications in the Highlands. He built 40 stone bridges and hundreds of miles of roads. The beneficial result is remembered in the lines of a popular rhyme:

> 'Had you see these roads before they were made,
> You would lift up your hands and bless General Wade.'

At the same time, the roads built by Wade served to guarantee the links between Fort William and Fort George. Their military value did not escape the Highlanders over whom they watched and they would have a part to play in the most famous of the Jacobite rebellions, that which the Jacobites began in 1745.

'The Old Pretender' lived until 1766, when he died in Rome at the age of 78, but it is his son, Charles Edward, 'the Young Pretender', the cause of defeat and a brutal pacification of the Highlanders, who is remembered today, and with a remarkable degree of affection. Charles Edward was 25 when, without his father's knowledge, he landed with seven companions on Scottish soil on 25 July 1745. It is customary to see 'Bonnie Prince Charlie's' venture in a romantic light but it was from the beginning foolhardy. He had, it is true, chosen his moment well; the War of the Austrian Succession had drained the country of government troops and George II's garrison in Scotland, under Sir John Cope, numbered no more than 3,000. Scotland had known peace for years, even if in the Highlands there was always the possibility of disturbance, and

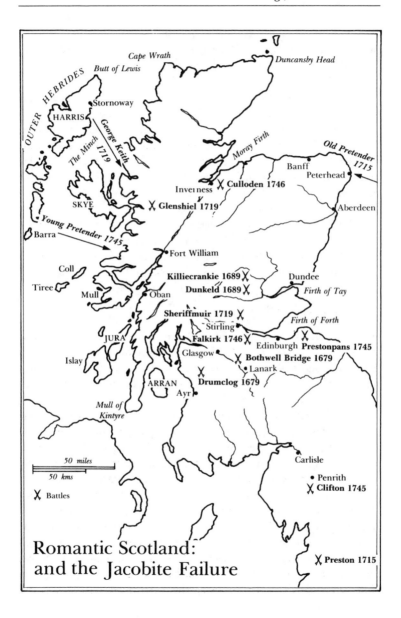

Romantic Scotland:
and the Jacobite Failure

'the Young Pretender' at first met with apathy when he raised his standard at Glenfinnan on 19 August. The Stuart name and his own attractive personality, however, worked to his advantage and when he secured the loyalty of Cameron of Lochiel, he could hope for further reinforcements. The government put a price on Charles' head and sent Cope against him. Argyll had understood the value of containing the Jacobites in the Highlands; Cope marched north to face 'the Young Pretender' but then remained at Inverness while Charles entered Perth. Charles now had, and to his credit took, the opportunity to march south, to the capital; the discomfited Cope, left in the north, had to transport his men by sea along the east coast. On 17 September, Charles entered Edinburgh and proclaimed his father king as James III. Four days later, Charles' army which Cope had described as a 'parcel of rabble', routed Cope's government forces at Prestonpans. Where he had previously been bold, Charles now vacillated, wasting five weeks in Edinburgh; he gained few recruits and the government, shaken by news of his victory at Prestonpans, prepared to meet him with two armies when he should eventually, as he must, push into England. There was no widespread enthusiasm for Charles and the Stuart cause in Scotland; indeed, as he was to learn, the Lowlands remained staunchly Hanoverian.

On 3 November 1745, Charles' army, numbering some 5,000 left Edinburgh and took the western route into England. General Wade, based at Newcastle, was prevented by the weather from reaching Carlisle, which fell to the Jacobites on 15 November. Charles pushed on through Lancashire and was enthusiastically received in Manchester on 29 November. The anticipated English support had not materialised, however, and when he reached Derby on 4 December, he was faced with the reality of his position. Two days later, he retreated north, away from George II's son, William Augustus, duke of Cumberland, whose army lay across his path to the south.

The story of the rest of the 'Forty-Five' is well known. Charles inflicted casualties on Cumberland's advance guard at Clifton near Penrith on 18 December 1745, then gained a victory over General Hawley at Falkirk on 17 January 1746. It was not Hawley that Charles had to fear, however, but the relentless Cumberland, still in pursuit. At Culloden, to the east of Inverness, on 16 April, the duke, methodical and with a disciplined and well-trained army, routed the prince. Cumberland proved at Culloden that the courage of the Highlanders, which had served Charles so well at Prestonpans, was no longer enough. He had prepared his men for the expected and feared enemy charge, his artillery and musket power were superior, and Charles, whose own courage was never in doubt, could not control the impetuous clans once the armies were engaged. There could be only one outcome to the battle. Twelve hundred Jacobites were killed at Culloden, against 50 dead on the government side. Worse than the battle itself was the brutality which followed. Cumberland ordered that the Jacobite wounded be put to death, there were 120 executions at various places in Scotland and in England, under the law of treason, 700 died in prison and over 1,000 people were sentenced to transportation. This time the clans were thoroughly disarmed and the tartan was proscribed. Cumberland became and remained 'Butcher'. 'The Young Pretender', a reward of £30,000 pounds offered for his capture, escaped to France after five months, aided by Flora MacDonald of South Uist and others less famous but as devoted to him.

The Other Scotland

Support for the 'Forty-Five' had not been widespread in Scotland and within 40 years of the escape of 'the Young Pretender' to France, Jacobitism was dead. By that time George III, who succeeded to the throne in 1760, had already granted a pension to Charles' brother, Henry, cardinal of York. Charles himself had died in despair and debauchery. Once a hero to the French, he was expelled by them after they had recognised the Hanoverian succession by the Treaty of Aix-la-Chapelle in 1748, and died without legitimate issue in Rome in 1788. It is now generally accepted that he visited England after the 'Forty-Five' but he now counted for little and was ignored. Neither in Britain nor abroad was he ever to find support; on the death of his father, the pope would not recognise him as king.

George III never visited Scotland but under him the country prospered in the intellectual and economic senses as never before. It was the writer, Tobias Smollett, who in his novel *Humphry Clinker*, referred to Edinburgh as 'a hot-bed of genius'. Certainly, in Edinburgh were to be found the likes of the philosophers Adam Ferguson, Dugald Stewart, and David Hume, the author of a *Treatise on Human Nature* among other works. There were also the scholarly minister of Inveresk, Alexander Carlyle, known as 'Jupiter', the historian William Robertson, and James Gregory, professor of medicine at the university. Some of these Dr Johnson met in 1773 through Boswell. Smollett might thus be forgiven his description of Edinburgh, but in Scotland as a whole there was also much evidence of an intellectual flowering. Adam Smith, professor of logic at the university of Glasgow, published *An Inquiry into the Nature and Causes of the Wealth of Nations* which was at once, and still is, an influential book. John Hunter of East Kilbride taught Edward Jenner, discoverer of the vaccine against smallpox. Throughout Scotland and in England the work of Scottish architects of this period can be admired; if the name of Adam is pre-eminent, James Gibbs, Colin Campbell and William Chambers also made their mark.

During the long reign of George III, which lasted until 1820, there was an acceleration in developments which changed the face of Scotland and the condition of its people as never before. In agriculture, the 'Honourable Society of Improvers in the Knowledge of Agriculture in Scotland' had been formed in 1723 by men intent on improving Scottish farming. They saw their task as giving advice and practical help to farmers. Word of their activities reached that unrepentant Jacobite, William Mackintosh of Borlum, twice captured and imprisoned for his adherence to the cause of 'the Old Pretender'. From his cell in Edinburgh Castle, he, as did many others, put his thoughts on agricultural methods on to paper. There was, however, a strong resistance to new ideas in farming and on occasion it took on a violent form; in 1724, in the south-west of the country, the 'Levellers' tore down the stone walls with which landowners had enclosed their land for grazing for cattle. Repression was used against the 'Levellers', some of whom suffered transportation, but they represented that hostility to change which was so characteristic of many Scots. But after the middle of the century, when peace returned after the end of the Jacobite rebellions, there was a wider acceptance of the need for change. The ideas of men such as William Mackintosh were revived and implemented. Henry Home,

Lord Kames, a lord of session, published *The Gentleman Farmer* in 1776 at the age of 80, the product of the thinking he had employed on his estate at Blair Drummond. James Small of Dalkeith introduced an improved plough and James and Andrew Meikle, father and son, sought better methods of winnowing and dressing grain. Agriculturalists came from England, the source of some of the new ideas, to study what was being done in Scotland.

Trade with the American colonies increased dramatically. In 1776, by which time the deepening of the Clyde was already in progress, Glasgow, the centre of the tobacco trade, had 386 ships engaged in it. The 'Tobacco Lords', such as John Glassford, prospered but, in general, were not to survive the outbreak of the American War of Independence. Glasgow, however, continued to grow; its population was approaching 100,000 before the end of the century. Although the balance of trade had shifted to the west, in the east, ports such as Leith, Aberdeen and Dundee, flourished. Despite the importance and size of Glasgow, Edinburgh remained the capital of Scotland; its provost, George Drummond, a native of the city, was a driving force behind Edinburgh's expansion. The creation of the 'New Town' came from a plan by James Craig, an architect, whose entry won the town council's competition of 1766. Improved communications helped trade and the prosperity of Scotland. John Macadam of Ayr and Thomas Telford of Westerkirk brought their talents to the building of roads; James Watt, born in Greenock in 1736 and better known for his work on steam engines, oversaw the construction of a stretch of canal for the carrying of coal into Glasgow. The Industrial Revolution, although not yet complete, was already well advanced by the end of the century. In cotton first and more slowly in iron, with the founding in 1759 of the Carron Company near Falkirk, there was marked growth. Now, increasingly, the population was to be concentrated in the western part of the Central Lowlands of Scotland. People from the east and the Highlands, dispossessed of their farms as land was enclosed for grazing. They sought and found work, of which there was no shortage, but had to live in conditions which were both degrading and harmful to health. As people moved to the towns from the countryside, they exchanged the poverty of their rural existence for the squalor of urban life. Even as late as the end of the first quarter of the nineteenth century, the trend of mortality in the principal cities of Edinburgh and Glasgow was still rising. Prosperity had come to Scotland but not all benefited from it either in economic or social terms. Scotland was relatively unaffected by the unrest in the American colonies which led to the War of Independence, but the French Revolution which began in 1789 had a greater and more lasting impact. France proved, it seemed, that reform of the system by those it repressed was possible by radical means. There was imitation of French models; societies were created for debate, the most prominent being the Society of the Friends of the People, dating from 1792. The Scottish radicals, in their somewhat naive admiration for what they thought was happening in France, aroused the fear of a government which was similarly watching events abroad but reaching very different conclusions. War with France was likely and any correspondence with the Jacobins, even the simple expression of sympathy for the French, was viewed as seditious by the government. There were arrests and trials of Scottish radicals when war broke out after the execution of Louis XVI. The judiciary itself was conservative and reflected in its conduct and judgements the prejudice and fear manifested by the government. Thomas Muir, a Glasgow lawyer, was one of those brought before the courts. He had gone to France, where he had already established contact, and on his return to Scotland was sentenced to 14 years transportation to Australia for sedition. Any suggestion for change, however minor, was viewed as dangerous and others followed Muir to be sentenced to transportation. Not all who met with such treatment were as fortunate as Muir himself; on his way to Australia he was taken off his prison ship by American sailors and made his way to his spiritual home, France, where he died in 1798. When, years after these events, Henry, Lord Cockburn, commented that 'the frightful thing was the personal bitterness' he was speaking, perhaps better than he realised, about persons and actions of which he could have only a distant recollection. The propertied and landed classes in Scotland had the means and the freedom to influence policy and utter criticism in the knowledge that they would be safe from prosecution. But others, less fortunate and unprotected by their social position, faced the law and, worse, its abuse by judges committed to the preservation of a system both corrupt and uncaring. No trial for sedition started from a presumption of the innocence of the accused; there was indeed some substance for the government's fear, as when, for example, a plot to seize Edinburgh Castle was discovered in 1794, but it does not excuse the excesses of judges such as Robert MacQueen, Lord Braxfield, whose bullying tactics gained him notoriety as a 'hanging judge'. Revolution did not occur in Scotland on the French model; the ambition of Napoleon made it plain to supporters of the French Revolution that the slogans of the earlier days had no longer any currency.

Robert Burns

It was in this period that the writings of the most famous and best loved of Scottish poets appeared. Robert Burns, born at Alloway in 1759, lived only to be 37 but today, as in his own times, his verse portrays universal sentiments and conclusions as to the nature of human life. He is read throughout the world and it is easy to forget the circumstances of the Scotland in which he worked. When Burns rode into Edinburgh in November 1786, he had with him a copy of his *Poems, Chiefly in the Scottish Dialect*, published by Wilson of Kilmarnock. Burns was rescued by the success of this volume from his intention to emigrate and was lionised by polite society in Edinburgh. He was not entirely at ease in Edinburgh and spent most of what remained of his life in Dumfriesshire where, having failed in a farming venture, he died in 1796. Burns' own life was often one of deprivation and unhappiness and this helps to explain his sympathy for the suffering of his fellow-countrymen. His belief in freedom and equality, in an age of repression, threatened to bring him into conflict with the authorities; when today Scots sing the words of 'Scots Wha Hae' they are often unaware that Burns had not dared to put his name to them for fear of retribution from the government. But Burns was a realist; he saw, more quickly than some, that the character of the French Revolution had changed and joined the Dumfriesshire Volunteers, raised against the threat of invasion from the Continent. Thus, Burns epitomises that love of Scotland which could push men into rebellions against the same government which they were so ready to defend when it was threatened from outside. He was a poet of the present, one who reacted to what he saw and felt. He died when Scotland was about to enter a period in which the past, romanticised and distorted, began to achieve a lasting and detrimental effect on the imaginations of his fellow-countrymen.

CHAPTER TEN

Myth and Reality,
1820–1914

'Henry the Ninth, Uncrowned King of Scotland'

At the opening of the nineteenth century, the dominant figure in Scottish politics, as throughout the years of unrest engendered by the French Revolution, was Henry Dundas of Arniston in Midlothian, first Viscount Melville. From a family which traced its involvement in the law back to James Dundas, Lord Arniston in the reign of Charles II, Dundas was the half-brother of the second Lord Arniston, president of the Court of Session. An MP at the age of 32, he was Lord Advocate for eight years before holding a number of offices in the administration of William Pitt 'the Younger'. Dundas had mastered early the art of ingratiating himself with those in power and thereafter achieved power himself. Not everyone found Dundas agreeable; George III thought him a pest. In an age when it was not uncommon for politicians to change sides, Dundas served in Whig governments before giving his allegiance to Pitt. Dundas was capable of reading the political signs and progressed where others faltered. He saw that through increasing his authority in Scotland he could carry weight in Westminster, where decisions were made. When Pitt became prime minister in 1783, on the fall of the Fox–North government, he made Dundas treasurer of the navy. Subsequently, until his resignation in 1805, Dundas was Secretary for War, First Lord of the Admiralty, and President of the Board of Control for India.

It was Dundas who watched over the increasing industrialisation of Scotland in the reign of George III. It was also he who so managed the country's affairs that it survived, without greater upheaval, the influences emanating from France. Such was his grip on the Scottish electoral system that it has been estimated that he exercised control, either direct or indirect, over no fewer than 36 of the 45 constituencies, and that of the Scottish peers all but three were of his persuasion. With this secure base, he succeeded in keeping the country Tory, even when, with Henry Erskine at its head, Whig opposition to him was growing in Scotland. Dundas remained in office until 1805, a symbol to many of corruption and of values now under attack. When he resigned, it was because of an investigation into his stewardship of funds while he was Treasurer of the Navy. He had fought off his political enemies for some 30 years; impeachment, although followed by acquittal, led to the end of his career. 'Harry the Ninth the Uncrowned King of Scotland' was commemorated in a monument raised to him in Edinburgh by members of the classes whose interests he had protected. Nothing, however, could project Dundas, who died in 1811, as the protector of the less fortunate of Scotland. It was the war against Napoleon which prevented more trouble in Scotland as social unrest continued to spread, rather than anything done by Dundas and his successors, among them his nephew, Henry, and his son, Robert, second Viscount Melville. The second viscount, accorded the position of 'manager for Scotland', although competent, never equalled his father's supremacy and could not guarantee the adherence of the Scottish representation at Westminister. With the end of the war after the defeat of Napoleon at Waterloo, Scotland, like England, witnessed clashes between government and a people reawakening to the urgent need for reform of a system which denied them dignity and a share of the prosperity which had come to Scotland.

THE 'RADICAL WAR'

The protracted struggle with revolutionary France and then with Napoleon had not removed the causes of social unrest. There had been a remarkable expansion in the textile industry after 1780 but the use of machinery affected the workers and redundancies ensued. Prices were high and wages inadequate. There was an influx of labour from Ireland and from the Highlands, where the clearances, with their emphasis on sheep farming and the removal of tenants, were now having a profound effect; such newcomers were willing to accept lower wages and thereby depressed the status of others. Agriculture was not exempt from difficulties; after Waterloo there was an end to the protection which it had enjoyed. If much distress was caused by bad harvests, some of those who lived on the land contributed to their own condition by their refusal to abandon old methods, long outdated and unproductive.

For some Scots, unwilling to join the drift to the towns in the central belt of Scotland where work was available, emigration seemed the answer. The Darien scheme had been a disaster; now Canada offered some hope and a challenge. The hope was to prove largely evanescent, and the challenge too great for the majority. Canada, it is true, had already been a satisfactory home for Scots; veterans of the Highland regiments, with some money and with land granted to them on their discharge from military service, had had advantages denied to their successors. These emigrants, misled unintentionally by reports from fortunate colonists in Canada, but just as often deceived by unscrupulous land agents, met a harsh welcome. They endured intolerable conditions on board ship, only to be landed immense distances from their intended homes or, once arrived there, found that the land could not sustain them. When, from 1803 onwards, the fifth earl of Selkirk, Thomas Douglas, as well prepared as he was well intentioned, dispatched various parties of Highlanders to Canada, most notably into the Red River area, the hostility of the Hudson Bay and north-west companies raised echoes of the opposition of the Spanish to the Darien settlers.

In Scotland, the violence which had threatened for so long erupted in 1820. It had already occurred in England, where, in 1817 Habeas Corpus was suspended by the government of Lord Liverpool, fearful of radical movements and bent on their suppression. During the 'Peterloo Massacre', at St Peter's Field in Manchester on 16 August 1819, 11 people were killed when the magistrates ordered troops to attack a crowd gathered to hear Henry Hunt. This was followed by the Six Acts forbidding meetings of more than 50 persons. That Liverpool and his cabinet had good reason for their concern appeared to be demonstrated by the betrayal of the Cato Street Conspiracy which attempted to overthrow the government, in February 1820, but neither Liverpool nor his colleagues would address the causes of unrest with the same intensity as they sought to punish radicals. Events in England had been disturbing enough but the 'Radical War' in Scotland, which came two months after the Cato Street Conspiracy, was potentially much more serious, although it was soon dealt with. It is likely that the malcontents in Scotland were affected by what was happening in England, and the repressive measures taken by the government there probably drove men already suffering economically into open violence in an attempt to improve matters. A call for a general strike met with a large response in the industrial west of the country and there were demonstrations and riots with some not inconsiderable damage to property and persons. The government called out the yeomanry and at Bonnymuir near Falkirk the insurgents were routed. Bonnymuir does not, because of the numbers engaged, deserve to be called a battle, but it brought the 'Radical War' to a close. Some 40 prisoners were taken by the government forces; of 24 sentenced to hang, 3 were executed.

The Reform of Parliament

The 'Radical War' of 1820 is largely forgotten today. It had little chance of overthrowing the government and at Bonnymuir the pretensions of its leaders, to achieve a military victory as a prelude to a political one, were exposed as unrealistic. But the demand for reform would not go away. It found expression in publications such as the *Edinburgh Review*, founded by the Whigs, Henry Erskine and Francis Jeffrey, and, with a wider audience, in the *Scotsman*, which first appeared in 1817. Under its editor, Charles MacLaren, the *Scotsman* made the point that opposition to government policies could be respectable. The Scottish educational system, in which the nation as a whole took a pride which would have delighted John Knox, produced a readership on a scale and of a kind not to be ignored. It was becoming less easy to 'manage' the people of Scotland than it had been in the days of the Dundas supremacy.

In 1830 George IV died. Unlike his father who in his 60 years as king had never gone to Scotland, he made a memorable visit in 1822. An important part in the visit was played by Sir Walter Scott; he created a spectacle which showed the king, clad in the Royal Stuart tartan, in a pleasing light. George himself entered into the festivities which Scott arranged and was pleased with his reception. But the king never displayed any true understanding of Scottish susceptibilities and ambitions and his death, except among those who shared Scott's view of history and of the king, seemed less important than events on the Continent which, as they had in 1789, were once again giving an impetus towards reform. In the year of the king's death, there was a revolution in France; Charles X was ousted in the 'July Revolution' and replaced by Louis Philippe as king. In Brussels there was a revolt against Dutch rule, Belgian independence was declared by the provisional government, and Greece was proclaimed an independent kingdom by the protocol of London. It seemed that no country was free of revolutionary stirrings. When, in England, the prime minister, the duke of Wellington, hero of Waterloo, pronounced that 'the legislation and system of representation possesses the full and entire confidence of the country', he was unwise and inaccurate. His replacement, the Whig, Charles, second Earl Grey, was committed to reform of the system embraced by Wellington. He produced, after delays and political bargaining, the Reform Act of 1832. The act, which became law in June, was followed a month later by similar legislation in Scotland. The 'Rotten Boroughs' of England are well known; the electoral system in Scotland was no less anomalous. In 1832 there was a redistribution of seats on a more rational basis, the number of Scottish MPs at Westminster was increased from 45 to 53, and the vote was given to £10 householders in towns and, in the shires, to £50 leaseholders. Further Reform Acts, in 1868 and 1885, would extend the franchise and increase the number of Scottish MPs to 72.

The Creation of a Scotland of Romance

By the time that George IV descended on Scotland in 1822, the only monarch to come north since Charles II's fleeting and unhappy visit in 1650–1651, Walter Scott was already established in the literary world. He had published the *Minstrelsy of the Scottish Border* 20 years before and the first of his novels, *Waverley*, appeared in three volumes in 1814. He was a prolific author, with 20 novels, narrative poems such as *The Lay of the Last Minstrel* and *Marmian*, a history of Scotland under the title of *Tales of a Grandfather*, *A Life of Napoleon*, and more to his credit. His work, enhanced by the mystery surrounding his practice of publishing anonymously, was hugely successful. He was weak in financial matters where he had been strong in his art, and his health was blighted by his determination to pay off his debts through a debilitating programme of writing.

Tory, Unionist, monarchist, protégé and friend of the leading landowner, Henry, third duke of Buccleuch, his neighbour in the Scottish Borders, Scott was the ideal choice to present a sanitised and partial view of Scotland to George IV in 1822. Scott worked hard to achieve the effect he desired; not even the weather, wet and windy when George entered Edinburgh in August, could spoil the occasion. To his task Scott brought the imagination and the depth of antiquarian knowledge which had always informed his work. In the context of the reception arranged by Scott, the sight of the corpulent Hanoverian king and his companion Sir William Curtis in the kilt, did not cause the amusement it might otherwise have done. If the kilt was suitable for the king, others, Lowlanders for whom it was inappropriate, could see no objection to it; perhaps this aping of the royal visitor was what the second Viscount Melville had in mind when he thought that by coming to Scotland George had conjured up 'determined and deep rooted monarchical feeling'. Something of the atmosphere of the visit can be found in the painting by David Wilkie, *The King's Entry into Holyrood*. In it, Scott, deservedly, is accorded a prominent place. The painting indicates that in Edinburgh, in August 1822 at least, the Highlands, the poorest and most backwards part of Scotland, was being given a role in the forefront of events, a role long denied it in government policy.

There is no reason to doubt Scott's honesty in all of this any more than there is to question his scholarship. But, the vision of his own Scotland which he laid before his own king, and that which he painted of its past in his writings, is deceptive and unauthentic. His greatness as a writer and as a leading figure in the Romantic Movement is not diminished by the suggestion that he misled his own, and subsequent generations, as to the true nature of life in Scotland. Scott was born in Edinburgh in 1771, a short time before the hand of Henry Dundas, first Viscount Melville, was to be felt in Scotland. He lived through the 'management' of the elections and the disruption of the French Revolution, he practised as an advocate and, by the end of the eighteenth century, was sheriff of Selkirk in his own borderlands from which he drew so much inspiration. He was not remote from events and the life led by the unfortunates of society. His association with the great of the land was natural and understandable, his desire to describe Scotland and facilitate an interest in its history admirable. But he put before the public a Scotland remote from what he saw about him, not merely in time but in its values and practices. When, for example, he wrote in his novel, *Waverley*, the lines 'My heart's is in the Highlands . . . My heart's in the Highlands a-chasing the deer', or in *The Lay of the Last Minstrel* he praised 'Caledonia, stern and wild . . . Land of my sires', he provided for Scots at home and those about to go overseas lasting memories based on fantasy rather than fact. Scott is not the international influence that Burns is but it is arguable that the portrait of Scotland and its people for which he was responsible has lasted longer. There is still a belief that his Scotland once did exist, in a better and simpler time, in the pursuit of which much misdirected and wasted energy is devoted.

'THIS DEAR PARADISE'

Scott died in 1832, the year of the Great Reform Act which attacked some of the abuses of the electoral system which he had been content to tolerate. It is tempting, but futile, to speculate on his reactions to that and the later Reform Acts which gave to the people of Scotland a voice which his society had denied them. Five years after his death, Victoria, daughter of Edward, duke of Kent, and Princess Maria Louisa Victoria of Saxe-Coburg-Gotha, became queen at the age of 18. She was to be the last of the Hanoverian monarchs and her reign was the longest in British history, spanning 64 years. In February 1840 she married her cousin, Albert, the younger son of Ernest I, duke of Saxe-Coburg-Gotha. Together they came to Scotland in 1842, landing at Leith on 1 September. Victoria soon grew to love Scotland, which she thought of as 'this dear Paradise', and she was a frequent visitor to Balmoral, as were her successors. She worked hard at developing her relationship with Scotland as she did at everything else. Her tendency to seclusion after the death of her husband in 1861 was viewed with rather more sympathy in the north, where greater store was put on correct behaviour, than in England. Victoria saw Scotland and its inhabitants in a way in which Scott perhaps would have approved; the Scot of Victorian times became, and remained, idealistic, almost a caricature. His other qualities, once the butt of music-hall comedians, are less prominent in a society which frowns on racial stereotypes.

John Knox was not forgotten in Victoria's 'dear Paradise' and many Scots were driven by a sense of duty to spread the doctrine of self-reliance and self-help, now, once more, so fashionable. Samuel Smiles, a medical practitioner from Haddington, wrote *Self-Help* and *Physical Education*. James Mill, whose father had been a shoemaker in Angus, moved to London in 1802 where he helped in the foundation of the university and contributed to the *Encyclopaedia Britannica*. The most famous of Victorian missionaries, David Livingstone, took Christianity and commercial principles to East Africa. Thomas Carlyle, born at Ecclefecchan, wrote *The French Revolution* and *Oliver Cromwell*, as well as other works of history, from a standpoint of moral strength, making his readers aware of the follies of men and their societies. Preaching was never far from the mind of the Victorian Scot and the foremost names

David Livingstone

of the period were not immune to the temptation to indulge in it. The Scots who went abroad and served as soldiers and administrators were themselves motivated by high ideals. In the army and navy others found a different but no less important means of self-expression during a reign in which the empire reached new boundaries.

For those who lacked the spiritual qualities of people such as Livingstone, there was Samuel Smiles to follow, and for Scots without hope or prospects at home there was emigration, as there had always been. Tobias Smollett had given his opinion in *Humphrey Clinker* that 'the spirit of rambling and adventure has always been peculiar to the natives of Scotland'. He went on to say: 'If they had not met with encouragement in England, they would have served and settled as formerly, in other countries, such as Muscovy, Sweden, Denmark, Poland, Germany, France, Piedmont and Italy, in all which nations their descendants continue to flourish even at this day.' The other side of the Scottish character, as it is often perceived, is also to be found in Smollett's novel. Humphry Clinker, 'a most notorious offender (stood) convicted of sickness, hunger, wretchedness, and want'. What was true in 1771 when the novel was published, was, it seemed, no less so in the middle and late nineteenth century when Scots, for whatever reason, were going overseas in large numbers. Few, however, would emulate the success and eminence of Andrew Carnegie. From Dunfermline, Carnegie went to Pittsburgh in 1848 and, after working on the railroads, made a fortune in iron and steel. Carnegie, however, shared one characteristic with his fellow-countrymen; he could not rid himself of that sense of guilt which was part of the inheritance from the reform of the Church in the sixteenth century. When, in later life, he returned to Scotland, he bought Skibo Castle and spent much of his wealth on libraries and other benefactions, believing that it was sinful to die rich.

The Disruption

The Church in Scotland could not be immune to events or to current thinking, although its capacity to influence the former and lead the second had somewhat diminished. There was always a danger that an obsession with detail and principle would lose the Church its preeminence at a time when, for the population at large, there were more immediate and pressing concerns. Scotland might continue to observe the teachings of Knox but the Victorians were given to a powerful belief in rendering Caesar his dues. Inside the Church itself there was disturbance as in the past. In 1712 the question of lay patronage, over which minds had been exercised for years, had been resolved against the practice of congregations choosing their own ministers. If this decision was accepted by the majority of the population, it met with rejection twice in the eighteenth century. In 1734 it was opposed by the Secession Church of Ebenezer and Ralph Erskine and, in 1752, by the Relief Church when Thomas Gillespie and others sought the 'relief of Christians oppressed in their Christian privileges' because of lay patronage. Early in the reign of Victoria the Church was further shaken by 'the Disruption', behind which lay the formidable Thomas Chalmers.

Chalmers was a remarkable man by any standards. Born at Anstruther in Fife in 1789, he entered the university of St Andrews when he was 11 and showed a precocious ability in mathematics. At 15 he was studying divinity and, as minister at Kilmenny and the Tron Kirk in Glasgow, he continued to improve his intellectual capacities as he believed all good ministers of God should. He was professor of moral philosophy at St Andrews and later of divinity at Edinburgh. He saw as his major task in the Church, the winning back to it of the poor and the ignored, and his evangelical fervour converted many to his thinking. When he understood that those who favoured lay patronage were likely to hinder his plans, he combined with others in what became known as 'the Disruption' of 1843. In May of that year, more than 400 ministers, over a third of the total number in the Church in Scotland, put their names to the Deed of Demission and left to form the Free Church of Scotland. An associate of Chalmers, David Stow, having already founded the Glasgow Educational Society, now founded the 'Normal College' for the training of teachers for schools set up by the breakaway organisation, and Chalmers became its first principal, The cause of the Free Church gained support; by 1847 they had over 700 of their own schools where posts were held by teachers who had been threatened with expulsion from their previous appointments because of their faith. In 1874, however, the Patronage Act was repealed and there began a gradual process of return to the Church of Scotland by those who had left it in a dramatic fashion in 1843. The exceptions were the so-called 'Wee Frees', an intractable minority who resisted reunion with the Presbyterians with whom they had broken. In 1892 the Free Presbyterian Church was formed; the activities of the 'Wee Frees' have since brought them much criticism.

An Age of Progress

During the reign of Queen Victoria the Industrial Revolution gathered momentum. Cotton lost its pre-eminent place because of the war between the states in America from 1861 to 1865. The prosperity of Scotland had by this time strong foundations in the development of the iron industry. In the Lowlands of Scotland the Carron Works had existed since 1759 but it was the invention of the hot blast-furnace in 1828 that allowed the greatest expansion. The furnace was the brainchild of James Neilson of Shettleston in Glasgow. The metallurgist David Mushet had, in 1801, realised the value of the black-band ironstone found in Lanarkshire and Neilson's invention put it to use. Railways covered Scotland as a result and, by the middle of the century, the canals and roads were unable to compete in the carrying of passengers and freight. In 1842 the Edinburgh and Glasgow Railway opened. The links with the south were ensured with the North British Railway of 1844 which provided the route from Edinburgh through eastern Scotland to Newcastle. In the next year the Caledonian Railway set about the task of providing a connection between Glasgow and the west of Scotland and Carlisle over the obstacle of Beattock Summit. Steel, what the English engineer Sir Henry Bessemer thought of as the 'Eldest Brother of Iron' was becoming cheaper in the 1870s. The firm of William B Beardmore & Company, at Parkhead in Glasgow, went into steel in 1879, as did David Colville, who had already made a modest beginning in 1860, the following year. The shipbuilding industry, after the adoption of steel and rapid and constantly changing demands, responded to change and the Clyde was an area of boom and an increasing workforce. There was no shortage of investment in what promised to be productive markets. Edinburgh was, as well as the capital of Scotland, the leader in banking. In industry the situation was different; Edinburgh, where opportunities for employment lay more in service trades, could never hope to compete with Glasgow where the manufacturing industry dominated. As far back as 1831, Glasgow's population outstripped that of Edinburgh's with 274,000 against 166,000. Under Victoria the difference, in this respect, between east and west increased dramatically. In 1801 it had been noted that in Glasgow lived some 5 per cent of the total population of the country; 90 years later, when Victoria was still on the throne, the figure had reached 20 per cent. In 1901, the year of her death, Glasgow and the surrounding districts contained almost 2,000,000 people out of a total population in the country of around 4,500,000. This growth had been achieved at a great human cost; in the east and south-east of Glasgow, where workers were concentrated in dwellings erected by landlords whose motive was profit, conditions were appalling. Employers, in general, did not follow the example set at New Lanark by Robert Owen; there, in the textile mills, he had put into practice his belief that humane working conditions, fine housing and schools, did not affect profitability. Low wages and unpleasant, sometimes dangerous, conditions were common. Outbreaks of cholera, smallpox, typhus and typhoid decimated families already weakened by starvation. Crime was an escape for many but punishment was cruel for the slightest offences. The political bitterness which some Scots had felt at the union of 1707 was now surpassed by the bitterness of men watching the sufferings of their families and the refusal by masters in factories and mines, who were themselves benefiting from the work of others, to improve conditions.

A New Force in Politics

James Keir Hardie was born near Holytown in Lanarkshire, where coal mines proliferated and the effects of the industrial growth of Glasgow and the west coast could not be ignored. In 1866, at the age of ten he was already, like so many, working in the mines. The sense of injustice he had from the stigma of his illegitimate birth, his poverty and lack of education, spurred him into agitation against the social conditions in which he lived and worked. The life of a union organiser, to which he turned, was a difficult one, and dismissal from his job in the mines was

Willie Auchterlonie, Winner of the Open 1893

the inevitable consequence of his skill as an agitator. But he learned much in the struggles between the miners he represented and the owners of the collieries. In 1888 he formed the Scottish Labour Party but could find no constituency in Scotland; instead, in 1892, he was elected for the English constituency of South West Ham in London. Scotland itself was not yet ready for Hardie and the Labour Party; the franchise was extended by the Reform Act of 1885 to householders and lodgers in the shires, but the Tories and Liberals continued to command the allegiance of the voters. In 1893, backed by Hardie, the Independent Labour Party was founded in England, and in the following year it absorbed the Scottish Labour Party. Its founder, Hardie, saw the wisdom of the decision and gave it his support. Four names are associated with the foundation of the Independent Labour Party. Of these three were Scots: Hardie himself, Ramsay MacDonald, later to be the first Labour prime minister, and Bruce Glasier. In their native country, moves were now made to create an organisation behind the Labour Party. The Scottish Trade Union Congress came into existence in 1897, almost 30 years after that in England. With the Independent Labour Party, the Scottish Trade Union Congress supported the Scottish Workers' Parliamentary Election Committee which was formed in 1890. The clumsy titles should not obscure what was happening; from protest and the urge of the new party's founder to implement his moral and religious thinking in politics, a powerful and durable organisation was developing, about to challenge the established parties, themselves not without problems.

At the beginning of the twentieth century Britain was at war in South Africa and Victoria was an old woman near the end of her life. War and the approach of a new reign are likely to combine, in any society, to produce a sense of unease with the past and with the existing system of government. Scotland was no different, and it had, as it always had, its men like Hardie who would question authority and the general opinion. There was, moreover, a wider sense that things could not remain as they were and this was not limited to the members of the Labour Party. Enlightened men had their place among Tories and Liberals and their beliefs found expression in legislation passed by the governments which the Labour Party could not yet displace. In the year of Victoria's death, the Factories and Workshops Act and the Education Act (Scotland) were passed into law. In its turn, in 1908, the Liberal government of Asquith brought in another Education Act for Scotland. There was a growing awareness of the role of government in ameliorating the conditions of the less fortunate: the 'People's Budget' introduced in 1909 by Asquith's chancellor of the Exchequer, David Lloyd George, aimed at ambitious social reform, to be paid for by a land tax, higher death duties and a supertax on incomes over £3,000. Great controversy followed and the House of Lords rejected the budget. The Parliament Act of 1911 resolved the constitutional crisis precipitated by the action of the Lords, whose powers were reduced. These and other legislative measures did not guarantee the future of the Liberal nor, as events would demonstrate, that of the Conservative Party in Scotland. In 1910, when George V succeeded his father, Edward VII, the Liberals enjoyed their traditional support in the towns of the east coast and in the Highlands. But their unwillingness to acknowledge the strength of the Labour Party, with some form of arrangement against the Conservative Party, would cost them dearly, as indeed would their own internal divisions which became apparent during the Great War of 1914–1918. The Liberals could continue to rely on some support from those disenchanted with the old ruling classes but they had to share this source of support with the Labour Party which was better equipped to benefit from it.

Scotland was far from Westminster, it is true, but leading figures in both the principal parties sat for Scottish constituencies. Asquith sat for East Fife, while his Liberal predecessor as prime minister, Sir Henry Campbell-Bannerman, was a Scot, as was the Conservative prime minister, Arthur Balfour. The Conservatives, also known as the Unionist Party since 1886, and officially since 1909 the Conservative and Unionist Party, was almost continually in power for 20 years from 1886 to 1905, under Salisbury and Balfour. The Liberals then held some power until the coalition of 1915 offered the Conservatives some role in government again. Thus, although in 1900 the Labour party in Scotland had not as yet made its mark on parliament at Westminster, the philosophy it preached was of such a kind as to have the necessary appeal to bring it to power, and its organisation was more dynamic than that of either the Liberals or the Conservatives. In 1906 Ramsay MacDonald entered parliament and in 1911 he became leader of the parliamentary Labour Party which had taken 42 seats in 1910. Under MacDonald the Labour Party increased its representation at Westminster until in 1923 it had 191 seats, enough to give it a majority and the opportunity to govern. MacDonald was both Prime Minister and Foreign Secretary in the Labour government of January to November 1924. Scotland had 29 Labour MPs by now. Whatever MacDonald's subsequent relations with the party, he had brought it to power and held it together through a war of which he himself disapproved. Labour, MacDonald thought, was by the time he had formed its first government, 'a party of the people' not of a class. In Scotland, then as in the future, the distinction was never as clear, and the continuing hold of the Labour Party in Scotland depends in no small measure on its association with class.

CHAPTER ELEVEN

The Loss of Identity,
1914–1960

The Scottish Tradition in War

The causes of the First World War, the Great War, and the events leading to it have been well documented and need no repetition here. On 4 August 1914, after Germany had violated the neutrality of Belgium in accordance with the Schlieffen Plan, Britain entered the war on the side of France and Russia. The Territorial Army was mobilised; of its 14 divisions 2 were Scottish, estimated at 5 per cent of the male population, almost double the average for Britain as a whole. Many in the Territorials were more intent on defence against invasion, of which there was a great fear, than of seeking to free Belgium from the Germans. Early naval actions indicated that the fear was not unfounded; German submarines sank three British cruisers off East Anglia and a dreadnought sank after hitting a mine. Admiral Jellicoe reacted by taking the Grand Fleet north to Scapa Flow. The east coast of Scotland seemed vulnerable to German attack, although no invasion came then or later. There was widespread support for the idea of a volunteer army, with Scots responding in large numbers to the call. As was the case with the Territorials, Scots supplied a high proportion of those who enlisted as Volunteers, about one in six of the first 200,000 accepted for service. Ahead of them lay the slaughter of the battles of 1916 and 1917, the Somme and Passchendaele. The exact number of Scots killed in the Great War is a matter of debate; a total of 74,000 was arrived at in 1921 by a rough calculation but it may have been as high as 100,000.

The enthusiasm of the Scots for enlisting in the Territorials and the Volunteer Army for service in the Great War derived from an old tradition. The Scots had an affinity for war both in their own eyes and in the eyes of others. How far back that tradition went it is, of course, impossible to say. Tacitus wrote of the natural bravery of the Caledonians in opposition to Agricola's legions. It may be argued that the tradition was at its strongest when the Scots themselves were in disarray in political terms, as for example when William Wallace led them, without the support of the magnates, against Edward I at Falkirk. At the greatest battle in Scottish history, Robert Bruce commanded an army in which his Scottish opponents refused to serve. The Scots might react to a name, to a warrior, to a cause, but the degree of their involvement was difficult to forecast, as was their commitment. Although their indiscipline, which was notorious, lost them engagements which they should have won, they were not always well served by their leaders; the sixteenth century alone saw two disasters which should have been avoided, Flodden in 1513 and Solway Moss in 1542.

Scots sought, and were quickly granted, a military life abroad. The Garde Ecossaise du Corps du Roi was started in the first quarter of the fifteenth century and was in existence until the French Revolution. The Green Brigade, Scots commanded by Sir John Hepburn, fought with Gustavus Adolphus; Hepburn, who also served under the Elector Palatine, ended his career as a marshal of France. Wise British governments turned the Scottish penchant for war to their own advantage; the Cameronian Regiment came from the followers of the fanatical Covenanter, Richard Cameron, killed at Aird's Moss in 1680, and the Black Watch Regiment was formed in 1739 from Highlanders employed by General Wade and was the first British regiment to wear Highland uniform. Regiments might be privately raised; the Seaforth Highlanders were the creation of the earl of Seaforth. In 1914, James Dalrymple, manager of the Glasgow Corporation Tramways, provided a battalion for the Highland Light Infantry from his staff.

When the Great War ended in November 1918, the British armies were commanded by a Scot, Field Marshal Douglas Haig, born in Edinburgh in 1861. Haig had borne the horrific losses on the Western Front with a stoicism which came from his religious upbringing. His reputation as soldier was almost destroyed by the Great War but was

A Scottish soldier from the Sutherland Rifles

later ably defended by historians. Whether he might have saved lives by resorting to different methods must remain a matter for debate. The Germans, however, had no doubt that Haig had won the war for the Allies because he possessed certain of the admired Victorian values, an unshakeable faith and a rigid adherence to duty. Others, his French colleagues among them, thought him dull, even stupid. The kind of war in which he commanded was dominated by the trenches, hardly appealing to the nature of his Scottish troops but their contribution, under the severe disciple on which Haig insisted, was an immense one.

THE EFFECTS OF THE WAR ON SCOTLAND

On 3 August 1914, as Britain was about to enter the Great War, Asquith's foreign secretary, Edward Grey, uttered a memorable phrase. 'The lamps', he said, 'are going out all over Europe.' He went on to add, 'We shall not see them lit again in our lifetime.' Grey had foreseen irreversible change but not all Scots agreed with his judgement. Those who rushed to enlist, like others elsewhere, were confident that the war would soon be over, certainly by Christmas, with Germany defeated and Britain once more the peacemaker. At the beginning of 1915 the war was not over but there was still an optimism abroad; Sir William Raeburn, a Unionist MP, was telling readers of the *Glasgow Herald* that the war had not produced the anticipated and feared effects on the economy and on life in general. Raeburn appears foolish today but in 1915 he was expressing a popular viewpoint. A capacity for ignoring the facts obscured the impact that war would have and, although Haig was a professional and well-trained soldier, he was not ready for what the battlefield had become. In Scotland, few were ready for the upheavals that a prolonged war caused. The textile trade, the coal-mines and the fishing industry all suffered; markets were closed and sources of supplies either jeopardised or lost. The availability of labour, naturally, was reduced with the Western Front needing replacements in greater numbers as the war progressed. The munitions industry did, inevitably, expand and helped to allay the fears of mass unemployment which Raeburn had ridiculed in the *Glasgow Herald*. Gretna was the scene of a huge development in the making of explosives but it was in the area around Glasgow where the biggest growth in the munitions industry occurred.

Social Unrest

War is often a unifying factor in a nation. To a very considerable extent that was the case in Scotland in 1914. It took courage of the kind possessed by Ramsay MacDonald to oppose publicly Britain's entry on the side of the Allies and he did not hesitate to resign his parliamentary seat because of his belief that the war was wrong. He was not alone in his stance; indeed, to some, he had not gone far enough. As the eighteenth century drew to its close the French Revolution had sparked off the radical movement in Scotland but, with its repression by the authorities and the knowledge that the aims of the revolution had changed with Napoleon, the task of government was made easier. During the Great War and in its immediate aftermath the situation was more complex, although the threat posed by social unrest is now seen to have been less than was formerly thought. The inspiration for unrest came from Russia this time, although the mutinies in the French army which followed the failure of Nivelle's offensive in 1917 and which were brutally, if effectively, silenced by Petain, also played a part. Over a period of seven years, beginning in February 1915, a series of episodes gave rise to what has recently been called the 'legend' of the Red Clyde. One such episode, a strike in January and February 1919, brought from Robert Munro, the Scottish secretary in Lloyd George's government, the opinion that the strike in Glasgow was nothing less than 'a Bolshevist rising'. Bolshevism engendered the kind of panic which Jacobinism had caused in the Scotland of Henry Dundas. John Maclean, a Glasgow teacher and Marxist, had already been imprisoned in 1918 after he had acted as honorary consul for the Bolsheviks in Glasgow. Maclean was treated by the authorities as Thomas Muir, the advocate, had been in the 1790s and, again like Muir, he became something of a folk-hero, a fate and a status neither really deserved. If there was to be revolution on the Clyde, there had to be stronger leadership than Maclean could give and a plan of action more coherent than it appeared on the surface. There were three strikes in 1915 before a period of almost three years when the Clyde was virtually free of trouble. If these strikes were part of a plan, it is a difficult one to understand. The appointment of William Weir, of the Cathcart firm of G & J Weir, as controller of munitions for Scotland in the summer of 1915 may, in retrospect, have been the most revolutionary action of the whole period. Weir was a young man, aged 36, energetic, and with ideas for improvement which did not always pay heed to the need for conciliation of the workforce. The engineers were struggling against inflation and blamed it on those who profited from the war, but Weir berated those who threatened to strike for twopence an hour. The 'tuppence an hour' strike of Feburary 1915, the first of several in the period under discussion, might have been averted by a more sensitive man. In his determination to carry out the brief given him by Lloyd George, Weir was understandably anxious to press ahead; the unions involved had a different approach to the problems with which he was dealing and his managers, some of them of great experience, did not share what they saw as his rashness. None of this, the strikes, Weir's provocations, the news coming from the Continent, the persistence of anti-war feeling since August 1914, the presence on Clydeside of Marxist thinkers, the role of the unions and the shop-stewards, can be entirely discounted. But the argument that together they did not add up to anything approaching a problem of the scale once envisaged is now hard to defeat. At the end of the war, the Clyde was quiet; Marxism had its martyr in John Maclean but very little else. The future of the Clyde, and of Scotland, lay with the Labour party, and Arthur Henderson's membership of the war cabinet had given it a voice in the highest councils in the land. There was trouble in Glasgow in 1919 with the 'Forty-Hours' Strike'. Robert Munro, as Scottish secretary still alert to the Bolshevik menace, prevailed upon his colleagues in government to send 12,000 soldiers, a hundred lorries and six tanks to Glasgow to quell the anticipated disturbances. On Friday 31 January, a huge crowd assembled to hear the thoughts of Emanuel Shinwell and William Gallacher, both to be eminent MPs, on the situation. As the police mounted a charge on the crowd, Shinwell and Gallacher acted with sound sense to control the crowd and to prevent a disaster and were arrested for their pains. With Glasgow full of troops the strike soon faded away. Short prison sentences were handed out to those who, like Shinwell, were believed to be 'ringleaders' of a plot. If there had ever been a Red Clyde, it was now over.

Euphoria and Reality

At 5 a.m. on 11 November 1918, in a railway-carriage in the forest of Compiegne, Matthias Erzberger signed on behalf of Germany the armistice which brought the hostilities between Germany and the Allies to an end at 11 a.m. on that day. Ahead lay the Paris Peace Conference and the Treaty of Versailles. In Britain, Lloyd George, the joint-leader with Andrew Bonar Law, of the Liberal–Conservative coalition which had prosecuted the war to a successful conclusion, made in a speech which he gave on 24 November, an undertaking which was to haunt him for the rest of his life. He asked his audience: 'What is our task?' He then supplied the answer to his own question: 'To make Britain a fit country for heroes to live in.'

It was a ringing declaration which brought the expected applause. Three weeks later, on 14 December, he called an election which his Liberal opponents, with Asquith at their head, dismissed scathingly as the 'Coupon Election'. Those candidates who represented the coalition received an endorsement signed by Lloyd George and Bonar Law, the 'c' of Asquith's contemptuous jibe. Asquith and Lloyd George, colleagues in government before the war, had been unable to work together during it, and their split meant a decline in the fortunes of the Liberal Party. Asquith's supporters, numbering just over a hundred, did not get the 'coupon' and in the election were thrashed; 484 candidates holding the coupon were returned to parliament. Lloyd George was prime minister and the party which Gladstone had thrice led into government never recovered.

The troops returning to Scotland from the Western Front are unlikely to have been as receptive to Lloyd George's undertaking as the audience which first welcomed it. Their ranks had been reduced by horrific losses and life in the trenches under officers, too often remote and uninterested in them as individuals, had instilled a certain cynicism in them. The Scottish people had heard promises before; few enough had been kept. In their absence on active service, the families of these heroes had gone on living in the disgusting housing which had been their lot for generations: 'gross overcrowding and huddling of the sexes together . . . occupation of one-room houses by large families, groups of lightless and unventilated houses . . . clotted masses of slums in the great cities'. These descriptions, taken from a report of the Royal Commission on Scottish Housing, of October 1917, were an indictment of a situation which the soldiers and their families recognised without any difficulty; they had learned what to expect of their landlords and of government, local and national. Yet their experiences cannot have left them entirely unmoved by Lloyd George's rhetoric; he had a skill in manipulating his audiences which had carried him far and there was a willingness to believe, when a long and destructive war was behind them, that he was expressing intentions which would be put into action. The soldiers had fought for their king while, in Scotland, their families had resisted the blandishments of the radicals. There was thus both cynicism and hope.

'SINGULARLY FEW PROBLEMS'

Much of the cynicism and despair prevalent among Scots after the Great War, as well as at other times, originated in the deeply ingrained belief that, with the true centre of power at Westminster, some 300 miles to the south, the likelihood of a sympathetic hearing in government circles for the affairs of Scotland was reduced. Nothing would ever entirely dispel this belief; its persistence would make it easy to categorise the Scots as labouring under the twin disadvantages of a suspicious, whining nature and an inferiority complex. The pawky Scot, careful of his money as of his speech, was, it seemed in this portrait, an inveterate grumbler, beyond pleasing. Yet it could not be denied that there was reason, as there was mischief, in some of the complaints emanating from Scotland. The reactions of Westminster to Scotland had varied since the Act of Union in 1707. As the duke of Queensberry assured his listeners, 'it is a great satisfaction to the Queen the Union is happily concluded'. But not long after, the question was asked at Westminster: 'Have we not bought the Scots?' This was a reference to compensation granted to the Scots as part of the negotiations preceding union. A more enlightened attitude was, of course, to be found but there continued to be an assumption that Scotland could take care of itself. Sir William Harcourt, Home Secretary in Gladstone's second ministry, was of the opinion in the summer of 1883 that, 'Scotchmen do their own business so well that the questions that come up for solution by the Central Government are singularly few'. Not everyone agreed with Harcourt; the Scot, Arthur Balfour, was soon arguing that, however bad the lawlessness in Ireland, it was worse in Scotland. Whether or not Balfour was exaggerating the gravity of the situation in Scotland, with the oversight of which he was responsible as chief secretary, the government had already, in 1884, sent a gunboat to Skye because of the 'Crofters' War'. Such an action was more appropriate to the stifling of rebellion in a colony. Both Harcourt and Balfour, political opponents, had to confront another frequent Scottish complaint, that Scotland was not being given its fair share of government expenditure. The so-called 'Goschen Formula', introduced in 1888 by George Goschen, chancellor of the Exchequer under Salisbury, went some way towards soothing the Scots. Scotland was to be allocated 11/80 as its share of the total of government grants; the figure was arrived at as an acknowledgement of the country's contribution to taxation. This general principle survived, as did the Scottish distrust of Westminster.

It was now that the Scottish Office was created. Since the Union, until 1746, Scotland had had, although intermittently, a Secretary of State. After 1746, Scottish affairs were handled by one of the Secretaries of State, then largely by the Home Secretary. In 1885, a Secretary for Scotland was appointed; in 1926, the title became that of Secretary of State for Scotland. The holder of the post has been described as 'Scotland's Prime Minister', an understandable disregard of the true position to which some secretaries themselves have not been immune. In fact, within the Cabinet, the post has a minor status. The ability of the holder of the post to influence events, and equally important, to be seen to be influencing events, is limited. Policy for Scotland does not come from the secretary or from the Scottish Office but, in theory, from the Cabinet which may have little time to devote to it. British interests are not automatically Scottish interests and, in a Cabinet with issues on a wider scale to occupy it and in a House of Commons where Scottish affairs do not of themselves absorb the attention of the majority of members, the role of the Secretary can be an unenviable one. The Secretary's 'constituents', that is the Scottish people, are not always tolerant of the difficulties of the position; if the Secretary represents a party in a minority within the country, the people will be loath to accord him a fair hearing. In essence, the Secretary is required largely to administer British policy decision in Scotland. During and after the Great War, the situation was particularly delicate. The nation was already divided by class and income, the building of the Conservative--Liberal coalition, the events surrounding the decline of the Liberal Party and the manoeuvres of those who eventually forced Lloyd George's resignation in 1922 by the withdrawal of their support. These problems accentuated by the stress of war, meant that now, perhaps more than before, the fate of Scotland was being decided at a Westminster where the traditional forms of government and party were no longer sustainable and Scotland's voice was, it appeared to many, being swamped. In the election of 1922, despite sweeping Labour gains, Bonar Law became prime minister at the head of a Unionist government. Lloyd George had been defeated and never again held office, although in 1940 Churchill thought long about including him in his government. The 'land fit for heroes' had not materialised under Lloyd George; his political reputation alone should have prevented an association in the public mind of the phrase with the accomplishment. Nor would it materialise with the Unionists of Bonar Law. Hope was placed in the Labour Party, which was the creation of a Scot, James Keir Hardie, with another Scot, Ramsay MacDonald as its leader. But it had, in 1922, yet to achieve the parliamentary power without which nothing was possible. When it did, in 1924, it lasted only a few months, dependent as it was on Liberal support, and preoccupied, inevitably, with its own survival. Exactly how far the Labour Party, despite its origins, was committed to the cause of Scotland was difficult to judge; it was still a party of class, not of the nation. The Communist Party of Great Britain was founded in 1920 and in the 1922 election Scotland returned, at Motherwell, Walton Newbold, one of the two Communist MPs to enter parliament in that year. But there was little question that the loyalty of the Communist Party of Great Britain lay with Moscow and its policies, in respect of Scotland as of elsewhere, would be determined there. The answers to Scotland's problems were not, then, to be found in the traditional political groups nor in those formed more recently. Scotland turned to nationalism and to the past.

Visions of Camelot

Home Rule for Scotland had been an issue at the forefront of politics in the 30 years before the outbreak of the Great War. The Scottish Home Rule Association was founded in 1886 by the Liberals but lacked the whole-hearted support of Gladstone. The association lasted in its first creation until 1914; the name was revived by the Labour MP, Thomas Johnston, secretary of state for Scotland in 1917. An indication of the pressure for some form of Home Rule can be gauged from the fact that between 1889 and 1913 ten bills came before parliament and to a division. Defeat was the outcome but, in 1894, the resolution was passed, 'that it is desirable, while retaining intact the power and supremacy of Imperial Parliament, to establish a legislature in Scotland for dealing with purely Scottish affairs'. The hope of progress disappeared as parliament's attention was engaged by Ireland and the Boer War, but in 1910 20 Liberal MPs formed the Scottish National Committee. It was proposed that the Scottish MPs, of whom there were 72, would remain at Westminster but that Scotland would have a separate administration and its own parliament. The proposal failed to find the necessary parliamentary time in the sessions of 1912 and 1913 and, in 1914, the Great War brought the episode to a close. After the war, Home Rule bills were once more put before the House. The idea of Scottish representation at Westminster with a purely Scottish parliament in Edinburgh was gaining ground; in 1924 such a plan was advanced by the Scottish Liberal Federation. More appealing still, however, was the suggestion of a complete separation from England, a case increasingly stated from 1927 by the Scots National League. On 23 June 1928, the anniversary of Robert Bruce's victory over the army of Edward II at Bannockburn, 614 years previously, the National Party of Scotland was founded. The 'Scottish Party' which advocated devolution, but not complete separation from England, joined with the National Party to form the new 'Scottish National Party'.

There was strong sympathy in Scotland for the nationalist movement but, significantly, that sympathy would not be translated into votes at general elections. The Scottish National Party (SNP) has been tolerated, often with amusement, sometimes with scorn, rather than supported by Scots. Any reference to Bannockburn strikes a chord even with those who would not consider voting for the SNP. But such an approach was not natural to the SNP despite the date of its creation. From its inception there was about the SNP a marked involvement of what became the Scottish literary establishment. The years of the Depression, from which Scotland took longer to emerge than England, were the years of the 'Scottish Renaissance', a term coined in 1925 by the Frenchman Denis Saurat. In the 1920s Hugh MacDiarmid, whose real name was Christopher Murray Grieve, was already at work; he was to be the outstanding figure, as a poet and polemicist. Neil Gunn, a civil servant from the north, published his novel *Grey Coast* in 1926, Eric Linklater and Naomi Mitchison were at the start of their long and productive careers. Osborne Henry Mavor, who held the chair of medicine at Anderston's College in Glasgow, was engaged, under the name of James Bridie, in writing plays such as *The Anatomist* and *Storm in a Teacup*, which brought him an audience far outside Scotland. Another of this literary generation to use a pseudonym, James Leslie Mitchell, was working against time, as Lewis Grassic Gibbon, to produce his trilogy, *A Scots Quair*. The nationalist movement, born in part out of such a literary background, was bound to reflect it, at some cost to itself. The literature of Scotland had for some time been dominated by the 'Kailyard' (cabbage yard) school with its concentration on a rural environment. Writers like James Matthew Barrie, Ian Maclaren and Samuel Rutherford Crockett, at the end of the Victorian period, were the masters of this genre. For them the Industrial Revolution, with Glasgow as its Scottish focal point, was to be ignored and the gentle simplicity of the country life, away from the big centres of population, emphasised by a disregard of the less agreeable facets of life. It was, in a later phrase, 'escapist', but nonetheless devoured by a nation which found relief in it from the grim reality of their existence. When, after the Great War, the literati of the 'Scottish Renaissance' were writing, they turned away and against the 'Kailyard'.

The founders of the SNP thus had, among their number, men and women with the literary skill to express their opinions on social issues. But it was less easy to achieve the political maturity and authority to bring round to those opinions the nation, with whose cultural and economic welfare they were genuinely concerned. The voice of the nationalist movement in the 1920s and 1930s might be articulate or, in the eyes of its opponents, garrulous, but it could not convince an electorate for whom matters of style and language, other than on the superficial level, meant little. It has been said that potential voters had their enthusiasm for the nationalist cause stultified by a speech from a nationalist candidate. The nationalist movement had in its ranks people who helped in the revival of Lallans or Lowlands Scots which they saw as imperative in the re-generation they planned for Scotland. This was not, however, an issue to grip the 'man in the street', the norm by which the success of all political philosophies is judged and measured in Scotland. The SNP lacked a broad base of support among what, for want of a better word, might be called 'ordinary people'; it did not attract the draper, the foundry-worker or the bricklayer. It was the Labour Party which, despite the 'utter and absolute capitulation', as Jennie Lee put it, of the General Strike of 1926 and the defection and treachery of Ramsay MacDonald, was securing the votes of the 'ordinary people'. The Labour Party was uneasy, even hostile, in the presence of nationalism. As late as the 1960s and 1970s, William or 'Willie' Ross, Secretary of State for Scotland in the Wilson governments, thought nationalism to be a major threat to his party in Scotland. Ross, although a Scot himself, was not to be seduced from his duty to the Labour Party and, as he saw it, to Scotland, by the siren call of nationalism.

Yet there was, and is, a latent nationalism in every Scot. The Tory cabinet minister, Iain Macleod, was wont, when requried to enter his nationality in a hotel register, to put 'Scottish'. His colleague and political chief, Harold Macmillan, was one proud to declare his Scottish ancestry, although the engineer in a Glasgow shipyard would find it impossible to identify with Macmillan's accent or attitudes. It has perhaps always been the case that support for the nationalist cause, sometimes of a financial kind and on a generous scale, has come more from outside Scotland than from inside it. It is not necessary to be born in Scotland to think of oneself as a Scot. Americans, Canadians,

John Logie-Baird, the inventor of television, in his workshop

Australians, descendants of the optimists, the proselytisers, the refugees and the victims of past centuries, demonstrate this. They indulge in Burns' Suppers and Hogmanay celebrations with the utmost seriousness and devotion to the opportunities which they offer and to the past which they commemorate. Nowhere, also, is there a greater awareness of the continuity of Scottish history than among those living thousands of miles away from its physical setting. The literary associations of the 'Scottish Renaissance' are likely to be unimportant; the Scotland to which Scots abroad adhere is that of the 'Kailyard' school.

Association Football

For the average Scot, uninterested in or bored by the niceties of political debate, nationalism assumes a real meaning when set in the context of Association Football. Scotland lays claim to the invention of the sport and with, perhaps more accuracy, to the invention of golf. Quite how football evolved is not clear; it is typical, however, of Scottish humour and of the football supporter's obsession with the 'Auld Enemie' that he should choose to believe his game originated in the medieval and laudable practice of kicking about the severed heads of the defeated English after a battle. In medieval Scotland the game of football was common at Fastern's Eve or Shrove Tuesday but the authorities frowned upon it. It was banned in 1424, during the reign of James I, and again, in 1491, when James IV was king, although it is recorded that the king himself indulged in the sport. Football was the game of the 'ordinary people', their devotion to it, in preference to Rugby Union and cricket, unassailable. The Scottish Football Association was founded in 1873 and in the building of Hampden Park gave Glasgow the biggest football stadium in Europe, where crowds in excess of 130,000 were common in the period between the two World Wars. Football became quickly and hugely popular; in Glasgow, apart from Hampden Park, Ibrox Stadium and Celtic Park, the homes respectively of Rangers and Celtic, the two most famous teams in Scotland, were capable of holding massive crowds. It has been suggested that the development of football on such a scale coincided with the problems of drinking and drunkenness. It is not without interest that, in 1873, the year in which the Scottish Football

Association was founded, there were over 150,000 arrests for offences connected with drinking in Glasgow alone. The problem of drink plagued football with the supporter taking his drink with him, not only as matter of course, but as part of a Saturday afternoon ritual which alleviated the harshness of the working week. Drink contributed to violence on the terraces and fuelled the bitterness of matches between Rangers and Celtic, where the 'Orange' faction among the former's following, confronted the Catholic element supporting the latter team. But football had not created the division betwen ultra-Protestant and Catholic which so affected the reputation of Scotland. The religious struggles of the sixteenth century and the use of cheap Irish labour in the west of Scotland during the industrial Revolution had done that.

It was in the international matches against England, played in alternate years at Hampden Park and Wembley Stadium, London, that passion for football reached its peak among Scots. On such occasion every Scot attending was a nationalist, the kilt was worn and the Cross of St Andrew was carried aloft. 'Scots Wha Hae' was sung and today the National Anthem is booed; the circumstances of the Jacobite Rebellion of 1745 at which time it was written, are often forgotten – but not by the Scots. Scottish football had its own Bannockburn, the 1928 match in London, when the Scottish team, the 'Wembley Wizards', won by five goals to one. Just as the victory of Bannockburn was believed to compensate for defeats at Falkirk, Neville's Cross, Dunbar and Pinkie, as well as an endless series of humiliations inflicted by English armies, so did Wembley in 1928 obliterate the memory of other sporting humiliations on the football field. Scottish football considered itself superior, only the best was accepted. In 1950, the Scots declared that they would participate in the forthcoming World Cup, which was to take place in Brazil, only if they were winners of the Home International Championship, in which their opponents were England, Wales and Northern Ireland. Following a defeat at Hampden Park by England the Scots did not attend the World Cup, despite pleas that they should reconsider their decision. There was much amused comment in Scotland when the English team, including the incomparable Matthews, in newspaper terms the 'destroyer' of the Scots, was defeated by the United States of America. Any defeat of the English was a delight to the Scots;

the extent to which they identify with nationalism during the football struggle with England is both the envy and the despair of those to whom nationalism is a political, not a sporting, subject.

It was later in 1950 that there occurred an event which caused widespread amusement but which was of more serious import for the SNP. The Stone or Scone of Destiny, used for the crowning of Scottish kings, was removed by Edward I in 1296 at the time of his rout of the Scottish cause under John Balliol. The removal of the stone to Westminster Abbey appears to have had less impact on the Scots than might be supposed since when offered it in 1328 in return for political concessions, they rejected it. The origins of the stone are unknown; a popular theory in the Middle Ages was that it was Jacob's pillow, mentioned in Genesis. It did become with time a symbol of Scottish nationalism and it was felt that it should be returned to its proper place, in Scotland. Roland Eugene Muirhead, active in the cause of Home Rule and an associate of Hugh MacDiarmid with whom he corresponded, volunteered in 1937 the idea that the stone should be recovered. Early in the morning of Christmas Day, 1950, four young Scots, three men and a woman, broke into Westminster Abbey. They removed the stone, which they discovered was already broken and, after many adventures, it was lodged in Arbroath Abbey, the scene of the immortal declaration of 1320. In April 1951, the stone was recovered from Arbroath by the police who, no doubt spurred on by the knowledge that the king, George VI, was reported to be 'greatly distressed' by the disappearance of the stone, had been zealous in the search for it. Ian Hamilton, Gavin Vernon, Alan Stuart and Kay Matheson, responsible for an exploit which did not meet with the entire approval of the Scottish National Party, were not prosecuted. This was a wise decision in the light of the general public sympathy and admiration for the four, in England as well as in Scotland, but one which deprived the nationalists of the martyrs so necessary to a cause such as theirs.

Scotland After the Second World War

The reaction of the president of the Scottish National Party, T. H. Gibson, to the removal of the stone or scone from Westminster Abbey sprang from his awareness that in recent years the SNP had enjoyed successes. To Gibson, the removal of the stone 'does not help the cause of Home Rule at all'. In by-elections during the war, the SNP vote reached as high as 40 per cent and, in April 1945, it won the seat at Motherwell. Home Rule, for which the SNP was working, featured on the platform of other interests. In the same election in which the SNP won Motherwell, the independent candidate for the Scottish universities, Sir John Boyd-Orr, who favoured Home Rule, was returned. The idea of a covenant, dear to Scottish hearts, had re-appeared in 1948, with a demand for Home Rule within a federal system. It was inspired by John MacCormick, a Glasgow lawyer, who had been secretary of the SNP before the outbreak of war. In appropriate style, it was put before the public and in all gained some 2,000,000 signatures. The success of MacCormick and his covenant, in the event, was not an unmixed blessing for the cause of Home Rule for Scotland. The Labour Party, returned to power after the 1945 election, was suspicious of the SNP and uncertain on Home Rule. When, in 1947, Arthur Woodburn replaced the sacked Joe Westwood as secretary of state for Scotland in Clement Attlee's government, he found reason to withdraw the vague approval which he had given to Home Rule during the war. In that same year, MacCormick stood as a 'National' candidate against Labour in the by-election at Paisley. MacCormick was defeated but he had polled over 20,000 votes against the Labour vote of 25,000. Woodburn and Labour did not forgive MacCormick for Paisley and the result confirmed Labour prejudice against the SNP. The Liberals had already gone into a decline in Scotland and were apathetic in the aftermath of the war; one observer remarked that 'the old fire of Liberalism, which had burned so ardently during the great days of the Midlothian campaign, was now almost extinct'. Neither Labour nor the Conservatives could be expected to look with equanimity on the rise of a third force in Scottish politics and the nationalist cause was, for some years, forgotten in the legislative rush of the first Attlee government. Social and economic change was on an enormous scale; the benefits of the welfare state had a particular relevance to Scotland in the view of many of its people, while likewise, the nationalisation programme transformed industries which had brought social problems as well as prosperity to the country. In such schemes, Scotland could not be seen for its own sake as other than part of a whole. The reforms introduced by the Attlee government, the shared experiences of the period of austerity, which were widespread, and of the Korean War in which Scots fought with distinction, underlined the fact that for more than a decade after the end of the Second World War Scotland's fortunes were tied to those of England, to the detriment of the call for Home Rule.

CHAPTER TWELVE

Scotland Today

Emigrants and Immigrants

Scotland has always exported its talents, its discoveries and its inventions; it has been a long and painful process and one which continues today. Talk of improvements in economic opportunity has tended to sound more persuasive in London than in Glasgow, whatever statistics are advanced to convince the listener. The current and insistent argument, that a return to the values of Queen Victoria's reign is desirable, will not be well received in Scotland. It was such values, in industry, which swept thousands into insanitary housing and into work which destroyed the soul and threatened the body. The south-east of England beckons where once the colonies and the Commonwealth appealed. Conversely, however, Scotland has a tradition of accepting, if not always welcoming, immigration. The influx of Irish labour into Glasgow and the west of Scotland has been mentioned. It continued into the twentieth century but, by the 1920s as the Irish Free State was being formed and Dublin had its own parliament, it was slowing. There had been tensions in which religious differences were prominent. The language of the Good Government League is an indication of the emotions of the early years of this century. Bewailing the fact that Glasgow was no longer a 'douce (sweet or respectable) Scottish city', the league maintained that Glasgow was now largely Irish and, moreover, had 'a very large semi-alien population'. In a city in which the 1931 census showed that 2 per cent of the population had been born in southern Ireland but 3 per cent in the Protestant north, much was made of that abiding fear, 'the menace of Romanism'. The language of the

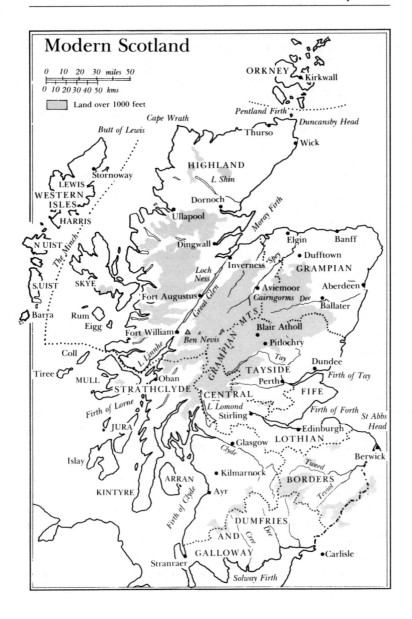

Modern Scotland

0 10 20 30 miles 50

0 10 20 30 40 50 kms

Land over 1000 feet

ORKNEY
Kirkwall

Pentland Firth
Cape Wrath
Duncansby Head
Butt of Lewis
Thurso
Wick

HIGHLAND
L Shin

Stornoway
LEWIS
WESTERN
ISLES
HARRIS
Dornoch
Ullapool

N UIST
Dingwall
Moray Firth
Elgin
Banff
Dufftown
GRAMPIAN
Loch
Ness
Inverness
Spey
S. UIST
SKYE
Aviemoor
Aberdeen
Cairngorms Dee
Fort Augustus
Ballater

The Minch
Barra
Rum
Eigg
Great Glen
Fort William
Ben Nevis
Blair Atholl
Pitlochry

Coll
L Linnhe
Tay
Dundee
Tiree
Oban
GRAMPIAN MTS.
TAYSIDE
Firth of Tay
MULL
STRATHCLYDE
Perth
FIFE
Firth of Lorne
CENTRAL
L Lomond
Stirling
Firth of Forth
St Abbs
Head
JURA
Edinburgh
Glasgow
LOTHIAN
Clyde
Islay
Berwick
Kilmarnock
Tweed
ARRAN
BORDERS
Teviot
KINTYRE
Ayr
Firth of Clyde
DUMFRIES
Dee
AND
Cree
GALLOWAY
Carlisle
Stranraer
Solway Firth

Protestant reaction was not to be moderated by facts. Alexander Ratcliffe of the Scottish Protestant League wanted, in 1927, to protect 'one of the most notable and certainly one of the most historical races on the face of the earth' from 'an alien race that would impose its culture, its traditions, and possibly its faith' on the hapless Scots of his imagination. All this was of that strain of exuberant oratory which had found a different expression and a different target in 1909 with the publication of *Our Noble Families*. This volume by Tom Johnston, Secretary of State for Scotland during the Second World War, attacked the Scottish nobility whose fortunes, Johnston told his readers, had been made from 'pillage, butchery and theft'. Johnston, like his mentor, Ramsay MacDonald, who wrote an introduction for *Our Noble Families*, achieved respectability and office in politics. Ratcliffe's party, after initial advances in local elections, declined; he was accused by his own supporters of being 'dictatorial'. The Irish and Catholic immigrants had, by this time, been integrated to a degree which he could neither condone nor understand. It is difficult to judge how strong, even at its height, was the anti-Irish and anti-Catholic sentiment in Scotland; those who watched the colourful parades of the Orange Order lodges which celebrated William III's victory at the Battle of the Boyne in 1690 were not all fanatics. Tenement living produced a sense of corporate identity against which religious bigotry flung itself in vain; the landlord and the colliery boss were the greater enemies of the working classes, whether they were 'Proddies' or 'Papes'. If these terms were used in the climate of the 1980s they would cause hands to be thrown up in horror but, in the years before and after the Second World War, were in common parlance and then tolerated with a measure of humour, later absent.

As immigration from Ireland declined, Europe was providing a fertile source of newcomers to Scotland. As before, the availability of cheap labour had its effect, with miners from Lithuania and Poland seeking employment in Scotland, as once the Irish had done. Pogroms in Russia under the last of the Tsars, Nicholas II, which involved the massacre of Russian Jews, brought an increase in the Jewish population in Scotland, as did the policies of Nazi Germany and the Second World War. Many of those who had fled from persecution in Germany because of their faith, or had escaped to Britain as their countries fell under Nazi

Neil Armstrong during the first moon walk in 1969

domination, fought at the side of Scottish soldiers in the campaigns which won Europe back from Hitler. After the close of hostilities in 1945 they stayed on to make their homes in Scotland. The struggle with Nazism, the deprivation and the violence of the war, the determination to make a better future, were experiences which these immigrants shared with the Scots and this shared history helped to ease assimilation.

The path of immigrants from what became known as the New Commonwealth promised to be less easy. In England in the 1950s and 1960s the policy of encouraging coloured immigrants from for example, the West Indies, to fill poorly paid and unskilled jobs would lead to tension. The acceptance of other immigrants like Ugandan Asians evicted from their homeland by the repressive regime of Idi Amin added to the racial mix. By the 1980s the situation had worsened; racial prejudices between the various kinds of immigrants as well as between black and white, language difficulties and a lack of the skills necessary for the securing of employment in a rapidly changing world, led to despair and reaction as well as a sense of growing alienation. Riots in Merseyside, Greater Manchester and London in the 1980s put Toxteth, Moss Side and Brixton into the headlines. The presence of the television camera brought home to Scots a realisation of the violence which they had been spared. It is impossible to say whether the Scots were more tolerant than the English. Certainly, assimilation in Scotland of such minorities as Jews, Poles and Italians had proceeded without overt problems. At the same time, however, it must be remembered that the percentage of New Commonwealth immigrants into Scotland was considerably smaller than in England, some 0.2 per cent of the population in the middle 1960s as opposed to 1.1 per cent for Britain as a whole. There was some evidence that by the 1980s, however, the situation in Scotland was changing. There were accusations that in schools colour was a growing issue and in the popular press Scots were being charged with prejudice as coloured footballers, such as Mark Walters of Rangers and Paul Elliot of Celtic, were met with abuse from the terraces at a number of grounds outside Glasgow. In this regard Edinburgh, which has so long considered itself the superior of Glasgow, became notorious. Where once, however, the football ground had been the centre of life for Scottish males on a Saturday afternoon, it was ceasing to be so with the advent of the television set, the motor car and the relatively inexpensive foreign holiday. Attendances at games dropped dramatically, although they rose again in the mid and late 1980s with the arrival of players from outside Scotland such as Walters and Elliot, and the capacity of Hampden Park, the home of the Scottish international team, had to be halved from that of pre-war days as the stadium failed to meet the growing emphasis on safety regulations. Football was still, with its ritual of the 'bus' collecting the supporters from street corners and the 'bevvy' before the kick-off, the incomprehensible and fashionably crude rival chants and the idolising of players, the singing of sectarian songs and the swaying at moments of excitement and emotion, the focus of the macho image so dear to Scottish males. But it was also an uncertain indicator of the thinking of the nation as a whole.

Devolution Rules and the Rules of Devolution

Devolution or, more commonly, Home Rule, had been, as already noted, an issue in the politics of Scotland for more than a century before the referendum (Scotland Act) of 1 March 1979. This, however, put the issue before the Scottish people and tested their commitment to it. The result of the referendum baffled at the time, and still baffles, attempts to interpret it definitively. The interpretation of the vote became almost as big a talking-point as the whole question of devolution itself.

In the years after the end of the Second World War Devolution came increasingly and significantly to be associated with the fortunes of the SNP, although the latter preached not so much Devolution as independence, a more radical solution to Scotland's ills. When the SNP was doing well, Devolution was much in the public mind, when the SNP met with a reversal, the cause of devolution suffered. The fortunes of the SNP began to improve in the early 1960s with the appointment of Ian Macdonald, an SNP candidate in the Glasgow Bridgeton election of 1961, as full-time organiser. Although he had failed to win the seat, he gained a very respectable 18.7 per cent of the vote and offered his services in a full-time capacity to the party. He increased membership, devised ways of increasing income and set up an efficient central office. In 1964, the SNP contested 15 seats in the general election won by Labour under Harold Wilson, three times the number contested in the 1959 election. Two years later, with 23 candidates presented, it captured five per cent of the total Scottish vote. Support for the SNP increased from 1966 onwards in both national and municipal elections, although the results were not uniformly encouraging. The SNP campaigned with skill, vigour and some wit, having in its ranks members who were at ease with the media, especially with television. The value of this in capturing the imagination, and with it votes, was becoming appreciated. Winnie Ewing captured Hamilton in the parliamentary by-election of November 1967 and Margo MacDonald, later to make a career in television, took Glasgow Govan in November 1973. The general election of October 1974, as a result of which Edward Heath's hold on the Conservative Party slackened, gave the SNP 11 MPs at Westminster and 30 per cent of the votes cast in Scotland. In the general election of 1979, which brought Margaret Thatcher to power, the SNP gained 17.3 per cent of the Scottish vote. This was a drastic drop from the October 1974 election but by now the other parties, because of the impact in recent years of the SNP, had had no alternative but to look again at Devolution.

The attitude of these parties to Devolution, in the years leading to the referendum of 1979 was, in general, as inconsistent as that of the Scottish people themselves. In a number of surveys asking what importance they attached to Devolution, the Scottish people gave support which varied widely from 10 to 61 per cent! In the Labour Party, the voice of Willie Ross, who thought Devolution like nationalism, 'shabby' and 'irrelevant', carried weight. The equivocations of the Labour Party lost its MPs Jim Sillars and John Robertson in December 1975. They and others created the Scottish Labour Party with its commitment to independence. The whole story of the reaction of the Labour Party to Devolution can find no place here, any more than can that of the Conservative Party. At the Conservative conference in 1968, a study party set up by the Scottish Conservative Party reported in favour of a Scottish Assembly and Edward Heath, as party leader, endorsed this recommendation. A later recommendation proposed a Scottish 'Convention' which would be directly elected and have as its brief to take over the work of the Scottish committees at Westminster. Although this became official Conservative policy in 1970, it did not find backing at the conference of 1973. Neither party could seem to settle firmly and permanently in favour of Devolution. There was a grave danger that the recurrence of the issue would alienate MPs, many of whom had little interest in Scotland, and it was not just English MPs who felt that to accept Devolution was to give in to a minority, that is, the SNP. It is noticeable, too, that the attitude of either party could depend upon whether or not it was in office or whether, while in office, it had the majority to carry legislation through. Devolution became complicated; independence had always seemed a simpler issue, although one with less hope of success. The public, who ultimately would decide, was not only rarely engrossed and more often bored by the debate, but also disillusioned by what it saw as squabbling and the disregard of what had once been a 'great' issue. A clear demonstration of the public's feeling came with the referendum of 1979. Five years before there had been a strong tide running for Devolution but in 1979, such was the change, that no more than 64 per cent of those eligible to vote on the issue bothered to turn out on the day. Of these there was a small majority in favour of Devolution but it fell well short of the necessary 40 per cent needed, a figure set by parliament. As many questions were asked about the nature of the result as had been asked about the nature of Devolution in the campaigns preceding the referendum. Ignorance of what Devolution, if the necessary 40 per cent of the electorate voted for it, would mean in practical terms was not limited to those outside Scotland; nor, more seriously for the ambitions of its proponents, was indifference and even hostility. Voters sympathetic to the concept could not overcome their loyalty to parties which feared that Devolution was the first but still avoidable step to independence, which was seen by many as the next, more sinister possibility. The Conservatives and Labour alike viewed with concern the advantages of Devolution to the SNP. Business interests came out against Devolution; the spectre of the withdrawal of firms from Scotland frightened workers. It was one thing to join in the nationalist slogans and to participate in the traditional anti-English propaganda, but it was quite another to vote for Devolution. A confused vote reflected a confused situation.

Devolution as an issue will not go away. It finds support among people of all political parties and of all classes in Scotland. Whether it can ever again reach the levels of support it had in 1974, when in October a survey showed that 76 per cent of those approached favoured some form of Devolution and members of all parties accepted the principle, has yet to be discovered. If another survey, that carried out by Mori in May 1987, is any guide, it may fail to do so. At that time, unemployment and the state of the health service were thought to be more important to the electorate than Devolution. Surveys such as these are not, of course, infallible, despite the effect they have on the thinking of politicians, and there will certainly continue to be some hope for the supporters of Devolution in the character of the Scottish people and their aspirations towards some form of break with England.

The 'Doomsday Scenario'

In the general election of 1979, the first fought by Margaret Thatcher as leader of the Conservative Party, the Labour government was defeated and the Conservatives returned to power with 339 seats at Westminster. Of these, 22 represented Scottish constituencies. In 1983, when Mrs Thatcher was again successful, the Conservatives secured 397 seats, 21 of them in Scotland. Four years later, out of 376 Conservative seats, 10 were in Scotland. Of the Scottish electorate, 31.4 per cent had voted Conservative in 1979; in 1987, the percentage was 24. In the same period of eight years, Labour representation in Scotland had increased from 44 seats in 1979 to 50 in 1987, and the share of votes cast had risen from 41.6 to 42.4 per cent. Scotland was out of tune with England, where support for the Conservatives had given them 306 seats in 1979 and 358 in 1987. These bald figures tell why, in 1987, there was talk in Scotland of a 'Doomsday Scenario'. Scotland, the argument went, would vote with increasing determination against the Conservatives while being governed by them for the foreseeable future. The prospect chilled and daunted the Scots, for whom personality has always counted for much. Themselves dogmatic, they could not support dogmatism in a leader, especially when that leader was female. Prejudice against Mrs Thatcher contributed strongly to the relationship of the Scottish people with the Conservatives in the years which followed upon the general election of 1979. There were other, more tangible problems for the Conservatives in their role in Scotland. With only ten Scottish MPs after the general election of 1987 there was great difficulty in providing ministers for the Scottish Office and in finding members for the Scottish committees of the Commons, for which a government majority is always required. With its lowest total of Scottish MPs since the general election of December 1910, when seven Conservatives were returned in Scotland, the Conservatives argued that their failure in Scotland did not affect their right to govern Britain, of which Scotland was but a part.

The despair which the 'Doomsday Scenario' reflected came from the economic as well as the political condition of Scotland. The distaste felt for Mrs Thatcher could not entirely conceal a sneaking admiration for one who refused to deviate from stated principles, even when they cost votes. Mrs Thatcher had made plain her intention to curb inflation and she stuck to that intention. Inflation would be curbed but only at the expense of growth and employment; Scotland, as usual, was hard hit.

The Chrysler car factory at Linwood in Renfrewshire, which had been saved by the intervention of Willie Ross in 1976 when the Labour industry secretary Eric Varley wanted it closed, was shut down under Mrs Thatcher. The name of the Ravenscraig steel mill, outside Motherwell in Lanarkshire, featured heavily in the media and in conversation as its fate was being decided in London. Its survival obsessed many Scots for whom the processes carried out at Ravenscraig could have little meaning. When in 1984, Arthur Scargill and his Scottish deputy, Mick McGahey, met their match in the Conservative government and the National Union of Mineworkers was defeated after a year-long bitter and on occasions ferocious struggle, an industry which now employed only 11,300 men seemed about to contract even more. At the height of the strike, Beadmore's Forge, where once the Red Clydesiders had been active, disappeared; there was no discernible reaction, other matters occupied the attention of Scots. In 1986, unemployment in Scotland was running at 14.4 per cent, as against the national average of 12 per cent. The Scots discounted the unemployment levels in parts of England, such as the north and the West Midlands, and made the comparison with the south of England, the stronghold of what was thought of as the new radicalism. It was the older industries, coal, iron and steel, shipbuilding and textiles which were worst hit in these years, and the sentimental picture of life in them, which closure conjured up, bore a limited connection with reality. Government rhetoric, in accents alien to Scottish ears, offered no comfort. The development of the North Sea oil-fields seemed to suggest a better future for Scotland. The SNP's 1973 campaign claimed: 'It's Scotland's oil.' To some degree it was; Westminster was now forced to pay heed once more to Scotland for political and economic reasons. But the benefits to Scotland were not easy to see. Jobs were created, in large numbers, but this was on the east coast and it was the west, more remote from the oil-fields and already affected by the decline in traditional industries, that was lagging behind. Devolution or independence once more appeared attractive in this context; if Scotland had its own assembly, it would be able to oversee the redistribution to Scotland of some of the revenue generated by oil. Scotland's future was being decided, it was once more argued, against the wishes and inclinations of its people. They had denied themselves the opportunity which devolution had given them in 1979, and were disenchanted with the continued existence of a system guaranteed by their indifference.

1990: An Anniversary

Glasgow has been designated European 'City of Culture' for 1990. A city known, unfairly, more for the notorious housing of the Gorbals and the sectarian rivalry between Orangemen and Catholics, than for its many beautiful parks, the Burrell Collection, and the Citizens Theatre, has worked hard to improve its image and it has been rewarded. The capital, Edinburgh, its International Festival established under Lord Provost Falconer in 1947 and secure in it reputation as the 'Athens of the North', has looked on with amusement and scepticism and, perhaps, some jealousy. Glasgow will be judged by severe standards in 1990. It is too

Springburn tenement

early to know whether the transformation of Glasgow will be maintained or whether Scotland as a whole is capable of a similar transformation. The vast expansion of the leisure industry in a country where once shooting, fishing and golf were the main attractions, and not all open to the majority of visitors, was not generally foreseen. To the descendants of emigrant Scots, now returning to see a land of which their knowledge can only be second hand, are added the Japanese who are investing their energy and their money in Scotland as tourists and business people. The Highlands and the south-west, two regions significant in historical terms but often neglected, have seen an impressive increase in the numbers of visitors. Scotland's historic houses, for many visitors all that is best and most memorable about Scotland, are beneficiaries of the boom in tourism. The unpopularity of nuclear power in the thinking of the public has opened the possibility of a new future for coal. The Highlands and Islands Development Board, created by an act of Parliament in 1965, had already reversed the trend of emigration away from its area. Clydebank, some 15 miles from the centre of Glasgow by road, was among the enterprise zones set up by the Conservative government in 1980. Conservatives could point to these and other developments in Scotland as evidence that it was not being neglected and that a prosperous future could be achieved. This argument, however, had little hope of acceptance in a Scotland alienated in 1989 by the introduction of the Community Charge or 'Poll Tax', a measure capable of arousing fierce opposition throughout the country and even among those who had Conservative leanings. The tax proved expensive to collect and difficult to enforce in the face of the belief that it was immoral and that Scotland had been selected as a testing ground for the tax.

As well as Glasgow's year of Culture, however, 1990 marks a little-known anniversary, that of the Treaty of Birgham, sealed on 18 July 1290 and confirmed at Northampton in August. The treaty, it will be remembered, was made to arrange the marriage of the young queen of Scotland, Margaret 'the Maid of Norway', and Prince Edward, son of Edward I of England. In it the separate nature of Scotland, with its 'rights, laws, liberties and customs' was guaranteed. Edward I was careful to insert, in two of the clauses relating to the rights of Scotland, a sentence upholding his own rights in respect of that country. The Scots and Edward would disagree over Edward's claim to overlordship of Scotland and in time would come to blows, a common interest in preserving peace giving way to rivalry and hatred. It was conveniently, and perhaps understandably, forgotten in Scotland that it was the Scots themselves, unable to resolve the problems they faced after the death of their king, Alexander III, who had invited Edward I's participation in their affairs. It is from the events preceding and surrounding the Treaty of Birgham 700 years ago that Scotland's dependence on England originates. The anniversary of Birgham is perhaps an appropriate time for Scots, once again, to look at that dependence and to decide whether, as in 1979, their indifference is greater than their commitment to the nationalist spirit of which they are so proud.

Rulers and Monarchs

(From c. 843 when Kenneth MacAlpin became King of the Scots and Picts to 1707, the Act of Union)

Kenneth I   c843–58
Donald I   858–62
Constantine I   862–77
Aed   877–78
⌈ Giric ⌉   878–89
⌊ Eochaid ⌋
Donald II   889–900
Constantine II   900–43
Malcolm I   943–54
Indulf   954–62
Dubh   962–66
Culen   966–71
Kenneth II   971–95
Constantine III   995–97
[Kenneth III]   ?997–1005
Malcolm II   1005–34
Duncan I   1034–40
Macbeth   1040–57
Lulach   1057–58
Malcolm III   1058–93
Donald III   1093–94
Duncan II   1094
Donald III (restored)   1094–97
Edgar   1097–1107
Alexander I   1107–24
David I   1124–53
Malcolm IV   1153–65

William I   1165–1214
Alexander II   1214–49
Alexander III   1249–86
Margaret   1286–90
Interregnum   1290–92
John   1292–96
Interregnum   1296–1306
Robert I   1306–29
David II   1329–71
Robert II   1371–90
Robert III   1390–1406
James I   1406–37
James II   1437–60
James III   1460–88
James IV   1488–1513
James V   1513–42
Mary I   1542–67
James VI (& I)   1567–1625
Charles I   1625–49
Charles II
(exiled 1651–60)   1649–85
James VII (& II)   1685–89
⌈ *William III ⌉   1689–1702
⌊ Mary II   ⌋   1689–94
Anne   1702–07

*Strictly speaking William II of Scotland

225

Chronology of Major Events

80–85	Campaigns of Agricola
84	Battle of Mons Graupius
85	Agricola built forts on Forth–Clyde line
122	Hadrian visited Britain, started building of wall from Tyne to Solway
c. 140	Antonine Wall
207–11	Campaigns of Severus
c. 400	Ninian active
c. 500	Irish 'Scots' founded Dalriada
c. 550	Anglian settlement in south-east
c. 565	Columba at Iona
c. 590	Kentigern (Mungo) active
597	Death of Columba
664	Synod of Whitby
685	Battle of Nechtansmere
794	Scandinavian raids first mentioned
c. 843	Union of Picts and Scots in kingdom of Alba
c. 890	Scandinavian earldom of Orkney
937	Battle of Brunanburgh
c. 960	Edinburgh held by king of Alba
1018	Battle of Carham
1034	Strathclyde part of Scottish kingdom
1057	Battle of Lumphanan
1072	Malcolm III submitted to William the Conqueror
1093	Malcolm III (Canmore) killed at Alnwick
1138	Battle of the Standard
1157	Malcolm IV surrendered Northern counties of England to Henry II
1174	William I captured at Alnwick
1174	Treaty of Falaise

1189	Quitclaim of Canterbury
1237	Treaty of York
1263	Battle of Largs
1266	Treaty of Perth
1286	Death of Alexander III
1290	Death of Margaret the Máid of Norway
1292	John Balliol King of the Scots
1295	Alliance with France
1296	Outbreak of war with England
1296	Battle of Dunbar
1297–98	Rising of Moray and Wallace
1297	Battle of Stirling Bridge
1298	Battle of Falkirk
1305	Wallace executed
1306	Bruce murdered Comyn, was crowned Robert I
1314	Battle of Bannockburn
1315	Edward Bruce invaded Ireland
1318	Edward Bruce killed at Dundalk
1320	Declaration of Arbroath
1328	Treaty of Edinburgh-Northampton
1329	Death of Robert I
1332	Invasion of Scotland by Edward Balliol
1346	Battle of Neville's Cross; David II captured; a prisoner in England until 1357
1357	Treaty of Berwick
1363	Failure of rebellion by Douglas, Stewart, and March
1375	Barbour's life of Bruce
1378	Start of Great Schism
1388	Battle of Otterburn
1396	Clan fight at Perth
1398	Dukedoms of Rothesay and Albany created
1402	Imprisonment and death of Rothesay
1407	Resby executed for heresy
1411	Battle of Harlaw
1412	University of St Andrews
1417	'Foul' (foolish) raid on Berwick and Roxburgh
1417	End of Great Schism
1425	Execution of Duke Murdoch
1437	James I murdered
1440	'Black Dinner'
1451	University of Glasgow
1452	James II murdered Earl of Douglas
1460	James II killed at Roxburgh

1468–69	Acquisition of Orkney and Shetland: Scotland now at fullest extent
1488	Battle of Sauchieburn
1493	Forfeiture of Lordship of the Isles
1495	King's College, Aberdeen
1496	Education Act
1503	James IV married Margaret Tudor
1505–06	Royal College of Surgeons founded
1507	Printing introduced by Chepman and Myllar
1512	Renewal of alliance with France
1513	Battle of Flodden
1528	Patrick Hamilton burned for heresy
1542	Battle of Solway Moss: death of James V, accession of Mary Queen of Scots
1544–45	Hertford's Invasions
1546	George Wishart burned for heresy. Murder of Cardinal David Beaton
1547	Battle of Pinkie
1554	Mary of Guise Regent
1559	John Knox returned to Scotland from continent
1560	'Reformation Parliament'
	First Book of Discipline
1567	Battle of Carberry
1578	Second Book of Discipline
1583	University of Edinburgh
1587	Execution of Mary Queen of Scots
1592	Presbyterian government first authorised
1603	James VI King of England
1607	James failed to achieve more complete union of Scotland and England
1609	Statutes of Iona
1610	Episcopal government restored
1616	Education Act
1617	Return visit by James to Scotland
1618	Five Articles of Perth
1633	Charles I's coronation visit to Scotland
1637	Scottish Prayer Book
1638	National Covenant
1639	First Bishops' War
1641	Second visit to Scotland by Charles I
1642	Start of English Civil War
1643	Solemn League and Covenant
1644–45	Montrose's Campaign

1646	Charles I surrendered to Scottish army
1647	The Engagement
1649	Charles I executed
1650–51	Charles II in Scotland
1650	Montrose executed
1651	Cromwellian occupation
1660	Charles II restored
1662	Re-establishment of Episcopacy and Patronage
1666	Pentland rising
1678	The Highland Host
1679	Battles of Drumclog and Bothwell Brig
1685	Succession of James VII
1688	'Glorious Revolution' in England
1689	Revolution against James VII in Scotland
1689	Claim to Right; Crown of Scotland offered to William and Mary
	Battle of Killiecrankie
1690	Presbyterian government restored
1692	Massacre of Glencoe
1695	Bank of Scotland
	Company of Scotland
1696	Education Act
1698	Start of Darien Expedition
1707	Union with England
1712	Toleration Act
	Patronage restored
1715	Jacobite Rebellion; Battle of Sheriffmuir
1735	First Secession
1736	Porteous Riot
1745	Jacobite Rebellion
1746	Battle of Culloden
1759	Robert Burns born
1760	Carron Iron Works in operation
1761	Second Secession, Relief Church
1766	James Craig wins competition for plan of new town of Edinburgh
1769	James Watt's first patent for improved Steam Engine
1771	Walter Scott born
1779	First Spinning Mills
1789	Outbreak of French Revolution
1790	Forth and Clyde Canal opened
1791	Henry Dundas became Home Secretary
1796	Death of Robert Burns

1803	Commissioners for Highland Roads and Bridges
1805	Melville impeached and forced to resign
1812	Comet steamship
1817	'The Scotsman' established
1822	State visit to Scotland by George IV
1822	Caledonian Canal opened
1828	Hot Blast invented
1831	Glasgow–Garnkirk Railway
1832	First Reform Act
	Death of Walter Scott
1843	Disruption
1846	Potato Famine in Highlands
1853	National Association for Vindication of Scottish Rights
1868	Reform Act (Scotland)
1872	Education Act
1873	Death of Livingston
1879	Gladstone's Midlothian Campaign
1884	Reform Act (Scotland)
1885	Secretary for Scotland appointed
1886	Crofters Act
1888	Scottish Labour Party formed
1889	County Councils established
1890	Forth Railway Bridge completed
1892	Free Presbyterians (Wee Frees) left Free Church
	Keir Hardie MP for South West Ham
1894	ILP absorbed Scottish Labour Party
1900	United Free Church formed
1906	First Labour MPs
1914	Start of First World War
1915	Labour unrest on Clyde
1918	End of First World War
1919	40 Hours Strike
1924	First Labour Government, under MacDonald
1928	National Party of Scotland formed
1929	Union of Church of Scotland and United Free Church
	Local Government Act
1930	Scottish National Development Council formed
1934	Scottish National Party formed
1938	Empire Exhibition, Glasgow
1939	Start of Second World War
1942	Beveridge Report
1945	End of Second World War
	SNP won Motherwell

1947	Coal Mines nationalised
1948	Railways nationalised
1948	National Health Service set up
1953	Royal Commission on Scottish Affairs reported
1958	Slump in Scottish Industry
1962	Scottish Development Department set up
1965	Highland Development Board set up
1967	Steel nationalised; SNP won Hamilton; Oil exploration began
1971	Upper Clyde shipbuilders crisis
1972	Scottish Economic Department set up
1973	Miners' Strike; three day week; Britain joined EEC
1974	Eleven SNP members of parliament
1974–75	Reorganisation of local government (Wheatley Report)
1975	Scottish Development Agency set up
1978	Scotland and Wales Act (Referendum to follow)
1979	Act fails to gain necessary support in Referendum; Thatcher PM
1980	Beginning of Steel Industry contraction
1981	Closure of Chrysler Car Factory at Linwood
1984	Start of Miners Strike (to 1985)
1985	Shipyard crisis on Clyde
1986	Closure of Gartcosh Steelworks; Announcement of replacement for rates
1989	Community Charge (Poll Tax)

Further Reading

BARRON, E.M. *The Scottish War of Independence* (Inverness, 1934)

BARROW, G.W.S. *Robert Bruce & the Community of the Realm of Scotland* (Edinburgh, 1976)

BARROW, G.W.S. *The Kingdom of the Scots* (London, 1973)

BLACK, J. & CRUIKSHANKS, EVELINE: *The Jacobite Challenge* (Edinburgh, 1988)

BRAND, J. *The National Movement in Scotland* (London, 1971)

BURN, A.R. *Agricola & Roman Britain* (London, 1953)

COLLINGWOOD, R.G. *Roman Britain* (Oxford, 1937)

CRAIG, D. *Scottish Literature & the Scottish People* (London, 1961)

DAICHES, D. *Sir Walter Scott & His World* (London, 1971)

DAVIS, I.M. *The Black Douglas* (London, 1974)

DICKINSON, W.C. *Scotland from the Earliest Times to 1603* (Edinburgh, 1961)

DONALDSON, G. *Scotland James V to James VII* (Edinburgh, 1965)

FERGUSON, W. *Scotland 1689 to the Present* (Edinburgh, 1968)

FISHER, A. *William Wallace* (Edinburgh, 1986)

FRASER, A. *Mary Queen of Scots* (London, 1969)

GRAEME RITCHIE, R.L. *The Normans in Scotland* (Edinburgh, 1954)

GRANT, A. *Independence & Nationhood, Scotland 1306–1469* (London, 1984)

HARVIE, C. *No Gods and Precious Few Heroes (Scotland Since 1914)* (Edinburgh, 1987)

LENMAN, B. *Integration, Enlightenment, and Industrialization, Scotland 1746–1832* (London, 1981)

LOGAN MACK, J. *The Border Line* (Edinburgh, 1926)

MacDONALD FRASER, G. *The Steel Bonnets* (London, 1971)

MacDOUGALL, N. *James IV* (Edinburgh 1988)

MACKIE, J.D. *A History of Scotland* (Harmondsworth, 1964)

McLYNN, F.J. *The Jacobite Army in England* (Edinburgh, 1985) *JACOBITES*

McNAIR SCOTT, R. *Robert the Bruce King of Scots* (London, 1982)

MITCHISON, R. *A History of Scotland* (London, 1970)

MITCHISON, R. *Lordship to Patronage, Scotland 1603–1745* (London, 1983)

NICHOLSON, R. *Scotland the Later Middle Ages* (Edinburgh, 1978)

PIGGOTT, S. *Scotland Before History* (Edinburgh, 1958)

SMOUT, T.C. *A History of the Scottish People 1560–1830* (London, 1969)
STEVENSON, D. *The Scottish Revolution 1637–1644* (Newton Abbot, 1973)
TURNER, A.C. *Scottish Home Rule* (Oxford, 1952)
WAINWRIGHT, F.T. (Ed): *The Problem of the Picts* (Edinburgh, 1955)

Historical Gazetteer

Numbers in bold refer to the main text

Famous Battles *(given in date order)*

MONS GRAUPIUS, 84: The confederate tribes of Caledonia were routed by Gnaeus Julius Agricola, the governor of Roman Britain, in the course of his campaigns to subjugate Scotland. **11**

NECHTANSMERE, 685: Brude, king of the Picts, defeated the Angles under Egfrith and halted the northward expansion of the latter. The battle was fought at modern Dunnichen, near Forfar. **19, 21, 25**

BRUNANBURGH, 937: Athelstan, king of the English, defeated the forces of Constantine II, king of Alba, and his allies, Picts, Scots, Irish Norsemen, and Britons. The site of the battle is unknown but is celebrated in an Old English poem. **27, 41**

LUMPHANAN, 1057: In the battle, fought in Aberdeenshire, Malcolm III defeated and killed Macbeth. In the following year Malcolm killed Macbeth's son, Lulach, at Essie. **44**

BATTLE OF THE STANDARD, 1138: The army of David I which had invaded the north of England, was heavily defeated near Northallerton by an Anglo/Norman force under William count of Aumale. **50**

LARGS, 1263: Alexander III drove off the Norwegians under Haakon IV, whose successor, Magnus IV, ceded the Hebrides to Alexander under the treaty of Perth in 1266. **55**

DUNBAR, 1296: The earl of Surrey inflicted a crushing defeat on the army of John Balliol, king of Scots, who was later forced to abdicate by Edward I. **63, 64, 111**

STIRLING BRIDGE, 1297: William Wallace and Andrew Moray defeated Surrey and High Cressingham, giving impetus to the movement for Scottish independence. Wallace was made Guardian of Scotland after battle. **67**

FALKIRK, 1298: Edward I defeated Wallace, who lacked the support of the Scottish nobility. Wallace resigned as Guardian and went abroad to argue the Scottish cause. **68, 69**

BANNOCKBURN, 1314: Robert I's decisive defeat of the English army under Edward II who was trying to relieve Stirling Castle. The battle did not end the war with England but allowed Robert the opportunity to extend his rule over much of Scotland and to raid into northern England. **76, 77, 78, 85, 204, 208**

OTTERBURN, 1388: The Scots, led by James Douglas, defeated the English under Henry Percy (Hotspur). Douglas was killed and Percy captured in a battle which became celebrated in ballads. **96, 103, 111**

FLODDEN, 1513: James IV was defeated and killed by the earl of Surrey after invading the north of England. The Scottish losses are estimated at 10,000, the English at 1,500. **114, 115**

SOLWAY MOSS, 1542: The army of James V, led by his favourite Oliver Sinclair, was routed by an inferior English army. James V, already ill, died soon after learning of the defeat. **115, 119, 120, 125**

CARBERRY, 1567: A confrontation between Mary Queen of Scots and rebel lords. Mary's army began to disperse and she surrendered to her enemies. **135**

PHILIPHAUGH, 1645: The battle which ended the campaigns of the royalist James Graham, Marquis of Montrose. Montrose went into exile but returned to Scotland in 1650, when he was captured and executed. **152**

DUNBAR, 1650: Oliver Cromwell defeated a superior Scottish army under David Leslie who was frustrated by the interference of the ministers of the Scottish Kirk. **154**

BOTHWELL BRIG, 1679: Charles II's natural son, the Duke of Monmouth, defeated the Covenanters who had earlier defeated James Graham of Claverhouse at Drumclog. **158**

KILLIECRANKIE, 1689: James Graham, by now Viscount Dundee, acting for the exiled James VII and II,

defeated William of Orange's army under General Mackay, but was killed at the moment of victory. **163**

SHERIFFMUIR, 1715: The Jacobites under the Earl of Mar faced government forces under the Duke of Argyll. The battle ended indecisively but the Jacobites retreated, bringing about the end of the rebellion. **169, 170**

CULLODEN, 1746: The Jacobite army under Charles Edward Stuart, the Young Pretender, was heavily defeated by the Duke of Cumberland. Charles, after many adventures, escaped to the Continent. Cumberland's actions earned him the title of 'Butcher' as he re-imposed government authority in the Highlands. Culloden was the last battle fought in Britain. **172–173**

PLACES

Aberdeen A royal burgh and bishopric at time of David I. Cathedral dates from 15th century. King's College, Aberdeen, founded in reign of James IV. Marishal College founded 1593. The university of Aberdeen was created from the two colleges in 1860. Aberdeen has associations with Edward I, William Wallace, Robert Bruce, the Covenanters, and the Jacobite rebellions of 1715 and 1745. **3, 67, 108, 116, 131, 175**

Abernethy Abernethy, in Perthshire, was the scene in 1072 of the submission of Malcolm III to William the Conqueror. **45, 46, 131**

Alba The name given to the kingdom, north of the Forth and Clyde line, of the Picts and Scots created by Kenneth MacAlpin. **23, 38, 39**

Annandale David I granted the

lordship of Annandale (Dumfries-shire) to Robert de Brus (Bruce) in or about 1124, and it remained in the Bruce family until the reign of Robert I (1306–1329). Annan itself had a motte and bailey castle early in the twelfth century and played an important part in the struggle for Scottish independence. **48, 57, 110**

Antonine Wall Built by Lollius Urbicus in the reign of the emperor Antoninus Pius (139–161), the wall stretched about 37 miles from Bridgeness to Old Kilpatrick. It was built of turf on a stone foundation and had 12 forts. Attacks from the north forced it to be abandoned before the end of the second century. **13**

Arbroath On 6 April 1320 by the Declaration of Arbroath the barons of Scotland wrote to the Pope, John XXII, stating their support for Robert I in his struggle to maintain Scottish independence. **81, 82**

Ayr William I created Ayr a royal burgh. Ayr had a leading part in the struggle with England in the fourteenth century; in 1315 Robert I held an important parliament there. John McAdam, the road builder, was born in the town in 1756. **84, 175**

Berwick on Tweed Berwick was much fought over by the Scots and English and was the scene of a massacre of the inhabitants by Edward I in 1296. Berwick never recovered its pre-eminent position as a port. By 1482 it was finally in English hands. **52, 61, 63, 64, 68, 71, 84, 85, 88, 91**

Bonnymuir The scene, near Falkirk, in 1820, of a one-sided skirmish between striking Glasgow weavers and a superior force of hussars and yeomanry. **182**

Buchan Roughly between the rivers Don and Deveron, the earldom became a possession of the Comyn family and was devastated by Robert I in a 'herschip' as he destroyed Comyn opposition to his rule. **74–75**

Carrick Carrick, in Ayrshire, passed into the Bruce family with the marriage of Robert, father of Robert I, to Margery, Countess of Carrick. In the early part of his reign, Robert, pursued by the English, sought refuge in Carrick. **72, 95**

Carron Near Falkirk, the Carron Company ironworks was set up there in 1759. **175, 189**

Dalriada The kingdom, in Argyll, of the 'Scoti', who emigrated from Ireland c500. The name Dalriada already existed in Ireland. The kingdom remained in existence until Kenneth MacAlpin joined it to Pictland. **19, 21, 39**

Dumbarton The 'fort of the Britons', and capital of the kingdom of Strathclyde, legend associated the famous rock with St Patrick. Dumbarton's position guaranteed it a role in guarding the western approaches to Scotland. It was held for Edward I by Menteith, traditionally the betrayor to the English of William Wallace. **26**

Dundee Dundee received a charter from William I and figured largely in the early Anglo-Scottish wars. Montrose sacked it in 1645. John Graham of Claverhouse lived near the town and took his title from it. **67, 175**

Dunfermline Scotland's capital during the reign of Malcolm III and became traditional burial place of Scottish kings. Malcolm's queen,

Margaret, installed Benedictine monks in the abbey. Dunfermline became a royal burgh about 1120. **83, 103, 187**

Edinburgh 'Edwin's fort', Scotland's capital is dominated by its castle, built on volcanic rock. The New Town, which was created from a plan by James Craig in the eighteenth century, gives Edinburgh an appearance of grace. The older history of the city centres in the castle, the Royal Mile, and Holyrood Palace. The Treaty of Edinburgh in 1328 gave Robert I his final victory over the English. The University dates from 1582–1583. **52, 56, 75, 79, 83, 85, 86, 91, 96, 108, 110, 111, 112, 117, 129, 148, 154, 155, 159, 161, 172, 184, 190, 195, 216**

Falkirk The setting for two famous battles in Scottish history: 1, the defeat of William Wallace by Edward I in 1298, 2, the victory by Bonnie Prince Charlie over General Hawley's government forces in 1746. **70, 72, 76, 77, 172**

Falkland Falkland Palace in Fife was favoured by the Stuarts. James V, who died there after learning of the defeat at Solway Moss, was responsible for much of the building of the palace. The Duke of Rothesay died in suspicious circumstances at Falkland in 1402. **103, 116, 131**

Galloway The lordship of Galloway in south-western Scotland was held by Devorguilla, wife of John Balliol and mother of John, king of Scots 1292–1296. Devorguilla founded Sweetheart Abbey and with her husband created Balliol College, Oxford. **22, 29, 48, 60, 61, 65, 75, 110, 113**

Glasgow The 'Green Hollow', Scot-

land's largest city and industrial capital, has as its patron Saint Kentigern (Mungo), who is said to have founded a church there. The University of Glasgow was founded in 1451. The city began to prosper in the eighteenth century with trading in tobacco, rum, and sugar. The Industrial Revolution added to Glasgow's importance and the city's population increased dramatically with an influx of workers from the Highlands and Ireland. **29, 30, 57, 60, 71, 73, 80, 117, 138, 149, 151, 175, 188, 189, 190, 195, 198, 199, 204–205, 207–208, 212, 216, 222–223**

Glencoe On 13 February 1692, 38 members of the MacDonald clan were massacred by government forces under Campbell of Glenlyon after the clan chief had failed to take an oath of allegiance to William III. **163–164, 165**

Gowrie Gowrie House in Perthshire was the scene in 1600 of a conspiracy to seize James VI. The Master of Ruthven and his brother the Earl of Gowrie were killed by James' followers. Doubt remains about the whole episode. **142**

Hermitage Hermitage Castle in Roxburgh originally belonged to the Soules family who held the hereditary office of butler to the kings of Scotland. In 1342 Sir William Douglas starved Sir Alexander Ramsay to death here and in legend one member of the Soules family was said to have been possessed by the Devil, for which he was said to have been boiled alive. Mary Queen of Scots almost died of fever at Hermitage which was later Sir Walter Scott's favourite castle. **90**

Holyrood James IV began the building of the Palace of Holyrood in the outer courtyard of the abbey which dated from the reign of David I. Under Charles II there was extensive rebuilding of the palace in 1671–1678; the architect was Sir William Bruce. **48, 97, 107, 109, 135, 148**

Inchtuthil   Agricola built the fortress at Inchtuthil in Perthshire to house the Twentieth Legion as the key to his planned occupation of the north of Scotland. The fortress did not long remain garrisoned as the Romans withdrew to the south. **9, 11**

Inverness   The scene of Columba's conversion of Brude king of the Picts to Christianity, Inverness later had a stone castle, built by David I. In 1427 James I locked up some forty opponents in the castle. Bonnie Prince Charlie blew the castle up before the battle of Culloden. The present building is used for county offices. **3, 67, 168, 172**

Iona   Columba, abbot from 563 to 597, founded the monastery which was the centre of the Celtic Church. From Iona monks went to Northumbria where they founded the monastery of Lindisfarne. The influence of Iona began to decline with the adoption of Roman practices, although it was the burial place of Scottish kings. Iona was sacked in the eighth century by Viking raiders. **28, 30, 31, 32, 33, 34**

Jarlshof   The site in Shetland of evidence of occupations since the Stone Age. **37**

Jedburgh   The abbey was one of David I's four great foundations in the Borders in the twelfth century. It suffered much during the wars with England. It was at Jedburgh that Alexander III married Yolande of

Dreux in 1285. Tradition has it that at the wedding feast a ghost warned the king of his death, which happened in the following year. **48, 52**

Kirkwall   Kirkwall in Orkney witnessed the death of Haakon IV after his defeat at Largs in 1263. The cathedral was built in 1137 by earl Rognvald and dedicated to his uncle, St Magnus, murdered on the orders of Haakon. **37**

Lanark   Possibly a royal burgh as early as the reign of David I, Lanark is traditionally the scene of the start of the rebellion by William Wallace who murdered the English sheriff, William Heselrig there. **65, 67, 92**

Lochleven   Mary Queen of Scots was a prisoner in Lochleven Castle after her surrender to the rebel lords at Carberry on 15 June 1567. The castle was the property of Sir William Douglas but Mary's escape was aided by two other bearers of the name of Douglas. **135**

Loudon   At Loudon Hill in Ayrshire in May 1307, Robert Bruce defeated the English under Aymer de Valence earl of Pembroke and thus began the campaign which led to his recovery of Scotland. **74**

Magus Muir   On 3 May 1679 the archbishop of St Andrews was murdered near St Andrews by Covenanters. **158**

Melrose   The abbey, in the Borders, was founded by David I. Alexander II gave Eskdale Forest to the monks and it was similarly favoured by Robert I, whose heart was buried there after its return from James Douglas' crusade. The abbey was destroyed by the English in the earl of Hertford's

'Rough Wooing' of 1544–1545. **48, 85**

Montrose Montrose Castle may have been the scene of the abdication of John Balliol in 1296. Andrew Melville, the proponent of presbyterianism and the opponent of James VI and I, was a pupil at the school in Montrose. **84**

Newbattle The abbey of Newbattle in Midlothian was founded by David I and suffered much at the hands of the English. **48**

Paisley Walter, hereditary Steward of Scotland, founded the abbey in the twelfth century. Paisley, in modern Strathclyde, probably had a school before the Reformation and later was famous as a thread-producing centre. **65, 99, 210**

Perth Perth played an important part in the wars with England and frequently changed hands. James I, who held parliaments in Perth which was then an administrative centre, was murdered there in 1437. Perth was the scene of the so-called 'Battle of the Clans' in the reign of Robert III. **56, 71, 73, 87, 90, 100, 101, 104, 108, 109, 128, 147, 168**

Sanquhar It was at Sanquhar, the seats of the Dukes of Queensberry in Dumfriesshire, that, in 1680, the extremist Protestant, Richard Cameron, made his 'Declaration' in which he renounced his allegiance to Charles II on whom he declared war. **158**

Scone The Stone of Destiny (Stone of Scone) was kept in the abbey until it was removed by Edward I in 1296. Kings of Scotland were crowned on the nearby Moot Hill, which is in the grounds of Scone Palace, built in the early part of the last century. **57, 61, 64, 73, 80, 82, 83, 86, 87, 92, 94, 97, 105, 209**

Skara Brae Skara Brae on the Bay of Skaill in Orkney is the most perfectly preserved Stone Age in Scotland. It was discovered in 1850 when a storm removed the sand under which it had lain for centuries. **5**

St Andrews The university, the oldest in Scotland, was founded in 1412 by Bishop Henry Wardlaw. In the castle the Protestant martyr George Wishart was imprisoned and Archbishope David Beaton was murdered. **48, 57, 71, 108, 121, 123, 124**

Stirling The castle, because of its strategic importance, changed hands many times during the wars with England. The battle of Bannockburn was fought as the English sought to relieve the castle. In 1452 James II stabbed the eighth earl of Douglas to death in the castle. Mary Queen of Scots was crowned in the castle chapel. **52, 68, 71, 72, 75, 76, 90, 106, 108, 113, 128, 151**

Strathclyde A kingdom of the Britons in the south-west of Scotland, Strathclyde later formed part of Cumbria and was the subject of frequent struggles. Its capital was Dumbarton. **19, 21, 25, 26, 27, 30, 34, 41, 43**

Turnberry Robert Bruce, later Robert I, was born in Turnberry Castle in 1274. The ruins of the castle can still be seen. **57**

Whithorn According to tradition, St Ninian is said to have built a church at Whithorn in Wigtownshire at the beginning of the fifth century. In the last year of his life Robert I made a pilgrimage to the saint's shrine. **29, 83**

Index